ReWriting White

ReWriting White

RACE, CLASS, AND CULTURAL CAPITAL IN NINETEENTH-CENTURY AMERICA

TODD VOGEL

Rutgers University Press
New Brunswick, New Jersey, and London

Library of Congress Cataloging-in-Publication Data

Vogel, Todd, 1959–
Rewriting white : race, class, and cultural capital in nineteenth-century America / Todd Vogel.
p. cm.
Includes bibliographical references (p.) and index.
ISBN 0–8135–3431–3 (hardcover : alk. paper) — ISBN 0–8135–3432–1 (pbk. : alk. paper)
1. American literature—Minority authors—History and criticism. 2. Literature and society—United States—History—19th century. 3. American literature—19th century—History and criticism. 4. Minorities—United States—Intellectual life. 5. Social classes in literature. 6. Ethnic groups in literature. 7. Minorities in literature. 8. Ethnicity in literature. 9. Race in literature. I. Title: Re-writing white. II. Title.
PS153.M56V64 2004
810.9'920693'09034—dc22

2003022258

British Cataloging-in-Publication information for this book is available from the British Library.

The publication of this book was aided, in part, by a grant from Trinity College, Hartford, Connecticut.

Manufactured in the United States of America

CONTENTS

ILLUSTRATIONS

ACKNOWLEDGMENTS

My debts are huge. When I decided to write this book, I knew that it would take a pound of my flesh. Little did I know that it would take flesh from others, too.

Librarians around the country cleared many paths for me. The University of Texas Interlibrary Loan Staff and Eric Novotny provided wonderful help at tracking down obscure volumes. Trinity College's interlibrary loan did likewise. Staffs at the American Antiquarian Society, Boston Public Library Rare Books and Manuscripts, Dartmouth College Library, Connecticut Historical Society, the Library Company of Philadelphia, Oberlin College Library, Williams College Library, Stanford University Cecil Green Library, Stanford University Rare Books, Stanford University Medical School Library, The University of California at Berkeley library, The Bancroft Library at the University of California, Wei Chi Poon of the Asian-American Studies Collection at California's Ethnic Studies library and Trinity College's Watkinson Library also provided great help.

Friends and colleagues provided ready friendly and intellectual support. They include Elizabeth Abrams, Bart Bracken, Vernon M. Briggs, David Claman, Cassandra Cleghorn, Judy Coffin, Athena Daniolos, David Dowell, Elli Finley, Bruce Forgrieve, Audrey and David Gow, Tim Marchell, Alexander Nemerov, Michael and Jo Nieman, Niki Parisier, Susan Pennybacker, Gunther Peck, Maureen Reed, Shawn Rosenheim, Laura Saltz, Laura Thompson, Patrick Walsh, Audrey West and Tim Wooldridge. Robert Levine, Janet Zandy, and Robert Fanuzzi have given me friendship and scholarly advice in time of need. The Center for Working Class Studies gave me an opportunity to try out an early version of a crucial chapter.

I've been blessed with an extended parental and sibling network, and they have all been wonderfully supportive. Herbert and Phyllis Vogel, Warren Boeker, Kirk Alland, Sisters Colette, Valerie and Carla, Mel and the late Virginia Gradiska, Jim and Dorothy Hust, and Henry Upton all let me know they were behind me.

I received needed advice from Rob Cox, George Forgie, Barry O'Connell, Bill Stott, John Kuo Wei Tchen, and Rafia Zafar. I benefited from readings of early sections of this book by Kevin Kenny, John Haddad, Jeffrey Meikle, and Maureen Reed. Readers of the dissertation that eventually became this book made enormously helpful comments. Robert Abzug, Robin Kilson, Elizabeth McHenry, and William Forbath generously spent time with me. Shelley Fisher Fishkin, who launched me into this material in a graduate class, provided advice and support much beyond the call of duty.

My colleagues at Trinity have been very generous with their time as the book reached later stages. Bettina Carbonell, Jan K. Cohn, Robert J. Corber, Jack Dougherty, Cheryl L. Greenberg, Joan D. Hedrick, Paul Lauter, Eugene Leach, Fred Pfeil, Barbara Sicherman, and Jenny Steadman all provided rigorous readings of sections that made the end result better. Thanks to Lisa Jerry, whose copyediting inched me toward the holy grail of concision and clarity, and Leslie Mitchner at Rutgers University Press for her support throughout the process. Thoughtful comments from Kevin Gaines and James Miller made this project better. Yuly Nosenzo helped with image permissions.

I also want to thank Henry Zalegowski for teaching me how to fly an airplane. I dedicate this book to Karen Hust, who makes me fly every time I catch her eye.

ReWriting White

Introduction

RECASTING THE PLOT

In 1899 James H. Canfield, chancellor of the University of Nebraska, found a value in John Bascom's work that we would consider odd today. Chancellor Canfield was "delighted" at the re-release of Bascom's book on rhetoric, the most popular of its kind during the period. Bascom published it thirty-four years earlier to link the laws of the universe, aesthetics, and language, and Canfield found the text useful for his social mission. "I used it when a student at college with greater enjoyment than almost any other text-book in its year; and I have used it steadily as an instructor," Canfield said. "It has peculiar *moral* worth, and has made a lasting impression on all who have come under its influence." Today, we might find it curious that anyone could become a zealot for a rhetoric textbook. A "lasting impression" may be plausible. "Enjoyment" looks like a stretcher. But "moral worth"?[1]

Yet the word "moral" is as crucial for us as it was for Canfield. *ReWriting White* is about how people with little moral standing in society use the performance of words—the heart of the nineteenth-century subject of rhetoric and Bascom's book—for moral, political, and social ends that might have confounded Chancellor Canfield. The writers and orators I consider here clearly used the content of their essays and addresses to bring change. But these African Americans, Native Americans, and Chinese Americans also transcended the meaning denoted by the language. These people performed their words; they acted out their message in a manner that demonstrated command of society's cultural capital. They exhibited their ability to create or interpret society's aesthetic codes with the choices they made about the structure of their essays, the forum for their orations, the very identity they crafted as racialized outliers in society. These performances gave new meanings to the words on the page. These cultural conjurers drew on narrative styles or occupied forums considered above their station by popular racial ideology. They fashioned a connotative meaning that hitched a ride with their stated meaning and shaped what their authors broadcast to the auditorium or wrote on the page.

Each writer uses a different technique, but the end game is the same. Antebellum black newspaper writers hop aboard the class-based language reform of the 1840s to make a place for free blacks in the republic. A writer named Edith Eaton poses as Chinese to perform as a different kind of Chinese American than the one in the public mind, and this one "deserves" rights in America. Essayist Anna Julia Cooper appropriates the tools of classical rhetoric to demonstrate an aesthetic sensibility supposedly foreign to blacks and to rewrite societal rules about gender and race. William Apess retells a seventeenth-century war history to place Native Americans at the root of the country's founding. He places himself on a Boston stage with a long history of performances and asks, "Who shall stand in after years in this famous temple, and declare that Indians are not men? . . . If men, then heirs to the same inheritance." Sometimes these marginalized people *spoke* their change. Sometimes they *became* it.

When I use the terms "racialized outliers," or "racial aliens," or "marginalized people" I mean people at the heart of this study, those whose race placed them outside society's mainstream. Each term describes a person or a group of people whose racial designation keeps them from enjoying full citizenship rights. This book inspects ways that, despite a national narrative of a free and open dialogue in which the public crafts the nation's direction, one's race dictates one's ability to participate, and the book asks how those excluded from participation, those not considered *white,* responded.

This study joins a growing body of scholarship that focuses on whiteness, a racial category packing a wordless power that will take a long time for literary and cultural critics to fully understand. In America, as Matthew Frye Jacobson has pointed out, whiteness's muscle shapes "notions of history, peoplehood, and collective destiny by which power has been organized and contested."[2] Its privileges are what "racial aliens" aim for even if the social behavior of whites is not. Of course, whiteness is a racial category, and it carries race's slippery characteristics: it changes with class tensions and with time; it goes unnamed in social discourse; and it provides legal, social, and economic privilege to its holders. That privilege may mean the ability to vote, entry into a certain railroad car or type of employment, or, as we will see, the right to hold forth before an audience. The accumulation of this privilege in the nineteenth century helped define a center in America, where individuals exercised these rights, and a margin, where they were denied one or all of these privileges.

David Roediger, who launched modern whiteness studies with *The Wages of Whiteness,* calls for whiteness scholarship that focuses on people of color and their reaction to the whiteness ideology.[3] This study provides a step in that direction. We can find much energy residing in work by people considered to be racial aliens—the places where race and power contours emerge—by looking at how they negotiate the gap that separates where they stand and the place of full citizenship in the country, by inspecting how they bridge the chasm created by whiteness.

Frederick Douglass used this chasm to infuse his orations with energy. He chose the country's premier holiday of citizenship to deliver "What to a Slave Is the Fourth of July?" In that speech he inspects the country's very meaning when some of its members are labeled so alien that they are, as slaves, considered to be *things*. "Do you mean, citizens, to mock me, by asking me to speak to-day?" he challenged his listeners. "The rich inheritance of justice, liberty, prosperity and independence, bequeathed by your fathers, is shared by you, not by me."[4] Douglass was not at that moment a slave, but the national narrative about blacks at the time maintained that none had the stuff of citizenship. This makes citizenship an interesting point of entry into understanding nineteenth-century race and discourse. Yet society has shifted its criteria of citizenship as technology, political parties, and community size have changed.[5] To consider what kind of cultural competence makes a citizen at a certain moment—an ontological status, an inner virtue, an informed mind, or a certain amount of property—tells us what a society cares most about in its participants. Focusing on people, like Douglass, who try to bridge the gap between those included and those excluded in citizenship and those allotted participation in those citizenship rights or restricted from it, helps us to understand the racial rules at work and the creative strategies employed to change them.

This work follows some well-established angles of inquiry and introduces some of its own. It examines, as Richard D. Brown does, the difference between the American ideal in which all citizens sit in the national parlor of conversation to guide the nation and the reality that excluded some. It looks at writers and orators who Cheryl Walker and others might say rely on "universal" rights or stake their claims by demonstrating the historical underpinnings of their subjugated position. It asks, as does Rafia Zafar, how black writers of early national and antebellum periods appropriated "white" discourses to write blacks into the mainstream of American literature.[6]

Together, these traditions stake out a rich terrain for analysis that includes republicanism and print culture, nation building and subversion, and discursive bargaining to claim rights. Each is crucial to look at how people of color write themselves into the national discourse, to ask why they use the discourses they use, and to question how they intended those audiences to read those discourses. But I also want to add what I consider another, equally important, angle: class. The writers I consider drew on class-based conventions of discourse to shift their position of power. The intertwining of race and class in the nineteenth-century often meant that people of color were *assumed* to be of lower class or at least not a part of the middle or ruling classes. Class positions, of course, brought with them class-based conventions of comportment and speaking. The performance of these class-based conventions by people of color—people who were reputed to be "brutish" or "savage" or "sinister"—on its face, challenged public expectations of a white republic which scripted that only white citizens with certain class skills could meaningfully participate in the national conversation. By placing themselves in a province mainly claimed by the white middle and upper classes, and by producing a product to engage that audience, the work of people of color, on the surface, still lived within the class-bound terms of the mainstream.

The writing and oratory of people of color improvise on mainstream discourse. To that end, this study continues the work of Henry B. Wonham, Carla L. Peterson, Shelley Fisher Fishkin, Robert Levine, Jeffrey Steele, and others who desegregate the American literary canon by examining the interplay between texts once considered per se "black" or "white."[7] The idea of "authenticity" has dogged the literary criticism of people of color and kept scholars' vision too narrowly focused. African American writers, for example, initially were left out of the canon because they dwelled on matters of race. African American women writers missed the rerouted canonical train because they dwelled too much on matters of gender. Furthermore, as Ann duCille argues, middle-class African American women writers lost out on still later revisions because they seemed too far from the "real" black experience. Any writer who deviates too far from what Zora Neale Hurston epitomizes—"the blues" in the vernacular sound or lifestyle—gets tagged with what duCille calls "historical conservatism." Writers of color who used a formal, mainstream English may cause some critics to question their "authenticity" or to wonder whether they became, through the digestion of their school rhetoric text, "hegemonized." One critic recently wondered if antebellum black writers "unreflectively accepted standard white English and Euro-American forms without questioning them." The implication, if we are not careful, is that standard English, the English used by those in power, is the "white" English that expresses opinions only of the powerful.[8]

This assumption is crucial to question. As we craft a multicultural curriculum and canon, we attempt two difficult things at once: to understand how the cultures of different groups cohere and to grasp how the cultural productions of different groups vary. Writers' stylistic choices do carry into the broader questions of how they negotiate their citizenship. But I demonstrate that what we have dismissed as conservative forms sometimes serve as vehicles for revisionary ideas. I shine a bright light on what we call racialized aliens' "standard white English"—their performance of words—to ask whether it was white and whether it was, indeed, standard at all for its time. Moreover, I ask what change they seek to make by simply showing off their cultural competence in verbal performance. How, in short, does the *act* of performing these competences countermand contemporary racial ideology and make a place for these people in the republic?

Constructing an approach that allows us to take these performances' cultural pulse requires historical evidence. Given that these writers and orators were outsiders, given that they were cultivating a revisionary ideology, how did their audiences receive them? Any critic would love to stumble on an old press clipping or journal entry in which the reviewer delivers a thumbs-up or thumbs-down reaction. But in the cases of people writing from the margins, assessments resembling modern movie reviews are few and far between. Instead, sometimes a reasonable estimation of reception follows by recrafting the rich fabric of contemporary culture. We can ask a few questions: How did the prevailing ideology of whiteness shape the audience? What expectations did the audience carry with it about the performer's identity? And finally, what expectations about cultural capital and race did the audience carry with it? What did readers or listeners of the black press, for example, expect when they encountered intellectual work by an African American?

One foothold into reader and listener expectations is to ask what kind of visual cues contemporary white Americans looked for when trying to plumb the inner depths of someone they did not know well. Phrenology, a popular reform "science" in antebellum America, offers one place to dig. For Native American William Apess, after reconstructing the auditorium in which he spoke, more questions abound: What kind of people normally spoke in that space? What kind of people attended? And what would be their likely expectations on arriving at the hall on that night? Anna Cooper knew, perhaps better than anyone in the audience, the kind of rhetorical rules society had informally established. A mapping of these rules—and an examination of how some marginalized people danced in and around them—provides a better appreciation for Cooper's achievement when she bent those rules to her will. Finally, visual clues about Chinese Americans in the popular photography of Arnold Genthe and texts by whites retelling their encounters with the Chinese allow readers to glimpse the expectations of a mainstream reader coming upon reportage by Edith Eaton's persona, Sui Sin Far.

By examining mainstream culture's expectations for marginalized people's cultural competence and by looking at the writer or orator's display of that competence, the gap that the performers had to jump emerges. Further, this investigation allows two additional unifying questions of these subjects: What kind of cultural competence did society demand before it granted someone the right to speak as a citizen? How did different groups choose to address this requirement? This focus gives a measure for understanding the similarities and differences across racial and ethnic groups, and it helps reconstruct a more complicated narrative of American literature.

New York newspaper editor Major Mordecai M. Noah complained that, should free blacks gain access to education and culture, then they will want full political rights and inevitably to "mix" socially with whites. A writer at *Freedom's Journal* marveled at the logic of "so great a stickler for the rights of man." Blacks with money and education would secure their rights, he vowed, and "had we daughters with the dowry of a fifty or a hundred thousand, we fear he would forget the law of rights and shades." The writer mixed claims of class and cultural capital to assert his rights in the republic—and to challenge Noah's racial ideology.[9]

Furthermore, this focus on language as cultural competence grounds the understanding of how power works in society. "Standard" language is, after all, the dialect of the group with power. And the "standard" literary canon is assembled by the same group. One path of struggle for marginalized people is to, at once, master "standard" English even while asserting their own value and priorities. For example, antebellum black newspaper editor James McCune Smith displayed his own cultural prowess even as the Supreme Court ruled that blacks were not citizens to revise the accepted narrative of American history.[10] In *The Souls of Black Folk*, W.E.B. Du Bois famously claimed to commune with Shakespeare, Aristotle, and Aurelius. Du Bois drew on this canonical cultural capital when another Supreme Court decision, *Plessy v. Ferguson,* ruled that blacks could not expect to share accommodations—including school classrooms—with whites. What are readers to do with these references to what was considered "standard white English" and Du Bois's assertion that, intellectually at least, he crossed the canonical color line?

But I am getting ahead of myself here. Another goal of this study is to cross that color line and continue the field's push past identity politics. A growing number of scholars have drawn on the variety of influences and languages used by different racial and ethnic groups. Historian Robin D. G. Kelley applies the term *polycultural* to denote an expression that blends various cultures to make its point. By examining how these writers first construct their identities and then borrow the master's tools—the "mainstream" connotative meanings generated by their performance of words—the reader more fully understands the tones of the polycultural chord.[11]

Accomplishing all of this requires steps outside traditional disciplinary boundaries. A concern with language alone—as a timeless element to analyze—renders a comparison of apples and oranges, given that definitions of race varied across time and group. A concern with time and place alone, however, flattens the expressive power that characters invested in their work. Meaningful distinctions arise only when we vary language, time, place, and racial formation in each moment and consider what Gary Okihiro calls "social formation." Okihiro self-consciously borrows Michael Omi and Howard Winant's idea of racial formation, in which race changes over time, to broaden the terms that vary and examine how race, gender, and class change over time and influence each other. This study uses a sociological definition of class, a sociological and historical approach to race and gender, and a cultural studies approach to the performance of words. Moreover, it draws on archival material to nail down how the lived experience of race, class, and gender unfolded.[12]

Perhaps as interesting as the similarities between these writers are the differences among them. For example, each racial and ethnic group designs its claims to overcome specific cultural and legal hurdles. In the late nineteenth century, Edith Eaton could not base a claim to American citizenship for the Chinese on centuries of contributions to building the United States, as Anna Julia Cooper could. The Chinese did not begin to arrive in the United States in large numbers until the cusp of the Civil War, and later the Chinese Exclusion Act of 1882 nearly clamped shut the pipeline of immigrants. In short, at century's end the Chinese enjoyed even fewer citizenship rights than African Americans. Edith

Eaton had to demonstrate specific qualities before anyone would even consider the possibility of Chinese-born U.S. citizens.

At the heart of these differences lies a key concept pioneered by Omi and Winant that complicates the organization of this book. Racial formation—the crafting of the meaning of race for a group—unfurls in a specific moment, in response to new economic, social, and regional circumstances. The idea that the definition of race changes over time may by now seem self-evident, but the implications run so deep, especially for work that seeks to compare experiences, that scholars have yet to understand them all.

Americans' changing view of the Chinese during the nineteenth century illustrates these complications. In 1850, Chinese working in California were nothing more than curiosities that might yield a profit. When San Franciscans gathered to celebrate the anniversary of George Washington's birth, the local paper welcomed the Chinese population's participation in the parade, and the writer, an "admiring gazer," described "our most orderly and industrious citizens."[13] A few years later, San Francisco's leaders proposed that, as a monument to Abraham Lincoln, the city build a college to teach language skills—not the English language but the *Chinese* language. The leaders believed that the city could serve the nation's imperial reach and prosper as a trading gateway to the East.[14]

With the completion of the transcontinental railroad in 1869, the Chinese laborers who built the system looked for other professions, and white workers resented the labor competition. In 1870, Bret Harte published his infamous poem, "The Heathen Chinee," about a devious Chinese card player who stuffed twenty-one jacks up his sleeve. By the 1890s, scientific racialism had made the devious little man from the East—devoid of character and willing to undermine free conditions in the labor force—a fixture in the white imagination. Samuel Gompers explained it simply in his 1902 pamphlet, *Meat vs. Rice: American Manhood Against Asiatic Cooliesm, Which Shall Survive?* He warned against the "swarms" of the lower race overtaking the land.[15] A useful curiosity had become a threatening swarm that "true Americans" had to exclude from the common polity.

I resolve this difficulty of changing racial definitions by dividing the chapters temporally and dividing the American nineteenth century into two parts: the antebellum and the postbellum. Part One, Public Virtue, examines how writers of color battled the racialized role the republic assigned to them simply because of skin color. The country had used whiteness to build a narrative of itself around republicanism, which placed its faith in an educated group who could gather to debate the day's key decisions. These decision makers supposedly had expressive and reasoning powers that allowed them to elevate the collective interest above their own, and writers of color found themselves excluded. For example, when stories about blacks showed them as brutes—people, according to the time, who did not have the ability to reason—how would a free black find political rights? I investigate the answer to this question by looking at free blacks' writing *about* language and texts as cultural artifacts or demonstrations of cultural capital. Similarly, how would Native Americans find political rights when all the stories about them argued that whites had to clear the land of noble savages who had no capacity for "civilization"? William Apess responded by retelling a popular story from the 1830s about the chief Metacomet, or "King Philip," in the King Philip's War of 1676. I inspect how Apess assembled his story of Philip by playing on popular renditions of the war, Native Americans, and the father of the country, George Washington.

Part Two of this book, The Virtue Within, examines the postbellum years, when talk of republicanism had dissipated, a new mass production reshaped society, and the culture reasserted a high and low division. "Virtue" in political terms (that is, the willingness to sacrifice one's own interest for the good of all, and the wisdom to know the difference), shifted subtly over time to a question of virtue solely in aesthetic terms: refined sensibility served as the sign of this wisdom. In these aesthetic terms, the discussion of whiteness and republicanism fused with racial ideology. Now scientific racism placed racial and ethnic groups—all "racial aliens" to the white men creating the definitions—in different levels of development. Here, blacks still belonged to a class of supposedly free laborers, and black women lived in an even more recessed world of easy virtue. Chinese in America, without legal standing because of the Exclusion Act and similar legislation, lived in communities walled off from all except gawking tourists. In the public mind they lived as quiet and dangerous shadow-dwellers.

The challenge for African American and Chinese American writers was to demonstrate their capacities as full participants in society. In late nineteenth-century America, this meant displaying an aesthetic competence. This competence does not refer to the Aesthetic Movement, when artists working after the Industrial Revolution rekindled their interest in decorative arts. Rather, I use the term aesthetic competence to signal the reigning popular sense of refined taste. How do racial aliens prove their refined sensibility, which might make them good leaders? One way, I argue, is to deploy elevated language or to emphasize abilities that popular lore denies them but links them to the powerful. I examine how Anna Julia Cooper, a black writer in the late nineteenth century, used the refined rules of classical rhetoric, and how Edith Eaton, a late nineteenth-century writer who assumes a Chinese identity, employed the persona of a sensitive neurasthenic to rewrite the rules of citizenship and make a place for herself in the national discourse.

The aesthetic competence of the late nineteenth century and the white republicanism in antebellum America share a common thread. Both rely on a demonstration of cultural competence as a barometer of inherent abilities. Anyone keen on strutting his republican prowess was sure to demonstrate the key definition of virtue—the ability to put the interests of the collective above one's own narrow concerns. A republican man of learning like Benjamin Franklin, for example, did not boast of a private library. The truly republican and virtuous man founded a public library where his books circulated among the many and everyone gained from the sharing. By the late nineteenth century, republican rhetoric no longer suited the more complex politics of the moment. Now, anyone who sought to join the public sphere, where one made laws and shaped public opinion, needed to show an appreciation of aesthetic norms, grounded in a bourgeois ideology that esteemed "highbrow" art. The higher sensibility itself—whether a political belief or the love of arts like symphonic music and belles lettres—signified that its possessors had the qualities of mind and spirit necessary for governing.[16]

Pierre Bourdieu uses the term "cultural capital" to describe how a social class forges a relationship between symbolic goods and one's position in society. "Cultural capital" gives us a way to link two symbolic goods in the United States: early nineteenth-century republican sensibilities and Bascom's late nineteenth-century aesthetic sense of high culture. Cultural capital is the set of skills that allows someone either to produce a work of art or to unpack artistic or aesthetic codes. Late nineteenth-century rules of rhetoric and aesthetics, of course, fit under this rubric. But the early nineteenth-century concept of republicanism fits here, too. Republicanism, as Gordon S. Wood has shown, was a sensibility that led individuals to act in the best interests of society. To act as a true republican, a man (and it was generally defined as a man in the public sphere), needed to achieve a certain amount of cultivation and refinement. This did not necessarily translate into formal years of schooling, but it meant possessing some inner quality or sense and the ability to express that sensibility with language.

How to get this cultural capital? Bourdieu argues that in the twentieth century the state allocates elite cultural capital through the educational system. The higher one's class position, the more easily a person can get both.[17] In the United States today, this class distinction gets translated into institutional differences. John Guillory argues that "institutional facts"—limits on access to such cultural production tools as education—have kept certain marginalized groups from acquiring elite cultural capital at the same rate as mainstream society.[18] But of course the late nineteenth-century ability to present oneself as able to appreciate beauty or work in the higher art forms all required a training or manifestation of these skills that society often denied racial aliens. Anyone familiar with nineteenth-century educational restrictions placed on blacks, Native Americans, and Chinese Americans recognizes this assertion.

Similarly, Ronald Takaki has shown how the American public ascribed traits of republicanism only to whites. The nation's founders saw republicanism as a state of being in which the mind is valued over the body. Whites identified with rationality. And they identified blacks and Native Americans as the opposite—brutes or cunning animals who could never possess the necessary virtue. The ur-republican Franklin, who considered himself a friend of the Indian, believed they lived lives notable for their "freedom from care and labour" and resisted "every attempt to civilize" them.[19] Lewis Cass, secretary of war under Andrew Jackson, argued that two centuries of contact with whites did nothing for American Indians. "As civilization shed her light upon them, why were they blind to its beams?" he asked. "Nothing but a dreary waste meets the eye."[20] Arthur Lee of Virginia reached back to Aristotle for his authority on blacks and virtue. According to Lee, the Greek philosopher declared that slaves lacked virtue, but none "were so utterly devoid of any semblance of virtue as are the Africans."[21]

So how do antebellum free blacks, characterized as brutes, or Native Americans, known as indistinct from hunted animals, show the qualities, the cultural capital, that allows them to lead others? To move the level of abstraction up one notch, how might racial aliens subvert the fusion of racial ideology and class in the making of culture that oppresses them? How can writers and orators who are stigmatized as belonging to "lower" racial or ethnic stock use the assets of cultural capital to make their point? What kind of point does the very appearance and wielding of this capital make in someone tagged a racial alien? How does it call into question class positions? Racial hierarchy? Gender roles? Citizenship?

Each part of this book groups a story of an African American with another person considered to be a racial alien. Because African Americans served as the foundation of the economy and because they played a crucial role in shaping Americans' understanding of whiteness and race in general, their history acts as a touchstone for comparison. With an understanding of how whiteness positioned blacks in society—and how blacks fought it—we can then move to investigating Native American rights in the antebellum world and Chinese rights at the end of the nineteenth century. The individuals at the center of these studies—the black press editors, William Apess, Anna Julia Cooper, and Edith Eaton—all use techniques in their storytelling and their identity-construction that allow readers to profitably inspect their efforts to overcome the gap between the country's stated ideas and the realities of race.

It seems to me that minority authors and orators use three important strategies when they "rewrite white" to subvert the racial ideology of whiteness. All involved the use of cultural capital to play on class markers in society. As the following case studies suggest, one strategy is to use "white" language to write about nonwhite experience; I call this the "supplanter tactic." Another, which I call "revisionist narration," is to use narration to revise the fundamental social myths on which the white nation builds itself. And the third engages white aesthetics and philosophers like Bascom directly by rewriting, again in "white" language, the society's definitions of race and gender and thereby refuting the notion of white aesthetics. I call this strategy "social theory."

In each of the four case studies that follow, the writers and orators adapt one or more of these strategies to step out of their race- and class-bound positions, and they redraft fundamental notions of what is American. Editors of the antebellum black press use a supplanter's prose to rewrite a whole class of people. They separate blackness from the idea of dim slave labor, which deserves few legal rights, and deploy a language that the mainstream middle class used to demonstrate its place in society. They thereby remade themselves from "brutes" into able candidates ready to engage in public discussion. William Apess, the antebellum Pequot essayist, used revisionist narration to change the idea of America itself by changing the nation's creation myth. He forces the audience to peer *inside* a Native American, to understand how he held the seeds of republicanism and forged the national narrative, and, hence, to appreciate what makes Native Americans good for the country. The late nineteenth-century essayist Anna Julia Cooper confronts aesthetic competence and Bascom head on, revamping social theory by using the professor's book of rhetoric to rewrite society's fundamental definitions of race and gender on the level of language. Edith Maude Eaton wrote under the pen name Sui Sin Far and in the style of a supplanter. But unlike the black press editors or William Apess, she does not pose as a republican model. Rather, she poses as a Chinese neurasthenic, an insider with both vision and sensibility that marked elite cultural capital. She then rewrites the everyday lives of Chinese Americans in ethnographies that reveal the beauty and dignity of a loathed people. Marginalized status unites stories in which ethnicity, race, and gender change. Racial formation, class, and citizenship collide, and the energy thrown off by this collision shows how marginalized writers made and remade race, how they played on class markers to write and rewrite white, and how, in the end, their verbal performances recast their roles in society.

PART I

Antebellum Revisions—Public Virtue

CHAPTER 1

Speaking to the Whiteness of the Brain

Of all the escapes from slavery, Henry Box Brown's wins extra credit for creativity: he mailed himself as dry goods from Richmond, Virginia, to Philadelphia, Pennsylvania. Like many other escaped slaves, Brown wrote a narrative about his path from chattel to free man. He ended the written narrative of his express shipping with a song he performed on a traveling tour, and his tune reveled in his passage: his descent into the box, the rolling of the rail car, and the chugging of the steamboat. Then the chorus exulted,

> Brown laid down the shovel and the hoe,
> Down in the box he did go;
> No more Slave work for Henry Box Brown,
> In the box by Express he did go.[1]

This may seem like a rather straightforward commemoration, but, surprisingly, Brown thought it necessary to explain his chorus's reference to the "shovel and the hoe." Brown says he refers to a slaveholder's version of Genesis in which God created not two people in Eden but four, two white and two black. In this southern Eden, it may come as no surprise that blacks attended whites. But in paradise, no one needs servants, for what is paradise if one's heart's desire is not delivered in just the instant that the heart desires it? To see black attendants with nothing to do drove whites crazy. They prayed that God would find the blacks "something," and they turned their gaze upward, Brown recounts. The sky opened and dumped two bags, one big and one small, onto the ground. Everyone ran to the drop, and the black man arrived there first. He seized the large bag, and the white man took the smaller one. "Lo! in the large one, there was a shovel and a hoe, and in the small one, a pen, ink, and paper," recounted Brown.

"Ever since the colored race have had to labor with the shovel and the hoe, while the *rich man* works with the pen and ink!"[2]

This last line of Brown's explanation is most interesting. In it, literacy's import in a slave's life becomes clear, and the racial division of labor emerges. But even more telling, as Brown marks the movement from manual to mental work, he does not say the "colored race" and the "white race"; rather, he says the "colored race" and the "*rich man*." Brown conflates race and class: the "rich man" becomes a synonym for white.[3]

Brown's "rich man" in place of "whites" reflects the antebellum American reality that workers, concerned about losing their class position, embraced a growing ideology of whiteness. I argue that black antebellum writers understood this conflation of whiteness and class in society, and they tried to defeat it. The story of their efforts and their ultimate failure traverses two odd provinces—the new style of popular rhetoric that swept the country between 1830 and 1850, and the cranial-mapping "science" of phrenology. Black writers had to decide how they would sound amid a class-inflected debate about language. They carved out a special version of the new "middling style," endorsed by the rising middle classes, and, like the middle classes, they tried to turn this language skill into cultural capital. This strategy helped black writers challenge a growing scientific racism, including phrenology, which "scientifically" placed blacks at the lower levels of humankind and made whites the standard by which all should be measured. The black writers' strategy eventually backfired; the racial ideology of whiteness captured the language debate and relabeled the class-based capital that blacks sought to employ as "white capital" or the "saxon tongue." But their resistance through the kind of language they deployed illuminates for us the relationships among antebellum race, class, and literature.

One way of seeing how language as cultural capital became a tool for antebellum blacks to pry rights from the nation is to examine the antebellum black newspapers. In the archives of the New York City papers, *Freedom's Journal* and *The Colored American,* and in Frederick Douglass's papers, *The North Star* and his eponymous Rochester journal, in the African Methodist Church's *Christian Recorder*, and in the Washington, D.C., *National Era,* we get a composite journal of the black abolitionist community's debates from the first paper's inception in 1827 to the Civil War. Of course, the editors talked about abolition, but they also tackled the day's key issues, such as citizens' obligations and rights in a republic, the required habits of civility, and the change in another key cultural barometer, language. That discussion of language swirled around two questions: Who should use certain types of language? And in what circumstances should they use them?

For antebellum blacks, language operated as a cultural code that represented one's place in society. Cracking that code yielded a more nuanced understanding of what, on the surface, today looks like a story emanating from a hegemonized middle class. These editors vested ultimate power in language as a tool in antebellum society. ("The black man's rights," observed one writer, were "swept away—as [was] the public thought—by the sweep of a pen or the utterance of a sentence.") This cultural code illustrates how the tool of language created power, and any understanding of Henry Box Brown's and other African Americans' literacy tropes expands. Language does not serve merely as a conveyor belt from slavery to freedom. "Freedom" amounted to a complex state for free blacks who confronted local laws restricting voting, a Fugitive Slave Law that made every black vulnerable to slave catchers, and a Dred Scott decision that wiped blacks off the American citizenship map. Language works outside the reading room: as a class marker in the antebellum world and as a means to reshape freedom in America. Watching popular culture, class, and race collide complicates the split between high and low culture developing in these years.[4] This analysis also reminds us that the black editors' retelling of the past does not reflect an obsession with myths and origins, but rather it reworks those origins and recasts history as an act of resistance.[5]

Race drove these editors into adopting a literary style that they believed would help them both to be persuasive and to generate the cultural capital necessary to elevate them in society—to give them rights in a republican social order; this picture offers insight into class and culture. William Charvat long ago established that early America considered oratory and language bulwarks of society. Rhetorical rule makers believed they served as societal watchdogs, who ensured good morals, strong character, and a broadly republican sensibility. Since Charvat others have examined how the performance of public oratory placed orators in the republican mold. This examination demonstrates how the performing of linguistic competence defied contemporary racial ideology and sought to make a place for marginalized orators and writers in the republic. Yet the strategy, in the end, did not work. When the editors deployed this cultural capital to combat racism, they fell into a class-based trap. The language originally designed to police class barriers in a white community, subsequently, employed race to justify those barriers. Two very different worlds appear in these writings: the world of opportunity that blacks hoped to create, and the world of racial hierarchy that most whites hoped to enforce.[6]

The racialized world figures in the reception of those who sought to express themselves with language that addressed the higher social registers. The British comedian Charles Mathews on a tour of the United States claimed that one of the premier thespians of the black community (and later all of Europe), the African-American Ira Aldridge, could not stick to his lines in *Hamlet.* Mathews reported that when the actor as Hamlet hit the line "and by opposing end them," "the similarity of the sound of the words reminded the black audience of the Negro melody of 'Opossum up a gum tree.'" Mathews claimed that Aldridge responded, "Well den, ladies and gemmen, you like Opossum up a gum tree better den you like Hamlet? Me sing him to you." In the carefully "correct" language of his memoir, Aldridge denies that the incident ever happened. "I need not say that the whole of the ludicrous scene," he said, "never occurred at all."[7]

Matthews could not believe either that blacks could do justice to *Hamlet* or that a black audience enjoyed *Hamlet* for its own sake. This suggests, counter to some arguments, that people did distinguish between high and low culture in antebellum America—at least when applied to black participants. Aldridge said that whites considered Shakespeare too elevated an indulgence for blacks, one that "licked nature slick outright." In other words, culture producers looked to language "as a mirror of the intelligent mind"; however, some of these same producers, as an audience, refused to believe that blacks could use the words of the bard properly or even distinguish between the artistic integrity of a pensive, brooding man and a large nocturnal rodent.[8]

To understand the reception of these black writers and orators we should understand the mindset or expectations that a white audience had of blacks and of free blacks' ability to deploy language. What did a white audience expect to come out of an African American's mouth? What framework did audience members use to understand what the person is saying and to understand its import? Could a writer or speaker outwit that mental frame? I follow David Damrosch's suggestion that we examine the metaphors of those involved to understand how they seek to assimilate the other and frame "ethnographically informed difference." This does not mean that this "ethnographically informed difference" is considered "well-done" or "accurate" ethnography. In this case, writings about scientific racialism and, more specifically, phrenology show a ridiculous, if popular, "frame." The glaring lapses in phrenological observations paint the racial ideology of the culture. Placing this ideology next to the work of the new language-style practitioners presents a closer look at the audience's expectations.[9]

A culture's racial ideology emerges in an examination of how people even as "enlightened" as antebellum reformers believed that mind and body fit together. Stephen Jay Gould shows how the growth of scientific racism in the early nineteenth century again and again "scientifically proved" that blacks were inferior beings, should serve only as stoop labor, and certainly could not rank as orators who could guide the republic. The majority of the American population seized on this "science" to limit black opportunity. Free blacks were hardly "free" in the common sense. They were free of slavery's chains, but northern society denied them rights accorded to everyone else. The *New York Enquirer* argued that free blacks could not be worthy citizens. States and cities introduced laws restricting free blacks' freedoms; for example, Cincinnati demanded a $500 bond from any black who wanted to live within city limits. The rise of the American Colonization Society threatened to send all African Americans out of the country. An Ohio commission later conceded that the state enacted "the most odious and oppressive laws, to degrade and depress."[10]

The early black press editors were keenly aware of their stunted freedoms and the ways pseudoscience affected their reception in society. *Colored American* contributor David Walker complained that whites "held us up as descending originally from the tribes of *Monkeys* or *Orang-Outangs*? O! my God! I appeal to every man of feeling—is not this insupportable?" The editors complained of jobs that allowed them only to be "hewers of wood and drawers of water," of schools that were closed off to them, and of a society that offered them only a place of "inferior subserviency."[11] Today we are interested in how this emerging scientific racism affected the *expectations* of anyone listening to or reading an African American's work. For instance, a writer and orator for *The Provincial Freeman* complained bitterly about the reception he received from a local newspaper. The *Norristown Republican* review said the black orator "appears to be an educated man and a fine speaker." But he quickly added that his style was "too sentimental and denunciatory" and "a little too harsh to be in good taste." The enraged speaker asked in the *Provincial Freeman* how one might be "too denunciatory" after the Dred Scott decision and after the Fugitive Slave Law "that converted the nation into one grand slave ground and men into blood hounds."[12] William Wells Brown saw how audiences could tune out a black speaker. He described the eloquent oratory of William Still, the abolitionist, in almost resigned terms. "When the head was averted, we heard, in well-modulated speech, such vigorous sentences and thoughtful remarks, that the identity of the speaker with the proscribed race was half forgotten; but," said Brown, "the biased eyesight revealed only a dusky son of Ham."[13]

Examining prejudiced expectations helps us understand the interplay of audience, speaker, and rights as the Republic felt the challenge of widening demographics. At the end of his study of the polite culture shaped in eighteenth-century America, David S. Shields notes that during the nineteenth century, the country's population became much more racially and ethnically heterogeneous, with more and more people who did not have a "recognizable place" in the conversation room of the national imagination. Shields asks, "Would the symbolic language of American civility be sufficiently flexible to incorporate them?"[14] The free black community's debates about civic language reveal their efforts to enter this room, participate in this symbolic language, and feel incorporated into the country.

The rules of language in antebellum years that detailed who may speak and the styles concerning how to speak changed at a speed that left much of the public reeling. In *Democratic Eloquence,* Kenneth Cmiel tells the story of how popular rhetoric changed between the eighteenth and nineteenth centuries and how Jacksonian democracy accelerated that change. Revolutionary Americans adopted a neoclassical rhetorical tradition that relied on refined language, not vulgar words, and the "literary arts," not common references. Cmiel argues that the growth of mass democracy in the early nineteenth century ushered in a new form of rhetoric that violated these neoclassical principles. Moreover, the move to mass democracy in the 1830s made many more people potential orators and sparked increased interaction between audience and speaker. This change, like the period's expansion of the middle class and the broadening of voting rights, threatened the elite who no longer held a lock on the privilege of speaker.

A new informality and bluntness undermined decorum and the authority of those elites. A writer dedicated to upholding standards railed at those adopting the new language: "In supposing their forefathers to have been egregious numskulls—these writers pounce upon the new mare's nest with greedy gusto, and bolt the eggs whole," he complained. "We are vexed with successive swarms of absurd neologisms" like a "plague of frogs." Why such concern? "The preservation of [a nation's] language in purity and vigor should be an object of religious and unremitting care," he said. When Andrew Jackson vetoed the charter for the Second Bank of the United States, for example, the president-of-the-people used this bluntness to rail against "aristocrats" and used a slang term—"Hydra of Corruption." One unapologetic aristocrat, Philip Hone, was offended. He complained by crafting an analogy that paired "mere" kitchen help with a gentleman gifted with cultural capital: "The language . . . is disgraceful to the President and humiliating to Every American. It smells of the kitchen, and resembles no more than that in which the foreign relations of the country are laid before the people than a scullion does a gentleman."[15]

Particularly frightening to Hone and others like him was the "low" rhetoric, embraced by the "common man," which found a wide public forum. This language employed colloquialisms and often dialect to express a folksy "truth" of the people. Perhaps the most famous exemplar is Davy Crockett, one-time congressman and humorist, who challenged Congress on the state of the nation's finances and the integrity of politicians. An extended quote from Crockett who spoke before Congress sets the register for "low" speech and illustrates how a group of people politically challenged their "betters." Crockett complained that Congress had

> riz the boiler o' my indignation clar up to the high pressure pinte, an' therefore I have riz to let off the steam of my hull hog patriotism, without round-about-ation, and without the trimmins. The truth wants no trimmins for in her clar naked state o' natur she's as graceful as a suckin colt i' the sunshine. Mr. Speaker! What in the name o' kill-sheep-dog rascality is the country a-comin' to? Whar's all the honor? no whar! an thar it'll stick! . . . What in the nation have you done this year? . . . You've spouted out a Mount Etny o' gas, chawed a hull Allegheny o' tobacco, spit a Niagary o' juice, told a hail storm o' lies, drunk a Lake Superior o' liquor, and all, as you say, for the good o' the nation; but I say, I swar, for her etarnal bankruptification!
>
> Tharfore, I move that the ony way to save the country is for the hull nest o' your political weasels to cut stick home instanterly, and leave me to work Uncle Sam's farm, till I restore it to its natural state o' cultivation, and shake off these state caterpillars o' corruption.[16]

How could a "fine gentleman," like Hone or a Washington senator, respond to that onslaught, keep his job, and yet remain a gentleman?

The rising middle class worried that bounders might challenge their place, too. Karen Halttunen has shown that this middle class looked to cultural forms as signposts that told them who truly belonged, and who did not. Families staged increasingly grand mourning ceremonies, and women began to pile hair on their heads in ways that might make the casual phrenologist believe that they had very attractive bumps. As Cmiel has charted, one of these cultural forms was language. This made sense to mid-nineteenth-century Americans, for, as a premier expert in philology said of language, "there is no better key to the habits and temper of a people."[17] Cmiel argues that a "new rhetoric," higher than Crockett and lower than Hone, gave the middle class access that the elite might deny them. But, at the same time, this rhetoric erected barriers designed to thwart any pretenders who wanted to seize a middle-class place. One language maven lamented the masses' effect on both politics and language standards. "Whilst the speech of the mobile vulgus in the great Republic changes almost from year to year," he said, "the extension of the right of suffrage to the very lowest and most ignorant classes have, moreover, favored the admission of so many vulgar and cant terms, that in politics, above all, the line between slang and solemn speech is not always perceptible."[18]

This new "middling" rhetoric carried a few defining characteristics that confused those policing the borders between middling and elite. Practitioners of middling rhetoric, such as Henry Ward Beecher, aimed to establish a rapport with the audience, employed a calculated bluntness, and bandied about inflated speech to increase their own senses of importance. Horace Greeley, whose directness as editor of the *New York Tribune* brought him many libel suits, called elite newspapers "mealy-mouthed" and illustrated the middling style's bluntness with this opening line: "Major Noah! Why *won't* you tell the truth once in a century, for the variety of the thing." Cmiel identifies several types of inflated speech. One used sound instead of meaning to rouse its audience. Another relied heavily on euphemism. To these writers and speakers, "*Limb* replaced *leg*," Cmiel said. "The word *corset* was deemed an insult. Servant girls were no longer *seduced*; they were now *betrayed*. The word *cock* became an anatomical vulgarism. After more than two centuries of use, the word *haycock* was replaced with *haystack*." The combination of bluntness and euphemism made heads spin. James Fenimore Cooper complained, "There has been so singular a compound of intelligence, kindness, natural politeness, coarseness and even vulgarity, in many of these persons, that I am often utterly baffled in the attempt to give them a place in the social scale."[19]

For Cooper and others, then, language was a kind of symbolic cultural code that signaled to others one's class position. Pierre Bourdieu's work to define a "linguistic habitus" can focus our analysis on how language, class, and race all combine in this code. Bourdieu argues that "linguistic habitus," that is, the unconscious habits that govern our daily speech, are difficult for cultural analysts to spot, but, once spotted, speak volumes. "The ways of looking, sitting, standing, keeping silent, or even of speaking," says Bourdieu, "are full of injunctions that are powerful and hard to resist precisely because they are silent and insidious, insistent and insinuating."[20] This "linguistic habitus," as we have seen with the "elite" language of Philip Hone, the "low" language of Davy Crockett, and the "middling" approach of Horace Greeley—is a form of cultural capital and registers the speaker's position in the cultural hierarchy. Phillip Hone felt pique at what he considered the invasion of the low. Cooper was upset that the old rules that allowed him to know exactly who was who were changing.

Nothing could be sweeter to free blacks than the news that, instead of birthright, the possession of a cultural code such as a speaking style could determine one's place in society. If one's manner of speaking illustrated the inner person, then perhaps it could get white society beyond skin color to examine the genuine attributes of blacks. Linguistic capital potentially offered the free black a path to expanded freedoms. One man's trip from slavery to freedom presented some hope that the possession of cultural capital could change one's status. In 1828, Abd al-Rahman Ibrahima, an African who had been enslaved for thirty years, was then set free when, by chance, he was discovered to be an African prince who could recite long passages from the Koran in Arabic. The ensuing debate over al-Rahman, no doubt partially fueled by the idea that he was a "prince," involved whether someone with so much linguistic capital could really be from such low "racial stock," a stock that deserved few, if any, rights.[21]

Early black newspaper editors clearly understood that the command of language, a command that far exceeds literacy, served as a mark of power. The writers in the black press continually called for education in writing and oratory as entrée to a higher station in the nation. The manual labor schools proved especially interesting to the free black community because those schools united mind and body by combining book work with physical work. This gave the free black newspaper writers the chance to create a united mind and body that did not inevitably reduce them to the slag heap of humanity. "Labor has received the anointing of the highest refinement," wrote one writer in *The Colored American,* "and healthy frames are proven to be the best accompaniment to high intellectual power."[22] "Enlightened" people understood that dark skin and strong biceps did not signify an inability to think. Like Henry Box Brown, William Whipper, encouraging the black community to work with pen and ink, instructed us along the way on the relation between education, literature, and cultural capital. "The station of a scholar highly versed in classic lore," Whipper said, "is indeed higher than any other occupied by man. . . . Every duty that is characteristic in the history of civilized man, should shine conspicuously in them."[23] The ideal man integrated the high points of civilization and made them part of his character. The importance of this cultural capital drove one writer in *Freedom's Journal* to demand that free blacks have a chance at an education. If blacks still cannot excel, said the writer, "then shall we be convinced that really we are of a different species . . . and that the Creator has, in his providence, designed for us 'hewers of wood' and 'drawers of water,' and 'beasts of burden,' for our fairer brethren."

Language often received special mention when an article extolled the virtues of a free black. William Wells Brown proudly reprinted a newspaper review in his short autobiographical sketch that said, "By dint of resolution, self-culture, and force of character, he has rendered himself a popular lecturer."

Brown boasted of a Scottish paper's assertion that he "lose[s] nothing by a comparison with the best educated and most highly cultivated of the Anglo-Saxons." A review of Brown's profiles in *The Black Man, His Antecedents, His Genius, and His Achievements* of model people of African extraction hammered home the importance of language and eloquence. He profiled established writers like Frederick Douglass, Alexandre Dumas, and Alexander Crummel. But he confirmed language's importance when he made verbal command a key feature in nearly all fifty-three people he profiled. Benjamin Banneker mastered Latin, Greek, and German, Henry Bibb evinced "eloquence," Henry Highland Garnett ranked among "first-class orators" with "complete command" of voice, and blacks as a group at one time stood at the "head" of literature. Everywhere he looked, Brown found "ardent lover[s] of literature" (Jeremiah B. Sanderson), "profound and original opinions" (Toussaint l'Ouverture), and "vigorous" writers (John Mercer Langston). In fact, Brown turned the tables on societal expectations. He asserted that some of his white neighbors did not possess the cultural capital necessary to hold his interest. "They are not very intellectual," he said. "They don't associate with my family; but whenever they shall improve themselves, and bring themselves up by their own intellectual and moral worth, I shall not object to their coming into my society." The ability to deploy Bourdieu-like "linguistic capital" and to use it to rise through society was clearly important to the black community.[24]

The black newspapers set out with gusto to discuss what *kind* of language African Americans should use. The reporters produced nearly one hundred columns on the importance of studying grammar and just how to do so. One writer called grammar the "fountain from which all [professions] flow." Another column called on a local school to modernize its pedagogy of grammar and adopt the "reformed and approved methods" for teaching current thinking. And in *The North Star*, Martin R. Delany even recommended a specific grammar text to use.[25]

Black writers' consciousness about language gives us today a grasp on how class and race converge. Free blacks, like the middle class, embraced the emerging middling style to gain a place on the public dais, but they made some changes, too. If Cmiel argues that middling stylists emphasized a connection with the audience, wildly inflated language, and earthy words, then the writers in the black press adopted two out of three. They valued any speaker who connected with the audience, and they often used inflated language. However, they left the most earthy language, the "boiler o' indignation" and "kill-sheep-dog rascality," to Davy Crockett. Instead, they stuck to words that stirred the "inner soul" of the listener.

The newspapers took enormous pleasure in broadcasting blacks' oratorical power and ability to connect with their audiences and the minds of America. One man recorded in his diary his response to listening to Samuel R. Ward, and he marvels at the newspaper writer and minister's ability to reel in his audience. "As he advances and launches out upon the subject," wrote the man, "he becomes more and more animated, and soon fastens the attention of all upon what he is about to say. And 'ere he finishes, the audience are in a great measure captivated by his appeals." In fact, Ward's success at capturing his audience brought him comparisons with one model of nineteenth-century America and led him to advertise himself as "the black Daniel Webster."[26]

One man claimed that Douglass's oratory connected with him so profoundly that the speech became the turning point of his life. "The crowds of people who were shouting themselves hoarse in their enthusiasm [for Douglass], fired me with the desire to become a public speaker," he said. "From that time I began to seek higher things in life. The spirit of manhood which lay slumbering in my breast began to awaken."[27]

William Wells Brown used inflated language—and a sentence that moves like a spring freshet—to drive home Frederick Douglass's oratorical power: "Few persons can handle a subject, with which they are familiar, better than he. There is a kind of eloquence issuing from the depth of the soul as from a spring, rolling along its copious floods, sweeping all before it, overwhelming by its very force, carrying, upsetting, ingulfing its adversaries, and more dazzling and more thundering than the bolt which leaps from crag to crag. This is the eloquence of Frederick Douglass."

In addition to highlighting "good" rhetoric—connecting with the audience and occasionally inflating language—black newspaper writers made themselves clear about what they did not want. Speakers who violated those rules were branded as people who associated with the lowest in society. They would never enter the pantheon of Daniel Webster, Edward Everett, and other great orators. High on the list was slang, and the newspapers attacked it mercilessly as bad behavior. It signified talk without meaning when one writer condemned "the empty slang of many of the literati" whose "boasting about 'truth, liberty, and progress'" amounted to "unmeaning twaddle."[28] It meant "vulgar caricature" for one writer in the *National Era* who decried the "doggerel slang" of the black-faced Christy minstrels. It stood for an ad hominem argument when Samuel Ward, debating the benefits of funding a children's home, aimed and launched the term "disgraceful slang" at the *Provincial Freeman*.[29] And it signified an orator who left his audience flat—or worse—in an article that complained about a man's lame statement in his "usual slang style," which called forth only "cowardice" from the crowd.[30]

The black press continually challenged readers to avoid slang and to enter the upper reaches of oratory. In *The North Star,* Frederick Douglass, who knew better than anyone how to connect to a crowd, argued that readers appreciated the high and are not called to low. Douglass surprisingly chose to reprint an article from another newspaper even though it lauds the proslavery legislator Henry Clay. But the point here for the abolitionist paper was not about slavery. Rather, it was about language:

> It is a great mistake to suppose that the people, even the most unculti-

> vated and ignorant, are fond of coarseness, vulgarity, or any expression of bad taste, in a public speaker. They demand strength, vivacity, wit, feeling; but they like it all the better when presented in a beautiful form; and when left to their choice, prefer the graceful drapery of a masterly artist, to the grotesque costume of a Harlequin. The slang of DAVID CROCKETT is listened to with curiosity by all classes, for any manifestation of life, originality, native power, is interesting; but after all, it is the polished eloquence of HENRY CLAY that commands the most permanent influence, and, in the long run, the most universal admiration.

Low rhetoric like Crockett's lacked the power to move people, the article claimed, or to connect the speaker with audience. This article eventually took an antislavery turn, with the Clay passage serving as the drum roll before a cymbal crash of applause for reformer Wendell Phillips's linguistic capital and oratory. "His classical taste, his thorough education, his courtly manners, his fine, spontaneous eloquence, is found among the ranks who are contending for universal freedom," claimed the piece. "Even those who are most at war with his principles could not withhold their testimony from the charms of his eloquence." The writer claimed that eloquence had power even when the audience was hostile to what the speaker was saying. In other words, the possession of linguistic capital itself made the speaker compelling. This was a good lesson, and good news, for antebellum blacks.[31]

Reading Bumps on the Head

But the middling rhetoric arose at the same time that other reforms swept the country, and these changes were not so kind to blacks. The middling rhetoric style arose from movements that also sought to unite the mind, the generator of language, and the body. Helen Horowitz's *Rereading Sex* illustrates how a new reform mentality embraced a "new science" that promised adherents prescriptions for living. These reformers dispensed with the ideas of "humors," or mysterious bodily fluids, and adopted the concept of "nerves," a tangible biological link between mind and body. Phrenology served as another means of imagining this link. Phrenology gave antebellum readers the way to reenvision society's hierarchy, to unite mind and body. Most important, phrenology gave the antebellum middle class a method of using physical characteristics to identify mental qualities. However, its racist foundations and applications carried disastrous effects for free blacks seeking a fair hearing. Phrenology helps us to understand the reception accorded blacks who employed the middling style.

Phrenology promised a "science" that predicted mental and personality characteristics based on head shape. In book after book on how to apply phrenology to your life, the leaders of the American version of the science, Orson Fowler and his brother, Lorenzo, identified thirty-seven different areas of the brain, each responsible for part of the character. "The general characteristics of the body and those of the mind harmonize with each other," claimed Orson Fowler. "Prominence of features, indicates strongly marked points of character; . . . beauty and proportion of body, indicate a well-balance character and fine feelings."[32]

Reformers with "the key insight" into the human abounded in antebellum America, so what gave phrenology its popular charge? This pseudoscience offered the opportunity to understand an area hitherto out of reach of thinkers and doctors. Scientists could see well enough that the heart was a large muscle that pumped blood and that the lungs acted like porous balloons to take in oxygen and disperse it through the body. But the brain lay behind a bone-hard skull and betrayed no physical hint of its inner workings. Phrenology gave these seekers a grip on understanding the elusive mind, and people deployed it as a tool for understanding an enormous array of things, from Renaissance art (Michelangelo's Moses had no "common sense") to birds (John James Audubon seized on the "science" to explain character traits of his subjects).[33]

This theory promised even more, though, than an understanding of art and the feather-headed. It held the potential to help people in their everyday lives. The Fowlers advised devotees to continually watch the shape of the head to monitor ways that their character changed. Following orders, Nicholas Biddle, of the Philadelphia banking family, carted casts back from Europe that contained more than a few made from his own head. This fact that one's own character could change drew the attention of the Jacksonian public. If one's character could change, then blood lineage, like Biddle's, did not tell the whole story, and one might rise up in society. Phrenology, in other words, valued individuals' exertion over elites' hereditary privilege. Indeed, people went to phrenologists to divine their strengths, so that they, in turn, could go out and get the training and work to develop those strengths. Orson Fowler devoted much of his *Illustrated Self-Instructor in Phrenology and Physiology* to identifying the occupations best suited to certain head shapes and advice on how those with certain cranial features ought to guide their lives. One man visited Fowler in New York, declaring that "in twenty minutes he described my traits with a clearness and vividness that would have astonished my most intimate friends." The man refuted anyone who questioned Fowler's prowess and claimed that "today I would give a large amount of money for a verbatim record of that interview." In the 1830s, a survey in Boston, the hotbed of phrenological thought, found that more than half the physicians were "favorably disposed" to the "science."[34]

In hindsight these imagined powers of phrenology arrived with a social cost; they bolstered the emerging scientific racism, created a physical hierarchy, and contributed to complex rationalizations for why race served unerringly as a sign of inferiority. Part of the black press fought this "racial science," but others, so surrounded by phrenology in reform movements, embraced it, bending the "science" to make blacks capable of achieving equality with whites.

The Fowlers' "model" heads, phrenogically speaking, show us what they

FIGURE 1.1. The Fowlers' exemplars: George Washington and Daniel Webster. *Courtesy of the Watkinson Special Collections Library, Trinity College, Hartford, Conn.*

thought counted, establish a standard for "model citizens," and give us a baseline for evaluating their claims about blacks. In the Fowlers' estimation, two American figures stand out: Washington and Webster. Another phrenologist agreed, calling George Washington "one of those rare specimens of humanity." The Fowlers claimed that Washington's features demonstrated "all the conditions of power, activity, and susceptibility; allow neither icy coolness, nor passion's burning heat, but unite cool judgment . . . with brilliancy."[35] Washington, they said next to an accompanying illustration of the president nearly bursting the buttons of his waist coat, was a perfect model of a "well-balanced organization" (see figure 1.1).[36]

In the phrenological pantheon with Washington sat the orator, statesman, and language reformer Daniel Webster. In the Fowlers' assessments of Webster we see speechmaking as a mark of quality and phrenology as a bodily indicator of one's language skills. Next to a drawing of Webster in the Fowlers' *Illustrated Self-Instructor* came the claim that his leonine face indicated remarkable attributes. The Fowlers called Webster the "lion of the North" who "rarely pounces on his prey, but when he does, so roars that a nation quakes; demolishes his victim; and is an intellectual king among men." Now that's power. [37] One newspaper correspondent linked Webster's head shape, intellect, and language skills. "In the higher walks of eloquence there is no man here who can contest the palm with him," he said. "He is of a large and firm stature, with a head that phrenologists will endorse as the seat of a gigantic intellect. . . . In his impassioned moment, he reaches an elevation of eloquence far surpassing anything that I have ever witnessed among his fellow senators and statesmen."[38]

Another writer claimed that one could not understand Americans as the most "talking and speech-making race" without understanding phrenology. The "science" "should be studied by every one, who is anxious to attain a correct knowledge of man, as a moral, intellectual and social being." Why is this understanding so important, if we are merely talking about public speaking? The writers' reasoning illuminates the charged link between the shape of the head, the mind, and the ability to move the public. "Eloquence," the writer says, "constitutes the means by which one mind acts on another. . . . The design of public eloquence is to make the minds of an audience harmonize, in all respects, with the mind of the speaker, to make them feel with him, think with him, resolve with him, and, if necessary, act with him, and thus surrender themselves entirely to his control."[39] Clearly such an important power as eloquence needed to be kept under guard. Orson Fowler gave readers a series of phrenological metrics that policed who could enjoy the power of eloquence, and thereby he helped shape a belief in African American inferiority. He claimed to find enduring differences between the heads of Europeans and those of Africans. In Fowler's *Illustrated Self-Instructor,* he devotes a section to the head-shapes of animals. The analysis moves seamlessly in an upward march along the scale of beings, from snakes to the ape family to "Africans" to "Indians" and then on to the "idiot," where we, presumably, get our first "white." The illustrator's angle for the profile of the orang-outang skull matches exactly the profile of the African on the adjoining page, with the cranial fissure, or parietomastoid suture, on the orang-outang charting the course of the African's sideburn (see figure 1.2).[40] Fowler likened his subjects' quality of hair to their mind and soul and declared that, "Coarse hair always accompanies coarseness in the fibres of the brain, together with coarse, harsh feelings, but that a delicately organized body, indicates and accompanies delicacy of feeling, &c." He says, "in short, that there is a unity of character running through the whole person, mentally and physically." In case anyone missed his point, he called it the "great law of our being that the texture of the body corresponds with the tone and character of the mind; that a vulgar soul inhabits a vulgar body."[41]

These "laws" quickly translated into an assessment of different races' amounts of cultural capital and made black skin a marker for low language skills. Blacks could never aspire to even "middling speech." The Fowlers suggested that the African American's head shape made the race suitable only for certain occupations. Blacks' "philoprogenitiveness" made them lovers of children and hence "our best nurses"; their large "approbativeness," a trait denoting one's "love of praise," made blacks "excellent waiters," although it also made them "fond of ornament and show." The proslavery *DeBow's Review* drew on phrenologists to support its "observation" about "the brain being smaller and the nerves larger

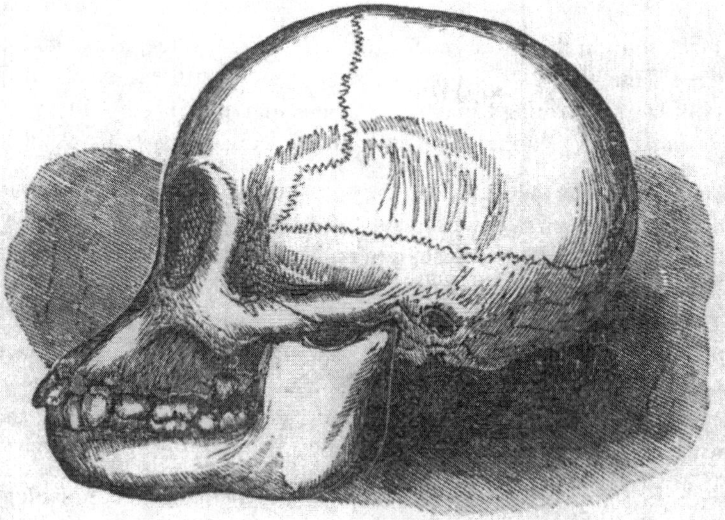

No. 37 JA[illegible], THE ORANG-OUTANG.

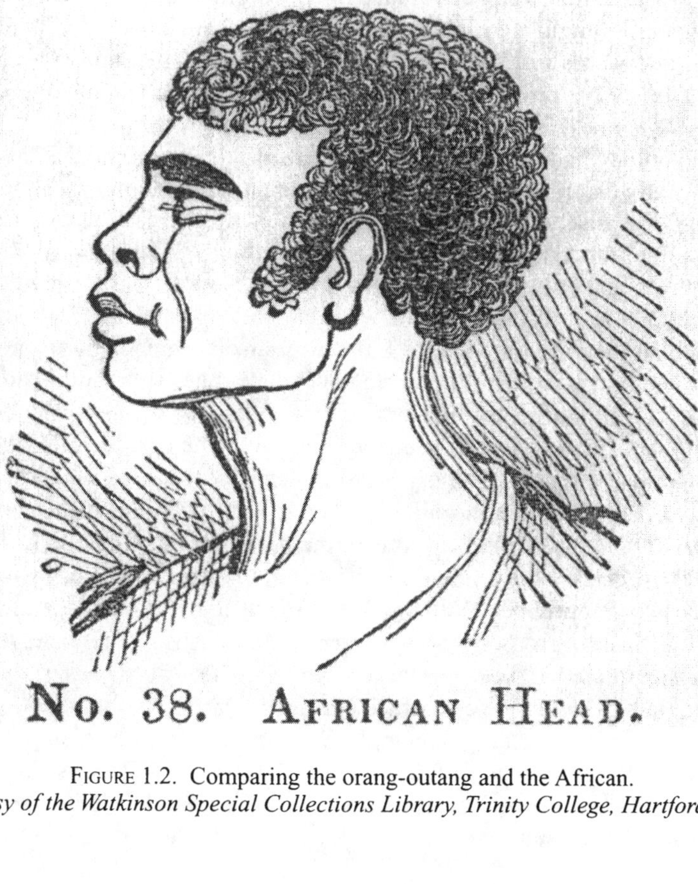

No. 38. AFRICAN HEAD.

FIGURE 1.2. Comparing the orang-outang and the African.
Courtesy of the Watkinson Special Collections Library, Trinity College, Hartford, Conn.

in the black than in the white race." Blacks had "full perceptives" and predictably "large Tune" but a "retiring Causality" that gave them excellent musical powers but "less reasoning capacity." [42] This meant they had no future as public speakers who could genuinely move the public. Fowler put it this way:

> So they talk, and talk much, but they construct their sentences in a manner differing from our own, and also employ a different class of words. In short they seem to have a cast of mind and tone of feeling, including intonations and gesticulations, differing materially from our own race. The fact is, there is an organization and a texture, both physical and phrenological, peculiar to the race, and which *characterizes* that race in all its ramifications and crosses, and which owes its cause to *parentage*, and descends from sire to son, from generation to generation, and which will last as long as the race lasts.[43]

So Fowler suddenly seemed less sanguine about whether one's phrenological attributes can change. Blacks derived their attributes from "*parentage*" and carried the attributes for ever or until the race became extinct. Furthermore, the shape of African American heads made them not only inferior in reasoning and thus deficient in linguistic capital, but it rendered them a people with different sentences and words that separated them from whites. Their addresses became merely "talk." What promised to be a tool for monitoring and making the best of oneself, becomes, for one racial group, a punishing sentence.

Phrenology had become so much a part of the reform mindset in the antebellum years that phrenological terms, despite a racist taxonomy, slipped into the public discourse, including even the writings of the black newspaper writers. Writers in the black press applauded individuals' "high forehead" or "expansive brow," and one writer even claimed a black speaker had a "massive head" that "a phrenologist would be proud to pronounce upon."[44] In *The North Star,* Martin Delany reported meeting a fourteen-year-old phrenology phenomenon in Ohio. The boy, who had little or no education, "passed his little hands over [Delany's cranial] organs, reading them with as much facility as Fowler," Delany said. Mary Ann Shadd Cary's *Provincial Freeman* seemed particularly taken with Fowler. Her paper reprinted Henry Ward Beecher's defense of phrenology, and it ran more than a dozen notices for the Fowlers' books or journals, calling his *American Phrenological Journal* "one of the best, if not the best, in the U.S."[45]

Clearly, black writers found phrenology's popular explanatory power useful for their own purposes. William Wells Brown found phrenological terms a helpful shorthand for describing leading people of African descent. Jeremiah B. Sanderson offered a "well-developed head," and the head-shapes of rival leaders of the Haitian revolution confirmed allegiances in Brown's mind. Dessalines, a despotic ruler, had a "dingy" complexion "and the lines of his features expressed the untamed ferocity of his character." Toussaint l'Ouverture, however, presented a "broad and well-developed forehead" that marked him "as one born for a leader." We do not know if these people were adherents to the "science" or merely lifted the language from those around them. Some certainly seemed to endorse phrenology.[46]

Without text in the papers explaining why the racial uses of phrenology did not bother Cary or a few others, we cannot know *why* people like Cary might give any space in their newspaper to the likes of Fowler and phrenology. But one possibility is that phrenology had become bundled into the large number of reform movements—mesmerists, Grahamites, and followers of animal magnetism—all of which offered the hope that nearly everyone can change for the better. If one willfully disregarded what Fowler said about blacks' inferiority and focused instead on his promises that people can change their condition, perhaps his treatises offered hope to blacks, too. Alternatively, it is possible that the terms of phrenology had become so embedded in the language that people who did not buy the whole "science" still used the vocabulary. After all, today we occasionally hear people describe someone as having a "strong jaw," or "weak chin," as if the description gave us some kind of insight into the inner characteristics of the person.

In 1839, a writer for the *Herald of Freedom* looked at a woodcut of Cinque, the leader of the *Amistad*, and got carried away with the similarities between the eye of one important phrenological model and the imprisoned leader of the slave revolt:

> The head has the towering front of Webster. . . . He has Webster's lion aspect—his majestic, quiet, uninterested cast of expression. His eye . . . looks like the black sea or the ocean in a calm—an unenlightened eye, as Webster's would have looked, had he been bred in the desert, among the lions, as Cinque was, and if instead of pouring upon Homer and Shakespeare, and Coke and the Bible (for Webster read the Bible when he was young, and got his regal style there) it had rested, from savage boyhood, on the sands and sky of Africa.[47]

Webster reigned as a standard, and this writer used that standard and phrenology as he tried to hitchhike a social promotion for a black man atop Webster's head. Yet curiously, the writer implicitly refutes Fowler's argument that these traits are inborn by pointing to the environment—not birth—to explain Cinque's cranial characteristics. If the environment created cranial characteristics, then everyone, maybe even blacks, had the chance to embody the magnificence of a Washington or a Webster.

More useful for understanding the white supremacy that writers and orators of color faced is to look at how these ideas of black inferiority affected cultural capital or, more specifically, the power to deploy language. If Fowler granted blacks a "large" language facility but claimed that they lacked the causal reasoning to say anything coherent or compelling, then black writers and orators were in a box. Prima facie, in Fowler's world, they had nothing to offer society. Whites thus felt justified in taking a dim view of blacks who wanted to raise their social standing. John F. Watson wrote in the *Annals of Philadelphia* that black residents were becoming a problem when they thought about societal roles any more elevated than servant or stablehand. "Their aspirings and little vanities have been rapidly growing," he complained. "Once they submitted to the appellation of servants, blacks, or negros, but now they require to be called coloured people, and among themselves, their common call for salutation is—gentlemen and ladies." Look at the ideas one white audience member carried with him when he went to hear the black abolitionist Robert Purvis. "We had anticipated a stubborn-looking negro, with a swagger, and a tone of bravado," he said. "In place of such we saw a tall, beautifully knit gentleman. . . . His foot and hand were symmetrical and, although his hair was gray with years, every limb was full, and every movement supple and easy." This writer not only expressed surprise at the appearance and performance of Purvis. He also combined a reading of Purvis's body—"symmetrical" foot and hand—with a reaction to Purvis as an orator so in command that he made "every movement supple and easy."[48] Purvis's audience realized that their eyes and ears were out of sync, so they carted their perceptions back in line with their racial ideology by calling Purvis "almost white." Purvis was able to convince this gentleman of his skill, but how many others could not be swayed? Forget whether blacks approach the eloquence or judgment of Webster or Washington. Never mind racial groups' enormous variation of characteristics. According to Fowler, blacks' heads lacked a shape that gave one good judgment or the ability to put together a well-reasoned oration as participants in a civil community. The head shape told you all you needed to know.

Phrenology Exploded

Few of the four hundred thousand free blacks in the United States could get an audience with someone even this open-minded. Free black writers and orators in the black newspapers sought to break the link between phenotype and cultural capital by modifying and reproducing a kind of capital—the middling style of rhetoric. This in part helped them in efforts to establish that phenotype, whether skin color or head shape, had nothing to do with one's capacity to wield cultural power. The cultural capital of oratory and the new "science" of phrenology come together in a New York address by the black editor James McCune Smith. Smith was the son of a bondwoman and attended the Free African School Number 2. He was a gifted student, and the black community pooled their resources to send him to college. No college that he applied to in the United States, however, would accept him. Smith attended the University of Glasgow in Scotland and stayed to receive his medical degree. He returned to the United States to serve as the physician at the Colored Orphan's Asylum, to help edit several black newspapers, including Douglass's *North Star*, and to lead the charge for black voting rights.[49]

On September 23, 1837, the twenty-three-year-old Smith, recently returned from Glasgow, gave a speech at New York's Philomathean Hall on Duane Street to a standing-room-only crowd. In his speech, Smith hammered at phrenology's fallacies. He stood before the audience with a blackboard and chalk and, on a table, a series of skulls for demonstration. He showed the audience how a skull might have a bump on the outside that did not ripple the inside surface. He showed them how the Fowlers' division of the "organ" appeared arbitrary and how the "natural divisions of the cerebrum" in no way reflected the separations supposed by phrenologists.

In a review the next day, *The Colored American* pointed out that, in walking out on the stage, Smith confronted believers in the new science and faced "the high wrought superstition of his audience against him." Given the claims that phrenology made about blacks, it might well have claimed that Smith faced an audience superstitious about *his own* abilities as an orator. But *The Colored American* claimed that the crowd lapped up Smith's presentation. The paper moved to the upper reaches of diction to express its thanks: "our soul feasted upon the exhibition of thought and learning," it exclaimed, and it titled its review "Phrenology Exploded." Two weeks later, *The Colored American* told its readers that calls for a repeat performance—and complaints from those who could not get in to the first talk—would prompt Smith to repeat his lection in the Broadway Hall.[50]

The *Commercial Advertiser* of New York agreed that Smith constructed a "forcible" argument, and the paper published a review that did more than applaud the content of Smith's performance. The reviewer responded to Smith's command of middling rhetoric and his claim for oratorical power:

> His modest demeanor, the ease of his address, the absence of all pedantry, and the facility of his elocution, were all calculated to bespeak the favor of his audience, among whom were a number of gentlemen belonging to the several learned professions, all of whom appeared to be interested, and indeed highly gratified. The arguments he advanced against the "science so called" denominated phrenology, were, some of them, entirely new, and all of them pertinent and forcible.[51]

Here Smith could stand as someone not only able to hold forth, as someone educated abroad, but also "modest," at "ease," and lacking "pedantry," even as he displayed a "facility" of elocution. His eloquence placed him in a class position with "gentlemen belonging to learned professions." This class position generated by his eloquence undercut conclusions that phrenologists advertised about blacks. And in this position, he influenced the opinion of people in the "learned professions." This review of Smith supports his aim to overthrow the popular idea of phrenology and seeks to change the audience's mind. The review concluded by calling readers to synchronize their eyes, taking in Smith's appearance, and their ears, hearing Smith's evidence and eloquence, and to question their beliefs about the inferiority of blacks. "If there be any who still doubt the competency or capacity of a man of color," it challenged, "they will have ocular and auricular demonstration that there is one at least, who has just claims to the character of a scholar and a gentleman." The writer had no doubt in Smith's capacity to acquire linguistic and cultural capital, even to become a scholar of that capital, and moreover to acquire the social capital of a gentleman.

This was exactly what the writers in the black press, like Smith, were aiming for. They hoped to use the power of language, their linguistic capital, both literally and visually, to erase the connection between black skin, servility, and the other characteristics that the new racial "sciences" like phrenology foisted upon them. These hopes surface in the assessments of fellow blacks and in the guise of the contemporary language stylists who instructed people on how to speak or write. But this same malleability of accepted language was setting them up for a fall.

Reform: The Language Whitener

George Frederickson argues that the rise of racialist thinking between 1830 and 1850 pinned two things together: a belief in American national greatness and a belief in special traits of the Anglo-Saxon.[52] American Romantics at the time applied this concept to linguistic capital and racialized the very locution that had been designed to include the masses. Kenneth Cmiel tells us that romantics, who valued the origins of things, sought the "roots" of language. They landed on short, hard, Anglo-Saxon words, which, they claimed conveyed intensity and "true meaning." As Emerson put it, "Guts is a stronger word than intestines."[53] Cmiel calls it "Saxon eloquence" and says that it "signaled not only a shift in *high* culture (classic to Romantic), but also a defense of an animate literary language against vulgar popular imitators."[54] In class terms, this "Saxon" movement embraced a more common vernacular but one that employed the "high" by creating a mixture that, while common, still settled at a level higher than Davy Crockett's "Lake Superior o' liquor." The door of reform thrown open by Jacksonian Democrats, where Crockett's neologisms animated the crowd, inched closed.

This language served as a window into the minds and souls of the middling class and as a force that united them. Popular philologist Maximillian Schele de Vere, said that "the language of a people" embodied "its spiritual life."[55] "The strong ligament of a common tongue," announced an educational report, "will never foster the subtle enmity to national unity that lurks in diversity of speech."[56] This veneration of the Saxon did not prevent popular philologists from admitting the influence of other languages. In fact, they basked in American English's ability to vacuum up the diverse tongues that appeared on its shore. Undeniably, place names like Flushing and Poughkeepsie came from the Dutch, while the Germans gave us "loafer, noodles, and sauerkraut." But Cmiel points out that philologists claimed that only African Americans did not contribute to the language (only in the 1970s did scholars recognize the African influences). American English, then, represented "an imperial cosmopolitanism of a chosen people," says Cmiel, and by the mid-nineteenth century the chosen people used this language to support imperialist ambition.[57]

These philologists believed that for language to effectively transmit a "spiritual life" or serve as the connecting "ligament," people needed to understand the Anglo-Saxon roots of words. In their eyes, American English took on a unique personality and spirit as it developed, and etymology became a kind of historical map of the conquered. Writers waxed ecstatically about the Anglo-Saxon roots of American language. Note the comments of a *Harper's New Monthly* editor: "Of all the honors that Anglo-Saxon literature has won, this is its noblest—this only is immortal—that its language, has constantly struggled to give a voice to . . . the highest aspirations that our redeemed nature can experience."[58] And Yale professor William Dwight Whitney contends that he "found the study of language proof of the existence of the 'favored races' [and to trace] 'the history of language' is to 'see how its growth has gone hand in hand with the cultural development of the race.'"[59] Vermont legislator and philologist George Perkins Marsh argued that the greatest authors of English used Saxon-derived words and presented percentages to evince a scientific precision: Shakespeare used 85 percent of Anglo-Saxon-derived words, Addison, 83 percent, and Swift 89 percent.[60] When Harriet Beecher Stowe sang the praises of the British reformer William Cobbett, she could think of no bigger compliment than to say, "the basis of his style was the old Saxon tongue, and it was as idiomatic and lucid as that of Franklin or Paley." The Saxon tongue, a white tongue unsullied by Africanisms, anchored what America had to contribute to the world. "In the variety of our idioms, the free movement of the language, there is, as in the race that speaks it, Saxon freedom," advised one philologist, "freedom that is not license, but law."[61] The American idiom had become fused to race; thereby society granted a special place and special freedoms in the republic to those whose race was white.

One black writer, who could take no more of these racially self-aggrandizing maneuvers, whipped up an operatic sentence to complain about speakers' and writers' glorification of the white race:

> Notwithstanding, almost every American writer or speaker, who would gain applause for himself, or a good hearing from his audience is sure, Paganini-like to play upon this one string, a fantasia on some national melody.—Now the Thema is "Anglo-Saxon Energy," (invading Mexico, perhaps), now, "Anglo-Saxon enterprise!,"—(re-opening the Slave trade!), then "Anglo-Saxon Piety," (with holding bibles from Slaves, and hating negroes generally!);—and so after variations on the martial, religious, mechanical and general superiority of the great Yankee nation, the audience are called upon to lend themselves, as stops to an organ, to be played upon, while the performer concludes with a grand Fugue movement, on "Anglo-Saxon blood."[62]

The writer had heard the tune time and again. He objected to the way middling rhetoric, by creating a connection between speaker and audience, made the crowd "stops to an organ, to be played upon" in the grand fugue of Anglo-Saxon domination.

Because so many freedoms had been attached to the uses of language, some white antebellum reformers plotted to broaden literacy skills beyond either the wealthy or the middle class. They sought to make the American idiom so approachable and easy to use that everyone would be literate. One group believed the solution was to make English easier to learn by simplifying its spelling. It proposed that Americans keep most of the letters of the alphabet but add nineteen new ones, six consonants and thirteen vowels. It printed every word as it believed that the word should be spoken. Indeed, when I first looked at the organization's newspaper, I thought the sheet was printed in Cyrillic. But after only fifteen minutes—aided by reading out loud to myself in the archives—I was able to navigate my way through the paper. This easy grasp of "English" is what the group hoped for. "Heretofore, learning has been hedged up and guarded as it were by a standing army," proclaimed the group. "We shall write for the people and not for the learned and the great. Let no one be astounded, either, if, after a time, he should find himself to know more than the Parson, or Squire Noodle the Lawyer."[63] On another occasion, the group declared that it was "rendering learning a *democratic* instead of an exclusive boon; of giving to the PEOPLE an easy access to the fountains of knowledge; of *guaranteeing to the son of every farmer and mechanic* an education ten-fold better, because truer, than the graduates of our colleges now obtain."[64] Within the first year of publication, the group had gathered "the extraordinary circulation of six thousand," according to the *New York Evening Post*.[65] The editor of the *Zanesville* (Ohio) *Gazette* proclaimed the mission to be "more important than the conquest of Mexico." Imperialism battles with a spelling book for attention.[66]

Editors of the black press saw the promise of this new orthography—thousands of poor blacks, who could not afford a formal education, would become literate, and, perhaps, gain the associated rights in society. The *National Era* (Washington, D.C.) gave the reform newspaper a favorable review and wished the paper and the reform "success."[67] When someone broke into the reformer's newspaper offices and absconded with its entire subscriber list, Douglass's *The North Star* printed condolences and requested readers to help the cause.[68] *The North Star* ran a glowing *New York Evening Post* article in its own pages. The article called the success of the paper, the "most striking and singular phenomena of the nineteenth century," and "it is undoubtedly the most perfect system of writing ever invented."

The promise, however, became tinged by racial thinking. The main newspaper of the new orthography movement claimed that it did not seek to divide the nation's "common brotherhood." However, it needed for the language to behave in a certain way if it were to create an entirely new system of spelling, one that corresponded *exactly* to the spoken word. Spoken by whom? The answer:

"This is a matter of the greatest importance; . . . [the language] must be under the direction of persons who have, all their lives, been accustomed to hear the language spoken in its purity."[69] Americans had to "banish provincialisms," said another report. The movement, by its nature, needed a "pure" language upon which to base its spelling, and it looked to England and the Anglo-Saxon stock for that purity. This was so important, in fact, that the newspaper called itself *The Anglo-Saxon.*[70]

The black press editors, then, suffered from the recoil of the reformer's misplaced cannonade. Like reformers who sought to bring literacy to the working class, they understood the power of language. They tried to use a class-based sign of worthiness, language, to move up through society's ranks and to disprove white society's conflation of skin color and mental prowess. But the very language they sought to use became more than a sign of class. It became a sign of race—the white race. Some writers for the black press seemed to go along with this move to locate the origins of the language in whiteness.

Abolitionists regularly used Anglo-Saxon as part of their lexicon. Their language illustrates how whiteness worked on a subterranean level to insinuate itself unnoticed. A look at the language they used when speaking on other matters illustrates how this belief wormed its way into everyday life of even the most well-meaning whites by reinforcing that they were constitutionally superior.[71] In *The National Era,* we see Harriet Beecher Stowe continually lauding the Anglo-Saxons for creating "the spirit of liberty" and praising British member of Parliament Charles James Fox for speaking "sturdy Anglo-Saxon sense; every word pregnant with meaning."[72] Likewise, the Philadelphia-based *Christian Recorder* wrote in "The Development of the English Language" about the "splendid reign" of Edward III and "a revival of the Anglo-Saxon genius."[73] And *Frederick Douglass's Paper* reprinted without comments the minutes of the 1854 Liberty Party state convention, the party that included Douglass and was designed to slay slavery. But when it reported that the abolitionist Beriah Green addressed the group, he "spoke, as he alone can speak in plain, and simple, yet most beautiful and forcible Anglo-Saxon."[74]

Some tried to use the Anglo-Saxon pride to snap whites to attention over the issue of slavery. Douglass's *North Star* reprinted a speech by Wendell Phillips that looked for solace in giving the American idiom an Anglo-Saxon root and considerable power. "I know the broad capabilities of the Anglo-Saxon language for sarcasm, reproach, and denunciation," Phillips said. But "another generation will wonder at the tameness with which we rebuked the slaveholder."[75] Another writer granted whites a proud heritage but also condemned the oppression they tolerated. For blacks, "the will of the white is law, and the Anglo-Saxon, priding himself upon his superiority," he said, "takes advantage of it to oppress the feeble race for his own benefit."[76] The racial pride of the Anglo-Saxon played on its presumed "superiority" to perpetuate injustice.

James McCune Smith appropriated these romanticized ideas of language and dug deeply into etymology himself to combat the Dred Scott decision, which stripped blacks of their right to citizenship in 1859. Supreme Court Justice Daniel wrote a concurring opinion to that decision arguing that blacks could not be citizens because ancient Rome, which provides the roots of American citizenship, did not allow slaves to be citizens. Shortly after the decision, a professor published an article showing that Daniel's own cultural capital had tripped him up. He had mistranslated a Latin word. The proper translation would turn the justice's argument upside down.

Smith pushed this inspection of the justice's version of history one step further. He took apart the meaning of the word *citizen* and dug into the roots of the word in ancient Rome. In a stunning display of linguistic capital, he used language history, an understanding of Latin and French (and his audience's fondness for word histories) to make his argument. He uncovered the Roman definition of private rights, or Jus Quiritium, and the Aristotelian conception of a citizen as "a partner in the legislative and judicial power." Smith then explained the thirteen Roman standards applied to citizens and compared free blacks to these standards. He found blacks' "right to citizenship is demonstrated as clearly as the meaning of the word itself." Further, he claimed the romantic's assertion of a deeper truth by asserting that blacks' "rights to citizenship of the United States is based upon a firmer foundation than legislative precedents, or judicial decisions, it is based upon the very meaning and definition of the term citizen; and in order to impeach that right it will be necessary to blot out from history the annals of lofty Rome, to erase from language the word citizen, and to efface from human polity the relation which the individual bears to the State, in a republic."[77] Smith mined the meaning of the words that had served as the very foundation for the Republic and used them to argue for free blacks' rights.

Smith displayed argumentative prowess, but free blacks understandably expressed frustration and disgust when they worked to cultivate their power of language and found society still denying them real participation. Black newspapers and books complained bitterly that society blocked free blacks from its higher jobs and thus closed off their rights as citizens in the antebellum North. William J. Brown said that the local carpenter and shoemaker refused him work. Then one man promised a clerk's job, but his boss refused to hire a black. "Other [white] boys of my acquaintance with little or no education were learning trades and getting employments, and I could get nothing," complained Brown. "If I possess the knowledge of a Demosthenes or Cicero, it would not bring to me flattering prospects for the future," he said. "To drive a carriage, carry a market basket after the boss, brush his boots, or saw wood and run errands was as high as a colored man could rise."[78]

In 1852 Smith, writing as Communipaw in the *Frederick Douglass' Paper*, also unleashed his anger. He entitled the article, "'Heads of the Colored People,' Done with a Whitewash Brush." Smith entertains a counterfactual history and imagines a country in which class and race do not limit people, in which Democratic party leader Cass does not support the Compromise of 1850, and in which President Fillmore does not sign the Fugitive Slave Act. Smith begins with an epigram from Anacreon, the fifth-century lyric poet from Greece, and he adds italics of his own to accent his point:

> Age Zographon ariste,
> Graphe Zographon ariste,
> Best of Painters, come away,
> Paint me the *whitewash brush,* I pray.

Smith says that he draws on ancient poetry in a quest to win a "post of door keeper, not to the Senate, (heaven save the mark!) but to the outermost enclosure leading to the Republic of Letters. That glorious commonwealth, perpetually progressive, free from *caste,* and Cass and Fillmores, which smiles upon all her citizens, if they be but true, which holds triumphant sway."[79] Smith used the cultural capital of ancient poetry for his gain. And what kind of gain was he looking for? Not a job, as William J. Brown sought. But for entrance into the "Republic of Letters"—a place where he might be free of class and race-based distinctions that kept him from assuming his role in the republic.

In the end, we are left with an understanding that members of the black press used a special class language, appropriated by the middle class to block pretenders; this move ultimately failed because, at the same time, American romantics were turning that middle-class language into a *white* language. The black press might have been addressing a formative shaping influence in American society—class—but it did not count on the combination of race and class that would keep them from full rights as citizens. This language could not overleap the structural hurdle of race.

But the hope did not die easily. After the Emancipation Proclamation a New Orleans writer called blacks "dormant partners" in America and emphasized African Americans' implicit republican ethos. He was excited that the new black paper among the freedmen would cultivate the republic of letters that created new participants in the government. "These, our dormant partners, are soon to become active participants in our system of self-government," he exulted. "To their hands, political powers will soon be entrusted." African Americans clearly were prepared to govern after the war, and more than six hundred served as legislators during Reconstruction. But they did not factor in one thing: the words that gave these black writers hope, the words of republicanism and freedom, embedded in the Declaration of Independence and in the day's discourse, were part and parcel of a whites-only language that, by the very definition of those who used it and claimed to protect it, excluded African Americans from the nation's conversation.

CHAPTER 2

William Apess's Theater and a "Native" American History

When William Apess stood before a crowd in 1836 at Boston's Odeon Theater, the Pequot essayist and Indian rebellion leader knew that he had tough acts to follow. Down the street, one of the most popular thespians of the nineteenth century, Edwin Forrest, had performed *Metamora: The Last of the Wampanoags* off and on before packed houses for nearly five years. The play starring Forrest, only one of dozens staged in the decade about the "extinct" Indians of the Northeast, told the story of the seventeenth-century King Philip's War between New England Indians and English settlers. These plays allowed white viewers in the Northeast to romanticize Indians along the Eastern Seaboard and to push them into a distant past, even as, farther south, Andrew Jackson defied the U.S. Supreme Court and ousted the Cherokees from Georgia.[1]

Apess, however, did not have to look far to refute a master narrative that put whites at the center of American history and Native Americans on the margins. He and others like him were still alive—and kicking. This member of the so-called extinct Indian tribe had only two years earlier led a revolt in Mashpee that sought to stop whites from poaching timber from the Massachusetts tribe's reservation. Apess massaged his identity as a "Pequot" Indian and became an honorary member of the Mashpees to lead the revolt. The rebellion landed him in jail for a month.[2] Now free, he rented the Odeon Theater to prove that Indians still had something to say. In those two January 1836 performances of the "Eulogy on King Philip," Apess offered a costumed performance as carefully staged as the Indian melodramas so popular with Jacksonian audiences. But he offered them in a completely different key. Instead of dishing up fair maidens and noble but doomed "red men," he created a new story—a new national narration that rewrote a story of white domination—and told it in a new way. Apess appeared not in feathers but in the garb of a Bostonian gentleman, and he began his speech by rewriting the story of Philip and the Pilgrims. He presented himself not as the half-terrible, half-quaint Indian his audience would have expected to see on stage, but as an authority with the full weight of oratorical tradition behind him. And his words carried contempt for the Mayflower set. "We find more manly nobility in [Philip] than we do in all the head Pilgrims put together," he declared that night at the Odeon.[3] By the end of Apess's performance he had punctured a veneer of whiteness that covered "official history" and left Native Americans out of the republic. And he put Indians, newly defined, at the center of the nation's very creation, by placing King Philip in the pantheon of the Founding Fathers, as the forefather of George Washington. Apess's oration that night reworked American history to make Native Americans, who had been erased from the annals, a vital part of it.

Setting the Native Stage

Archival sources about the Odeon, the history of the nineteenth-century American theater, and Native Americans (along with early American references to Indians in popular culture) show that the first act of Apess's performance took place before the audience stepped into the theater. By choosing a forum, a topic, and a form of presentation that resonated with the audience—and then artfully overturning their collective expectations—he aimed to put American and Native American history on new ground. He also sought to build a new foundation for Native American political rights. In Apess's second act—his delivery of the "Eulogy"—the Pequot essayist drew on a discourse of republicanism that the black press found so useful and on the history of Founding Father George Washington to make Native Americans the cornerstone of United States history. Jay Fliegelman in *Declaring Independence* argues that "true oratory represented and reiterated shared beliefs" that "maintain[ed] a shared cultural world. . . . [It] provided a circumscribed scene for human action and created consensus by calling forth the universal nature of man."[4] Apess's performance accordingly bent signifiers of both mainstream and Native American culture and also brandished high and popular culture to forge a new history and tradition for both Native Americans and immigrants from Europe. Our reading of the "Eulogy," then, must begin long before the curtain rises at the Odeon on January 6, 1836.[5]

Apess told a story about the Indian chief, Metacomet, who was dubbed "King Philip" by the whites because of his pride and upstanding posture. The King Philip's War, which engulfed the Northeast in 1675, was one of the most brutal wars in American history. As an encroaching white population bought tribal lands, the Indians became dependent on white commerce and goods, and the whites began to demand that the Indians recognize English sovereignty. Philip joined with the Nipmucks, Pocumtucks, Abenakis, and Narragansetts to fight against the whites. Apess's tribe, the Pequots, did not rally around Philip. They banded with the Mohegan, Massachusetts, and Nauset Indians to join the English side.

During fourteen months of war, Philip nearly drove the English into the sea. His army destroyed more than half the English towns, and the war killed a larger proportion of the white population than any American war since. But the losses on Philip's side were still heavier. The English ambushed him in a swamp and shot him. They dragged his body through the muck, quartered him, and then displayed his head on a pole in Plymouth. A young Cotton Mather made a pilgrimage to Plymouth to see "the exposed Skull of that blasphemous Leviathan," and, upon seeing it, he took a souvenir: Mather reached up to Philip's desiccated skull and, as if he were peeling a drumstick from a roasted chicken, tore away his jaw. Mather, Jill Lepore notes in *The Name of War,* metaphorically silenced Philip. Few, if any, tellings of the war that differed from the Puritans' version survived.[6]

In the nearly 150 years between Mather's souvenir and the Odeon oration, white views about Indians set the stage for Apess's performance. Roy Harvey Pearce and Robert Berkhofer, Jr., tell the story of white Americans trying to figure out how to live with yet totally subjugate Native Americans. During the eighteenth century, colonists increasingly identified the Indian with ancient cultures—people in an old savage state closer to nature. Sometimes they were Greek Spartans, and sometimes they were the lost tribes of Israel.[7] By the time of the Revolutionary War, colonists believed that the environment shaped human nature, and thus they had to rip Indians from their way of life to "civilize" the "savages." As the colonists conquered and "civilized" the wilderness, they believed they had cleared the way for savage and civilized destinies to converge.

But, of course, the "civilizing" of Indians failed in whites' eyes, and after the Revolutionary War, as the country sought to create a unique identity, it changed how it thought about Indians. Whites composed this story about themselves and their conflict with the Indians: they represented civilized progress, and savage Indians could not change to keep up with this progress. They had to be conquered. The Indian became distant and unredeemable, childlike and doomed—a sad but necessary chapter in the nation's history. About a decade before Apess delivered his oration, Timothy Dwight had given up hope when he described members of Apess's tribe as torpid brutes in decline. "All the vice of the original [Pequot racial stock] is left. All its energy has vanished," he said in *Travels in New York and New England.* "Children frequently behave well; but when grown up [they] throw off all that is respectable in their character and sink to the [degraded] level of their relatives."[8] An "improved" environment, apparently, did not create a better Indian. Apess grew up in a world in which one of his country's most influential speakers believed that he and his people were spent. Indeed, young William believed that to call someone an "Indian" was to call them something "disgraceful."[9] When one of Apess's foster parents grew angry at him, he whipped the young William and cried, "I will learn you, you Indian dog."[10]

This shift in cultural beliefs hurt Apess well beyond the whippings. He described in his autobiography, *Son of the Forest,* how he was taken from his

Indian grandmother, who beat him severely and broke his arm in three places. The town gave Apess as an indentured servant to a white family, who fed and clothed him and gave him all the schooling he received—six winters of classes. William, like many youngsters, rebelled and planned to run away. The family discovered his plan; instead of chastising him or attempting redemption, the family sold his indenture to yet another family. There young Apess had more troubles, and again the family sold him. Before Apess reached the age of twelve, he was at a third house. But here Apess's devotions to the Methodists, who were challenging the Congregationalists' power in early America, rankled the family, and William ran away to fight in the War of 1812.

No one knows how Apess became so well read and eloquent. But by the 1830s, he was an itinerant Methodist preacher and went to the only remaining Indian town in Massachusetts, Mashpee. The Mashpees adopted Apess, and he joined with them to write an "Indian Declaration of Independence," making themselves "free and equal" and the sole judges of what hay and wood was harvested from their land. The governor threatened to call out the troops to put down what he considered an insurrection. On July 4, 1833, Apess and others had an altercation with whites trying to take wood from their land, and here he earned his thirty days' jail time.[11]

By the time Apess brought Philip's story to the Boston stage three years later, the country waged most of its battles with Indians far away from the most populated areas. The general public in the Northeast believed, like Timothy Dwight and Apess's foster families, that Indians had nothing to offer society. The true Indian was extinct and exotic. He could be found only on stage, where Native Americans ranked as the most popular subject of American theater in the 1820s and 1830s. In fact, the seemingly ubiquitous Major Mordecai Noah began what became an antebellum theater fad. The man whose scurrilous editorials prompted antebellum blacks to start a paper and who fought to shut down African American Shakespeare productions piqued the American appetite for Indian theater with his drama, *She Would Be a Soldier; or, The Plains of Chippewa,* in 1819. Noah's play about a young girl who runs away to join the army to fight against the French and Indians proved to be a hit, taking in more than $2,400 in its first two performances.[12]

The public hungrily sought romanticized stories of this "safe" enemy. Down the street from the Odeon in Boston, less than two years before Apess's oration, audiences at the Warren Theatre thrilled to the machinations of *The Fire Warrior—Destruction of a Race* (figure 2.1). The playbill advertised that producers pulled out all the scenic and mechanical stops for this extravaganza. When the curtain opened, a party of Indians canoed peacefully across the River St. Marks at sunset. In scene five, U.S. troops arrived, ambushed, and pushed back the Indians. This skirmish merely set the stage for act two, which, the playbill teased, showed "Assemblage of the Warriors of the Kenhagee—and WAR DANCE!" Soon, the Indian village was in flames under the moonlight, with "the Red Glare of the Burning WIGWAMS reflecting on the Arms of the Troops—

The Fire increasing until the entire destruction of the KENHAGEE RACE, completes the TRIUMPH. . . .” The producers, eager to extend their run, posted playbills three days later that claimed *The Fire Warrior* “has been received with the most unbounded applause.”[13]

Even in homes, whites sang of doomed Indians. One songster of the period delivered a paean to their “extinction.” “The last dying echo was heard in dismay,” crooned people in their parlors,

> For the steel of the white man has swept them away,
> Has swept them away.
> And I, and I stand alone as the last of my race
> Upon this earth I feel I no more have a place
> Since my home, friends, and kindred are driven away
> For the steel of the white man, has swept them away.[14]

In whites’ eyes, the steel of their forefathers had raked the ground clean.

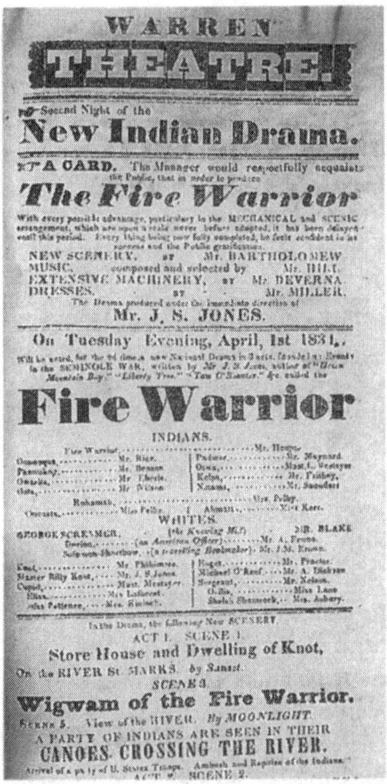

FIGURE 2.1. Warren Theatre playbill: *The Fire Warrior*. Destruction of the Kenhagee Race “completes the triumph.” *Boston Public Library/Rare Book Department, courtesy of the Trustees.*

Exhibiting Philip's "True Colors"

The period's runaway theatrical hit about Indians during this time was the story of King Philip, played by the supreme contemporary actor, Edwin Forrest. Forrest found the play in the late 1820s by staging a playwriting contest, in which he offered $500 and half the proceeds of the play's third performance to the winner. He asked some of the nation's top literary names, including William Cullen Bryant, to choose a truly "American drama."[15] John Augustus Stone won the competition with a story about King Philip, whom he called, *Metamora: The Last of the Wampanoags* (see figure 2.2).

The play captured the audience's imagination from the first scene when Forrest stepped on stage. The crowd heard "Zing!" an arrow left Forrest's bow, and a panther about to molest a fair maiden crumpled to the ground. The Jacksonian crowd could sneer at characters that included posers and an aristocrat, Lord Fitzarnold, who sought to entrap a lovely white woman, Oceana, in a marriage she abhorred.

The star, Forrest, played a Metamora who was simple, brave, noble, and not of this world. Metamora believed that whites had ensnared his people. Simple similes of speech reflected his unaffected noble character as he told the audience that "the race of the red man has fallen away like the trees of the forest before the axes of the palefaces."[16] The same icon in American landscape painting that suggested a powerful fear of the loss of the wilderness also meant the end of the noble savage. When another Indian betrayed Metamora by lying to a white tribunal, the chief's righteous indignation rose. He stabbed the Judas in front of all. The white's artificial laws couldn't contain the noble savage Philip, yet his action made him culpable before the white law of the land. The war began.

House raids and other bloodshed sent the white town into disarray, and the aristocrat Lord Fitzarnold did nothing to protect the settlements. Instead, he tried to blackmail Oceana into marriage. But never fear, Metamora appeared just as the British fop assaulted the maiden. "Hold! Touch her not!" he cried (33). When Lord Fitzarnold tried to buy the chief off with gold, Metamora would have none of it, and he killed the conniving Fitzarnold (34). But the Indian's path followed a slippery downward trajectory from there, and in his wisdom, Metamora foresaw his own people's doomed future. After he learned that his child had died in the war and that the Indians had taken heavy casualties, he announced, "The red man's power is broken now, forever" (37). Whites surrounded Metamora. The noble Indian killed his wife to keep her out of enemy hands and then, like a true stoic, shot himself.

Some reviewers howled at the production, and one reached for comparisons to African travel narratives and wildlife to describe Forrest's performance:

> Upon the approach of an enemy [the] ferocious baboon, standing upright on his hind legs, his eyes dilated, his teeth gritting and grinding, gives vent to divers snorts and grunts, and then, beating his breast fiercely with his hands till it sounds like a muffled drum, utters a loud

FIGURE 2.2. Edwin Forrest as King Philip in an "American Drama."
Courtesy of the Watkinson Special Collections Library, Trinity College, Hartford, Conn.

> roar. . . . What a singular coincidence! The similarity need scarcely be pointed out. Substitute the words 'great tragedian' for 'ferocious baboon,' omit the word 'hind,' and you have as accurate a description of Mr. Forrest in *Metamora*.[17]

But this was the minority opinion. Major Noah's *Morning Courier and New-York Enquirer* called the play "a new era in the histrionic art."[18] Forrest's biographer, William Rounseville Alger, sniffed that the "rapt silence, the copious tears, and the all-shaking plaudits of the unprecedented crowds" answered critics.[19] For the first time, said Noah, "an aboriginal of our country, was exhibited in his true colors."[20]

Forrest performed *Metamora* nearly eleven thousand times by 1854 and continued the productions until 1887. At the Tremont Theatre performance in Boston, five blocks from Apess's Odeon, spectators "crammed" the house to see the new piece. The last performance would be the biggest, argued the *Evening Gazette* reviewer, who reached to Hamlet's description of Gertrude's early love of the king to describe the audience's true devotion to the play: "The people Hang on it, as if increase of appetite/ Had grown by what it fed on."[21] Alger claimed that Indians attended *Metamora* at the Tremont and "were so excited by the performance that in the closing scene they rose and chanted a dirge in honor of the death of the great chief" (240).

Forrest's staging did not end in the theater. He crafted his life story to make himself an "authentic" performer of the doomed race. He declared that he injected "realism" into his portrayal of Metamora. His biographers claimed that it was a role that he had studied for all his life. Forrest's youth, one biographer explained, "was a world of dreadful fascinations and volcanic outbreaks, extravagant pleasures and indescribable horrors,—a world whose heroes are apt, as the proverb goes, to die with their boots on." This rough-and-tumble world made Forrest deep and mysterious, he said. "And the young actor with his professional eyes drank in many a revelation of human nature uncovered at its deepest places and in its wildest moods."[22] One of the strongest influences on the adolescent Forrest was Chief Push-ma-ta-ha, chief of the Choctaw tribe (126). The chief incited Forrest to study the Indians and "their genius and fate" (128).

Under Push-ma-ta-ha's wing, "he adopted their habits, shared their food, slept in their huts, mingled with the chiefs of their tribes, smoked the pipe of peace, and left the print of his own moccasins on the hunting-ground in the gloom of the dense forests, and the crack of his rifle echoed along the rockysides of the hills and lakes," claimed another adoring Forrest biographer. "Everything that could be absorbed by one nature from another, was absorbed and embodied and represented."[23]

Forrest may have believed that he was portraying a true-to-life, but extinct Indian. Forrest's biographer prepares us for the harsh reality of contemporary Indian life in America, if only to increase our amazement at his subject's acting skills. "The North American Indian seen from afar is a picturesque object. When we contemplate him in the vista of history, retreating, dwindling, soon to vanish before the encroachments of our stronger race, he is not without mystery and pathos," Alger wrote. "But studied more nearly, inspected critically in the detail of his character and habits, the charm for the most part disappears and is replaced with repulsion" (127). Alger enjoyed the romance of the Indian, the Indian he could conjure in his head and put in the background of a history now dominated by whites. Those still around proved an unsavory reminder of a once noble race. Stay back or the magic wears off.

Forrest's own experience verified this judgment in his own mind. When Forrest and his wife, Catherine, saw Indians on a trip through Michigan in 1843, the magic was gone. "We walked on shore, saw a sufficient number of Indians to satisfy all reasonable curiosity, and in a condition which tends to destroy the romantic ideas we are apt to form of them" (383), Catherine wrote. The "truly American" figure was nowhere to be found. Nothing remained to keep Forrest and his wife, and they left. Even the era's most sympathetic Indian hero was disappointed in them.[24]

Forrest's simultaneous identification with and contempt for Indians were nothing new to American society. Philip J. Deloria has shown recently how this process of transforming the Indian from redeemable savage to the routed savage of Forrest and Apess's time required a series of appropriations. Whites distanced themselves from Indians after they conquered them, but they, like Forrest, did not dispense with Indians and Indian identity altogether. White Americans used the Indian to craft their own identity. Revolutionaries, for example, kept Indians at arm's length as "savages" but, at the same time, used the image of the "wild Indian" to justify a break with England. White Americans "went native" and internalized the "wild Indian" to emphasize that they were beholden to no one and could revolt against monarchy. Deloria traces throughout American history how "indianness" became crucial to defining "Americanness."[25] Indian dress at the Boston Tea Party allowed whites to be "American" and "independent" at the same time. Protesters in the Whiskey Rebellion in 1792 borrowed customs from the Indians and posted their demands to the new government in the form of a "treaty." And the Tammany societies used Indians to create symbols of a long noble history and buttressed its claims as the keystone of the nation's political life. They "played Indian" but kept their distance at the same time. Into this tension between "other" and "American"—where Americans identified themselves as not-Indians but like Indians—Apess stepped when he walked onto the Odeon stage. And in this ideological masquerade, five blocks from *Metamora*'s Tremont, he sought to infuse his change into the national story.

Upstaging the Native

If white America defined itself by posing as Indian and distancing itself from Indians, then William Apess toyed with this unstable identity. The sight of

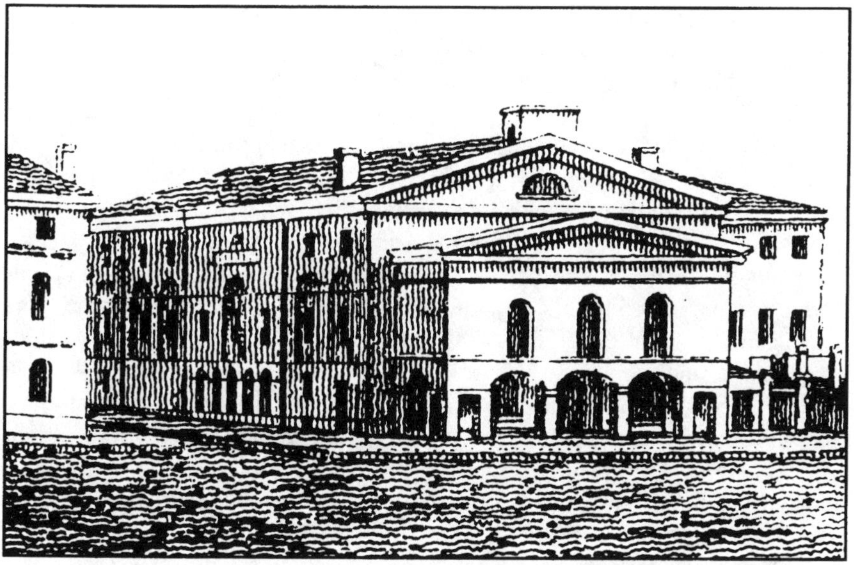

Figure 2.3. Abel Bowen's drawing of Bulfinch's plain theater, The Odeon.
Courtesy of the Watkinson Special Collections Library, Trinity College, Hartford, Conn.

the Pequot Indian on stage at the Odeon Theater must have pressed that fragile equilibrium in his audience's mind. For Apess had chosen not just any theater for his address; he chose the venue closest to a symbol of American revolutionary ideas. The Odeon was the oldest theater in Boston, designed in 1794 by the most American of celebrated American architects, Charles Bulfinch, who also designed the statehouses in Massachusetts, Connecticut, and Maine. The theater did not sport the colonnades and filigree of European houses. Rather, Bulfinch's brick structure offered a characteristically federal design. He placed only a few corinthian columns in the front along with double-pilastered windows. In a reconstruction after a fire in 1798, Bulfinch made the theater even "plainer" still (figure 2.3).[26]

To build the theater, Bulfinch worked witipJohn Quincy Adams and Paul Revere, and his creation opened as the Federal Street Theatre, with a band playing "Yankee Doodle" and "General Washington's March." Bulfinch and Adams were among the early owners, and a nineteenth-century chronicler of the theater claimed that it had "the most respectable citizens" as stockholders and that the public regarded it "as the triumph of taste and liberal feeling."[27] The building's financial backers—and thus the building itself—gave off the trappings of truth and aesthetic beauty. The stage spanned thirty-one feet with columns flanking each side. Bullfinch and his designers, who feared the new republic judged theaters frivolous, did their best to give the structure an official stamp; above the stage and podium, they painted crimson drapery with the arms of the Union and of the State of Massachusetts. Lest the setting look too solemn, they painted a ribbon dangling from the arms that read, "All the world's a stage." Here, beneath the seal of the state that had recently imprisoned him and the arms of the Union that denied his right to exist, Apess combined the official and the theatrical.[28]

Apess notified the public in a newspaper ad that at the Odeon—this building constructed by the city's finest and reflecting the most coveted architectural virtues—he, an "Indian Preacher," would take his turn to recast King Philip.[29] Apess's Native American ancestors may have sided with the English against Philip, but on this night, all sides joined, and Apess posed as a "representational *Indian*" to remake Philip's history, and, at the same time, remake America's story about itself. In the very staging of his performance, Apess challenged beliefs that extinct Indians could never responsibly participate in the community. Apess announced that he would tell his own story of Philip and thereby offer the nation a new history, and he did it in a forum that thrilled to its very foundations with the symbols of a free and equal people. In taking this stage he deliberately joined the company of those who guided the nation and shaped the nation's history.[30]

Yet perhaps Apess's most brazen act on that January night in Boston was not that he assumed the stage. Rather, it was in act two, when he anchored the Native American Philip firmly in United States history; Apess transformed Philip into the republican forefather of George Washington and thereby became the cornerstone of the nation as his audience knew it.

The audience could not have expected this brassy rhetorical move from an Indian standing under the federal and state seal. Audiences everywhere had been primed by popular belief that Indians were eloquent but simple-mindedly so.[31] Like nineteenth-century African Americans, Indians lacked the racial qualities that would allow them to amass cultural capital. They could never speak originally or to a deep truth. Indians "speak from nature, not from education," stated one writer in that arbiter of taste, the *North American Review*. "They utter what their subject inspires and never advert to approved models as their standard."[32] Apess not only "adverted" to approved models, but he also used them to his own advantage by bending the form and the signifiers of the day. He showed the audience that he was not only eloquent but also analytically keen. And that their whitewashed history was wrong.

With Forrest's *Metamora* firmly in the public mind and Bulfinch's cornice decorations overhead, Apess told of a different chain of events. Of course, Apess's version said nothing of an "Oceana" or a "Lord Fitzarnold." And he did not present an Indian who stood out from the rest of his people as a simple noble savage. In constructing his own version of events, Apess stuck closer to what historians now consider the historical record. He reminded the audience that Indians saved whites from starvation by supplying them food. Some whites, in their need, even became what a Jacksonian audience would have considered "degraded" by hiring themselves out as servants to the Indians. The initial connection between these two people was not of white benevolence toward a benighted Indian. Rather, the sides were reversed. The Indian helped the white. "And for all this, they were receiving the applause of being savages," mocked Apess.[33]

Apess did not flinch in outlining white atrocities. *Metamora*'s Philip spent much of his time saving women like Oceana from panthers and aristocratic ne'er-do-wells, but the whites were not so gallant. They killed more than seven hundred Naragansetts, many of whom were women and children. "When a people calling themselves Christians conduct in this manner," he said, "no pity at all ought to be had for them" (299). Philip's son did not get the "noble" death of the son in the *Metamora* play. The son of Apess's Philip was sold into slavery (301)—the worst fate a white Jacksonian audience could imagine.

Perhaps the biggest difference between *Metamora* the play and Apess's King Philip was the character of Philip himself. *Metamora* presented Philip as the last of a race who was purer and more upright than Indians who survived him and the whites who brought "civilization" to the country. If *Metamora* made Philip into the "noble savage," then Apess made Philip a "noble republican." Barry O'Connell notes Apess's use of republican rhetoric on another occasion,

FIGURE 2.4. William Apess. *Courtesy of the American Antiquarian Society.*

the Mashpee revolt, and in Apess's call in the "Eulogy" for each generation to make its own laws and revolution, if need be. "Different laws must be enacted, and all men must operate under one general law," Apess said.[34] But anyone reading the oration's beginning cannot help but notice one catch. Apess did not begin his oration with traditional "republican" figures. He invoked a traditional favorite of the Whigs, George Washington. Why would Apess begin his speech on Philip as republican hero with "the immortal Washington"—a perennial icon of conservatives in the tradition of Hamilton?[35]

The George Makes Land

The answer lies in Apess's design for the oration. He aimed to do more than construct a new version of the King Philip's War. He also sought to revise American historical ideology and symbols. Apess used republican ideology and the history of Founding Father George Washington to realign the foundations of American history. Apess constructed a Washington icon who was neither the Whig nor supplanter of the Indian, but rather champion of republican rights. And the very characteristics that made Philip great in Apess's eyes in turn animated Washington. Philip begot George. George served as the country's foundation. So Philip and Native Americans, in turn, helped build the country.

In Apess's day, the memory of Washington—which had been out of fashion for a generation—enjoyed a renaissance. Shortly after the Revolution and Washington's death in 1799, Federalists took up Washington as the nation's father who controlled the excesses of the new democracy. Biographers and essay writers cranked out material about Washington and cited the Farewell Address that Alexander Hamilton ghosted for him to prove that the first president was the enemy of divisive political parties and the rabble mob.[36] Rembrandt Peale combined the Washington of several busts and portraits to create what he considered to be the "national" likeness of the president (figure 2.5). Museums used oval frames around their portraits, and Peale, eager to memorialize the "Great Washington," painted one, ringing the president. A trompe l'oeil stone sculpture of oak leaves refers to "strength of mind," and Phidian Jupiter at the keystone recalls "almost universal worship."[37]

By the 1820s, the Whigs believed they had cast the Washington character in stone, as immovable and solid as Peale's trompe l'oeil frame. What more was there to say? The volume of books and speeches about Washington fell by half. Conservative politicians held up the same figure at the centennial of Washington's birth in 1832. Nearly one hundred members of Congress gathered with Daniel Webster at the Barbour Hotel in the capital to toast over dinner and wine a Washington they defined by his farewell address. He "inculcated the duties of 'respect for the authority, compliance with the laws, and acquiescence in the measures' of the Government." But the Whigs no longer controlled the image of Washington. Other voices had begun to make themselves heard.[38]

FIGURE 2.5. Rembrandt Peale's *Patriae Pater* (1824). George Washington's legacy given a *trompe l'oeil* boost. *U.S. Senate Collection.*

In the 1830s, several events revived interest in Washington outside Whig circles. Jared Sparks edited the manuscripts of Washington's letters, which gave writers new sources for biographies. Publishers released new editions of earlier work, and the centennial celebrations of Washington's birth fueled public interest. Writers doubled their output about the first president in this decade. People gushed with the enthusiasm of earlier years. "He is unlike all other heroes," claimed one children's book during the era. "Everything respecting Washington should be made familiar to the people. The first word of infancy should be mother, the second, father, the third Washington."[39]

Such enthusiasm made Washington a handy reference for anyone with a point to make, and Apess worked up his own revisions. The president's centennial birthday in 1832, just four years before Apess's oration, prompted speeches and parades throughout the land. Washington, D.C., began the day with a one-hundred-gun salute and closed all businesses until noon. Outside the Capitol, speakers gave a huzzah but wasted no time making what they would of the hallowed figure. Jacob Flint, pastor of the First Church and Society of Cohasset, said that Washington, who was a deist, "held fast the whole substance of pure and undefiled religion."[40] Thomas B. Fox, before the Washington Light Infantry Company in Newburyport, gave a centennial speech that at first looked like something Webster delivered—the standard fare of Washington and patriotism. But about halfway into the oration, he swerved off the party line and asserted that Washington-inspired patriotism did not allow the government to break treaties with Indians. Patriotism in his memory "does not understand where savage civilization gets the right to nullify the independence of civilized savages."[41] Fox was alluding to Andrew Jackson's expulsion of the Cherokees from Georgia. Speakers made what they wanted of the founder: Washington now offers communion; Washington now condemns the imperialists.

Philadelphia held one of the largest celebrations for Washington's birthday. More than twenty thousand people marched in the civil and military procession that queued for more than four miles. For at least two hours the procession steadily moved through the city as "nearly the whole population of Philadelphia and many thousands" from the country watched.[42] Perhaps most interesting about the procession is the freedom that Philadelphians felt in how they honored Washington. A broadside from the procession shows how each of the city's trades marched, with more than 250 brickmakers, 350 hatters, and 450 cordwainers in tow (figure 2.6). The stonecutters made the route with the block they intended to use to carve a monument to Washington. More than 250 tobacconists threw cigars to the crowd from a coach decorated to show the stages of tobacco production. Their standard displayed on one side Washington conversing with an Indian, and on the other, an Indian smoking the peace pipe. And the firemen marched with their engine "preceded by an Indian in full dress, with nose and ear rings, bow and quiver full of arrows." The victualers marched with oxen: on one horn hung the trade union's coat of arms; on the other, a portrait of Washington. The Whig icon was now a poster child for the working people.[43]

The Indians in the tobacco and firemen's contingents point to another representation of Washington that must have keenly interested Apess: Washington also represented the cleansing of Indians from the Northeast. Washington's myth in schoolbooks and many sermons began not when he controlled the Continental army and fought for American independence, but when he fought for the Brit-

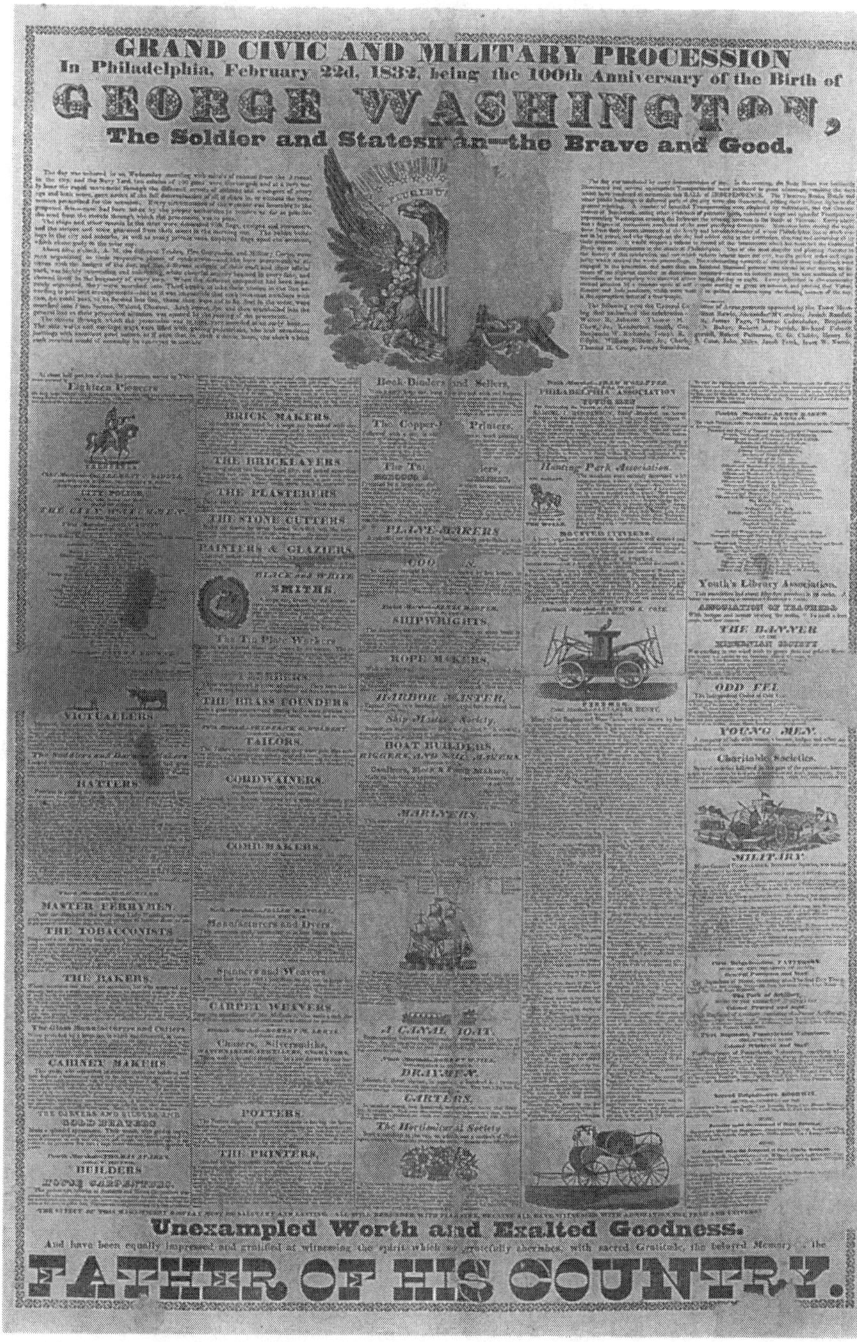

GRAND CIVIC AND MILITARY PROCESSION
In Philadelphia, February 22d, 1832, being the 100th Anniversary of the Birth of
GEORGE WASHINGTON,
The Soldier and Statesman—the Brave and Good.

Unexampled Worth and Exalted Goodness.
FATHER OF HIS COUNTRY.

FIGURE 2.6. Philadelphia parade broadside: George Washington, the soldier and the statesman; Indians tag along. *Courtesy of the American Antiquarian Society.*

ish with General Edward Braddock in the French and Indian War. Early Washington biographies recounted how he advised Braddock in 1754 that Indians badly outnumbered them and that they should postpone a battle. The arrogant British officer casually tossed aside Washington's recommendation, and the ensuing battle destroyed Braddock and nearly his entire contingent.

But Washington went unscathed. The physician on the battleground said, "I expected every moment to see him fall; . . . nothing but the superintending care of Providence could have saved him from the fate of all around him." Washington dodged the expert Indian marksmen, and his coat collected four bullet holes. "His safety, in the midst of such attacks, astonished his savage enemies, and they called him 'The Spirit-protected man, who would be a chief of nations, for he could not die in battle,'" a children's book enthused. "Thus did even the savages own a divine power in his preservation."[44] Never mind that Braddock could not have accepted Washington's recommendation to postpone a fight—the troops were a mere eight miles from his target, Fort Duquesne, and could hardly turn back. And never mind that Washington fought this war against the French as well as the Indians. Children learned that Washington, with God's hand on his shoulder, met native savages, and he prevailed. In case readers thought this only a story of survival—and not the ultimate defeat of the Indians—a page later the story tells them that despite the Indians' apparent victory there, "a few years since . . . the great Cumberland road, made by the government of the United States, was to pass directly over the spot" of the battle.[45]

Washington not only defied Indian dangers, but he also helped mark European settlers' clearing of them from the land. Charlotte Barnes's play about seventeenth-century Pocahontas included a tableau vivant with a cameo by George Washington. In one scene, Pocahontas envisions the civilizing white man arriving on Indian shores. The ship *George* approaches, clouds roll in, and Pocahontas awakens. As the clouds disperse, they reveal "the form of Washington—[and] the Genius of Columbia stands near him . . . 'To paint the future on my mental sight,'" exclaims Pocahontas as she "starts up clasping her hands in thankfulness." She continues in her grateful blank verse, "Improvement's course, *unebbing*, shall flow on . . . I hear the universal world declare, / In shouts whose echo centuries prolong / The Father of his Country!"[46] Washington marks the passage of the land from Indians to "civilization" and apparently even the Indians are grateful. In her preface, Barnes thanks Edward Everett and declines the "affectation of pedantry" of naming the more than twenty history texts that helped her stick close to what actually happened. Her scene makes another point clear about American history: George's ship comes in, and he begins to set the land right for whites.[47]

We see the linkage of George Washington and Indian removal all the more clearly in the famous statue of Washington, commissioned for the centennial of his birth in 1832, that sits in the Smithsonian Institution today (figure 2.7). Horatio Greenough spent more than four years carving Washington and other likenesses from a forty thousand–pound block of marble. He based the design

FIGURE 2.7. Horatio Greenough, *George Washington* (commissioned 1832). His sword "cleared the ground where our political fabric was raised." Smithsonian American Art Museum, Washington, D.C. *Photos: Smithsonian American Art Museum, Washington, D.C./Art Resource, New York (right); Karen Hust (left).*

on Phidias's statue of Zeus at Olympia, submitted it to Congress for approval, and made changes after receiving suggestions from public figures like Charles Sumner and Samuel Eliot Morse.[48] Greenough delivered a Moses-like Washington, clad only in a draped cloth. Washington's right hand pointed heavenward and his left offered the grip of his sheathed sword, the symbol of a war hero coming to lead in peace. The nearly naked Washington proved too evocative for antebellum hero worshipers, and Congress refused to allow Greenough's statue to take its place in the rotunda. They shunted it outside, where it sat exposed until Smithsonian officials moved it to their museum.[49]

Most interesting for our purposes, however, is not the front of the statue, but the back and sides. Congress commissioned the statue for the Capital Rotunda, and Greenough wrote Sumner that he labored hard to make the sculpture interesting from all sides.[50] He wanted visitors to view Washington and his message from every angle. "I have thought it my duty to make that on which

Washington is seated mean something with reference to the country—It is too large to be left dumb," he said.[51] Behind the Mosaic national leader, Greenough put two figures propping up the corners of the chair—Columbus, the white discoverer of the continent, and an Indian chief. Columbus connected America with Europe, Greenough said. The Indian chief is there "to shew what state our country was in when civilization first raised her standard there."[52] Greenough planned for the bas-relief on the Indian's side to carry the inscription from Virgil, "Magnus ab integro saeclorum nascitur ordo" (The great sequence of Ages is born anew). The Indian stood there noble, almost regal, but nevertheless, his fate was clear: whites would move him away. Washington saved the continent from savages who were in a state of precivilization. Or, as Greenough explained to his friend Samuel Eliot Morse, "We raise this monument because Washington's face and form are identified with the salvation of our continent." Greenough even tells us how Washington saved the continent—his sword "cleared the ground where our political fabric was raised."[53] Before Washington's left hand extended the sword in peace, the right hand used it as a scythe to shear the Indian from the land. The parlor song's refrain becomes encased in forty thousand pounds of marble: "the steel of the white man has swept them away, swept them away."

Washington, then, was not associated in the minds of Apess's audience with a republican friend of Indians. He was credited with clearing North America of Indians. Greenough himself showed this link with his next project, *The Rescue,* otherwise known as the Pioneer group (figure 2.8), which stood at the east entrance of the U.S. Capitol until 1958. Congress commissioned the piece a year after Apess's oration, in 1837, and hoisted it into the portico on its completion in 1853. A muscular savage, barely clothed, threatens a mother and child. He raises his hatchet and props his knee on an altar that provides a scalping table. A white hunter towers over the savage and takes control of the hand that wields the hatchet. The Indian looks up, outmatched, and subdued. Civilization wins. "I have endeavored to convey the idea of the triumph of the whites over the savage tribes," said Greenough of his statue, "at the same time that it illustrates the dangers of peopling the country." Whites overmatched the murderous Indian. And the Indian here did not even rank as a person.[54] Only whites "peopled" the continent. But perhaps most interesting is the association some viewers made on seeing the sculpture. One reviewer called the hunter "perhaps the noblest type of native manliness that ever issued from the imagination of the sculptor." And he added, "There is a sublime Washingtonianism of sentiment and character in the figure. It is just the attitude and the head that the youthful Washington would have presented. . . . The freedom, firmness, ease, and natural grace and inherent force of this magnificent form, are those of one conscious of an irresistible ascendant."[55] George still conquers.

That did not deter Apess. Perhaps the nation's revisionist history that created a white republic by conflating the founding of the country and the conquest of Indians merely spurred him on. Apess did not give his audience long to settle in their seats before he let them know what he intended to do in his

FIGURE 2.8. Horatio Greenough, *The Rescue* (commissioned 1837). "A sublime Washingtonianism." *Photo: Architect of the Capitol.*

oration. Within the first minute of his performance, he told the audience that his subject's war prowess was not as transparent as "Philip of Greece, or of Alexander the Great, or like those of Washington" (277). Rather, Apess brought before the audience a figure that the "civilized" world sought to repress. This figure required care and patience to understand. But, Apess promised, the figure rose to the occasion. For "as the immortal Washington lives endeared and engraven on the hearts of every white in America, never to be forgotten in time—

even such is the immortal Philip honored" (277). Yet this is no matinee idol, someone to be valued for his melodramatic effect. Rather, Philip was a bona fide great, and Apess sought to show us how. Philip was someone who everyone—not just the "degraded"—could appreciate. "So will every patriot, especially in this enlightened age," insisted Apess, "respect the rude yet all-accomplished son of the forest, that died a martyr to his cause, though unsuccessful, yet as glorious as the *American* Revolution" (277). So Apess made the stakes clear; he aligned himself and the Pequots with King Philip the Wampanoag; he rented a hall that housed some of the early nation's great performances and that dripped with the high seriousness of culture and state. In this setting Apess put Philip's cause on behalf of eastern seaboard Indians on a par with the American Revolution. In a printed version of the talk he even italicized *American* to emphasize his point. Every patriot of the revolution—every "enlightened" mind—should understand.

Apess wasted no time in showing just how great Philip was. He compared the keenness of Philip's battle at Pocasset with the shrewd Washington's iconic crossing of the Delaware (297). Philip's soldiers became hungry and destitute, just like Washington's men at Valley Forge, but the Wampanoag found ways to help them (297). And in nearly every conflict, Philip was at least as battle savvy as the great Washington (305–306). In the end, Apess could draw only one conclusion for his audience: "I shall pronounce him the greatest man that was ever in America" (308). His words lifted the conquered Philip from savagery to par with the most revered of America's heroes, the pinnacle of greatness in the country. No longer was Washington the conqueror of Indians. No longer were the terms savagery and civilization placed on a continuum that moved from Indian mounds to Mount Vernon. Indeed, because the qualities that made Philip great also made Washington great, the Indians became a *necessary precursor* to the first President. Indians like Apess were no longer the children who looked up to father Washington.

Jay Fliegelman has explored how oratory in the Early Republic created a shared milieu that reframed human action and prompted consensus. William Apess created just such a shared cultural world by putting his cultural capital on display. He took the stage of the Odeon Theater and participated in the nineteenth-century notion of oratory. He drew on the designs and expectations of the audience in his first act by choosing a stage and a setting that overturned the traditional and racial portrayal of the eloquent but simple Indian. And in his second act, Apess trotted out the tried and true characters of King Philip and George Washington only to reshape them into a new national mythology that gave northeastern Indians a place in American history and, by extension, American society. William Apess used this standard setting and popular beliefs about the meaning of cultural capital to reshape central American beliefs and the nation's rhetoric of whiteness.[56]

After Apess delivered his "Eulogy," he published the talk in Boston, and he put this epigram on the title page: "Who shall stand in after years in this famous temple, and declare that Indians are not men? If men, then heirs to the same inheritance."[57] By posing that simple question and supplying its declarative answer William Apess entered the temple and, in a complex oratorical performance supposed to exceed the ken of Native Americans, rewrote the national narration. Now Apess sought the rights of those who had raised the very temple itself.

PART II

Postbellum Revisions – The Virtue Within

CHAPTER 3

Sharpening the Pen

RACIAL AND AESTHETIC TRANSFORMATION

Around the time that William Apess delivered his oration, Charles Mathews performed the act of a language cop. Mathews's concocted story about Ira Aldridge moved seamlessly and unwittingly from Hamlet's lines to a possum's tale and thereby policed borders about who could use what kind of language. His tall tale also presages late nineteenth-century developments in which "aesthetic competence," the ability to discern "high culture," replaces in importance "republican competence," the ability to act as a republican citizen.

The change moves the public discussion on racial aliens' ability to participate in society from one location to another. Republican discourse can be demonstrated with the public expression of action or language, such as Franklin's establishing a library or the crafting of an uplifting oration. We move from someone who puts the good of the whole above narrow interests to someone who distinguishes high culture from low. The change is important. Before the nation's founding, working-class whites shared a discourse with elite whites on what it meant to be a republican citizen. After Reconstruction, however, the number of people participating in this discourse shrank and so did the discourse's power. An evolving hierarchy of cultural forms created a special class in society for "high culture" events. This class possessed the elite cultural capital necessary to pass judgment on the aesthetic abilities and sensibilities that qualified a person for citizenship.

As a result, not only did fewer citizens participate in the rule making about who was in and who was out, but an aesthetic sensibility, which is still more subjective than the broad public actions of republicanism, left those who practiced it from outside the inner sanctum still more open to elite fault finding.

This class-bound and subjective turn in taking someone's measure as a citizen, portended by Matthews's and Aldridge's argument, helps us to understand the strategies chosen by writers of color in postbellum years to counter the power of whiteness.

Before the war, Mathews, like the newspaper editor Major Mordecai M. Noah, could not believe that blacks enjoyed *Hamlet* for its own sake and that they were not simply mimicking whites who pretended to be blacks in the minstrel productions. In Matthews's account, Aldridge's immediate switch from Hamlet to minstrelsy demonstrated that the performer could not make a "clear" aesthetic discrimination.

Major Noah used this kind of thinking to even more insidious effect and turned his judgment of blacks' aesthetic competence into a judgment on their qualities as human beings and, by extension, their competence to handle political rights. Noah reigned as the premier theater reviewer in antebellum New York. When blacks there formed a theater for the production of Shakespeare, *National Advocate* editor Noah went on the attack to write reviews against a production of *Richard III.* He claimed that he was not just protecting the bard's work; he was protecting the republic from unworthy citizens and voters. In Noah's mind, the Shakespeare productions were part of a movement to liberalize voting standards for blacks at the 1821 New York Democratic Convention.[1] In "African Amusements," Noah reprints a playbill for the African American production but first perversely jumps to politics. "They now assemble in groups; and since they have crept in favour in the convention, they are determined to have balls and quadrilled parties, establish a forum, solicit a seat in the assembly, or in the common council," Noah wrote. He then added a claim so unrealistic that it could only have been calculated to kindle fear in his readers: "They can outvote the whites." Noah equated the display of African American elite culture with political activism. The bard led directly to ballots. The next day, Noah warned readers that increases in the black population would make them "formidable indeed."[2]

Everywhere Noah looked at black productions, he saw trouble. He began his review of one black Shakespeare production not with the actors or the interpretations elicited by the director but with the audience. He contrasted their "grotesque" racial features with their natty attire: "The gentleman, with his wool nicely combed, and his face shining through a coat of sweet oil, borrowed from the castors; cravat tight to suffocation, having the double faculty of widening the mouth and giving a remarkable protuberance to the eyes; blue coat, fashionably cut; red ribbon and a bunch of pinch-beck seals; white pantaloons, shining boots, gloves, and a tippy rattan."[3] Here, Noah writes about cultural value of the production in terms of the black body. The *Advocate* critic does not "prove" blacks' inability to appreciate Shakespeare by quoting the audience's conversation, by examining a black writer's criticism on Shakespeare (imagine what would happen to his pet theories should he encounter James McCune Smith!), or by investigating any other form of expression. Rather, the writer looks at the *body* of the audience member. When the fashionable clothing does not reinforce what Noah is looking for, the black body itself becomes the sign that the man cannot appreciate Shakespeare or beauty. The gentleman may put on fine clothes, but he cannot erase the "wool," the "shining" face, the "protuberance" of his eyes. In other words, Noah makes the body, like Orson Fowler's head bumps, point to mental thickness and cultural primitivism. Thus, this body could never responsibly wield voting rights.

Noah's paper sought to dismiss the *Richard III* production by arguing that blacks lacked the cultural capital to do justice to Shakespeare. It dredged up charges that had been around since before Phillis Wheatley and surrounded the slandered Ira Aldridge: blacks could only mimic, whether in clothing or theatrical production. "People of colour generally are very imitative, quick in their conceptions and rapid in their executions," said Noah, again sounding as if he had paid close attention to Fowler. "But it is in the lighter pursuits requiring no intensity of thought or depth or reflection," he added.[4] When people who lack "reflection" get the right to vote, they endangered the entire republic.

Whites convinced the New York police to close down the African American theater for being "disruptive." Newspapers joyfully hounded the actors, and the *New York Evening Post* reported that "the whole dramatic corps were actually taken to the watch-house, with all their tinseled honours upon them." The *National Advocate* printed a sneering epitaph: "And thus were many of our ebony friends excluded from a participation in those innocent recreations to which they were entitled by virtue of the great charter that declares 'all men are equal.' These imitative inmates of the kitchens and pantries, not relishing the strong arm of the law thus rudely exercised, were determined to have some kind of amusement."[5] Noah at the *Advocate* did not miss the chance to point out that the black actors had the right neither to challenge their racial and class positions with "innocent recreations," which kept them working menial jobs, nor to pretend that they had the cultural capital necessary to stage—and appreciate—Shakespeare.

Aldridge took Noah's hint and fled the American audience's hostility. He became one of England's finest Shakespearean tragedians but bitterly remembered the obstacles he faced in the United States and the distance between the nation's professed ideals and its practices. "The sons of 'the star-spangled banner' which 'Liberty upreared,'" Aldridge wrote in his memoir, "designedly conspire to humiliate and keep in degradation the race over whom that banner waves in vain, as though they feel convinced that the only difference between the Yankees and their slaves, lies in their relative social positions." By staging Shakespeare, blacks threatened to bridge that difference. "To allow the blacks the chance of improving their condition," Aldridge observed, "would be the sure means of raising them in every respect to a level with the whites" (10). Then, sounding like an antebellum W.E.B. Du Bois, Aldridge asserted that through his understanding and interpreting Shakespeare he became a fully developed person and demonstrated the full humanity of his black brethren. He wrote:

> It is impossible to regard one man of colour as being of extraordinary faculties, possessing a soul capable of appreciating, and endowments equal to the representation of immortal Shakespeare's great relations, and not sigh in serious contemplation of the wrongs of thousands of his countrymen, treated by their paler brethren as mindless, heartless, soulless, feelingless clay, bearing the corporeal impress of humanity, but cruelly or thoughtlessly denied its spiritual attributes. (5)

Aldridge, like Noah, draws a direct connection between the mental ability to exercise aesthetic competence and the understanding of conflict at the heart of the United States. How could this "soul capable of appreciating" Shakespeare be treated as "mindless, heartless, soulless, feelingless clay"? In short, how could they be treated as chattel? To Aldridge, the appreciation of Shakespeare's beauty epitomized the republican citizen; sympathy with Shakespeare's characters lead one to look beyond narrow self-interest and grapple with the injustices of caste in which African Americans found themselves confined. How? By pronouncing wrong whites who treat blacks as "feelingless clay" and "soulless." In this way, Noah did get something right: Aldridge's acting Shakespeare was a political statement. Black possession of the cultural capital required to stage a production of the bard called into question the racial and class hierarchy on which the United States built itself. It amounted to a republican statement, a bid for full citizenship. In a claim that presages the later half of the century, Aldridge created that connection not only with the general public but also within himself and, pace Matthews, within his soul.

Cultural Production Splits—and Takes the Classes with It

The story of Aldridge and the black Shakespeare company demonstrates that cultural production and the cultural capital required to stage the work was a political statement for some. The story also refines our understanding of cultural production in the nineteenth century. We see that although high and low cultural forms often mixed during the early part of the nineteenth century, society did place limits on those who could participate. Levine's account of nineteenth-century high and low culture documents how a cultural hierarchy emerged in America between 1840 and 1900. As "high" and "low" culture became separated, a gulf developed between popular taste and refined art. That refined art then required its consumers to receive training and direction in interpreting high art from society's elite. After 1840, the elite increasingly built fancy symphony halls for their orchestras. Light opera moved to its own venue and customers. By 1900, the elite was instructing the rest of society on the "proper" way to appreciate composers like Beethoven and playwrights like Shakespeare.

As Levine constructs the story of America's transformation to a cultural hierarchy, he admirably avoids a wooden model in which the elite faces no resistance as it imprints its ends into the lower classes. Yet, he misses some key restrictions that race placed on cultural production. He says that the elite's control of high culture "was by no means an absolute monopoly. The symphony hall, opera house, and museum were never declared off limits to anyone."[6] But as Ira Aldridge—or even Major Noah—would testify, some of these venues and the corresponding cultural capital they offered *were* off limits to blacks. Indeed, when one black man tried to take his family to the New York Zoological Institute, the organization's policies stopped him. People of color could enter its gates only when acting as maids or servants to white families. Race created impenetrable barriers in some people's access to cultural production or the skills to interpret it.[7]

These stories prepare us to understand a critical change in American culture after the Civil War. The language of republicanism finally dropped from the public discourse. The process began shortly after the Revolution, and continued, slowly, throughout the nineteenth century. In politics, as Gordon S. Wood and Charles Sellers show, and in culture, as Karen Halttunen and Kenneth Cmiel demonstrate, market-based and class-based ties were first superimposed on republican discourse. Later, as republican discourse's usefulness became less prevalent—and thus less useful—it faded away.[8]

The foundations were laid before George Washington had left office. During the revolutionary years, the Founding Fathers committed the new nation to develop itself through traditions of republicanism and uplift. The patronage system of a monarchy no longer divided society's spoils. Rather, the new Republic relied on virtue—a willingness to put public good over individual advancement—to hold the fledgling society of competing groups together. Workers who cultivated virtuous habits could train as apprentices, rise to the levels of masters, and eventually become their own bosses. No man was the master.[9]

Benjamin Franklin offered himself as a model for a virtuous citizenry and emphasized a personal definition of virtue. Virtue might make people rich, but more important, in Franklin's eyes, it prepared them to govern. The most virtuous citizens, those who best mastered self-discipline, frugality, and industry would serve as the country's leaders. Franklin believed that anyone who demonstrated the ability to master virtue—no matter how humble their origins—could lead.[10]

However, as soon as the Revolution was won, money and markets put their stamps on virtue. With a growing market economy, society increasingly stitched itself together with economic relationships. Commerce was "the greatest tie one man can have on another," wrote George Washington to James Warren in 1785, only two years after revolutionaries signed their peace treaty with England.[11] Merchants and capitalists tried to explain how serving one's own self-interest and serving the Republic could be accomplished at once. Virtue, "the most fragile element," of the new nation's order had been left behind; self-interest began to guide affairs and middle-class self-help reflected the change.[12] Instead of using economic advancement to care for the collective good, as Franklin urged, individuals pocketed the money for themselves alone. In 1839, R. W. Pomeroy's *The Young Merchant* promised that "the steady and constant acquisition of that wealth . . . affords the means of independence and active benevolence; the power of rewarding merit by giving employment, patronage and good advice."[13] Pomeroy promised that if you succeed, then *you* can hand out the "patronage." Despite this shift in the antebellum world, the rhetoric of Jacksonian democracy, sometimes in the homespun argot of Davy Crockett and sometimes in the bland promises of the stump speech, kept circulating and promising power to the common man. But workers knew better. They felt the increasing pressure of a market system and a threat that competition from slaves could drive them out of jobs. White workers increasingly feared the market would wipe out their citizenship rights, David Roediger argues, and they created the language of *herrenvolk republicanism*—a white republic.[14] As we saw in chapter 1, free blacks gripped tight the republican promise, but they used a class-based language to advance republican claims.

As America moved toward the Civil War, the governing ideology changed and with it the nature of cultural capital. Mass transportation and production expanded the market economy and ended the supposition that workers would some day rise up to become their own bosses. Republicanism, as it had been defined and redefined from the revolutionary pamphleteers to the politicians on the cusp of war, was dead.

Key to understanding this transition, as Eric Foner points out, is that the republican promise to white workers and rights for newly freed blacks in the South were linked. The Republican party was founded in 1854 with the ideal of securing both republican rights for workers and encouraging industrialization. But in 1876, Foner shows that the party dumped workers' rights and devoted itself to serving industrial interests. Indeed, with the 1876 presidential election, the party turned the republican rights dictum on its head: the government quashed the rights of the many in the interest of the few. After presidential candidates tied in the 1876 election, Republicans negotiated for the election of Rutherford B. Hayes in return for ending a Reconstruction that protected black rights. Shortly after taking office, Hayes's government used federal troops to end the railroad strikes of 1877 and protect corporate owners' interests. The nation, and its racial and class rhetoric, had taken an important turn. A broad-based government pledge to protect rights, however imperfect, gave way to a much narrower hierarchy in which the government protected increasingly large economic entities. Republicanism, as a term of art agreed on by society for all whites, faded from the public discourse.[15]

Cultural capital similarly lost its reliance on republican sensibilities as such. But this capital was still important. Levine traces how, after the war, ideas about high culture, and thus high cultural capital, increasingly became the province of the elite. The elite funded art museums, built opera houses, and constructed concert halls, all as ways to elevate culture *above* everyday life. They sought to make it, as Levine says, "an oasis of order and culture," away from the "noisy" and "rude" members of the working class. This move to what Levine calls the "highbrow" encompassed more than built spaces sequestered away from the working classes. To gain admission to these higher precincts, one needed specialized knowledge that "few could hope to master." Lecturers popped up to train people how to "cultivate taste" in music, on appreciating opera, and on how to comprehend Shakespeare. Cultural capital—the ability to understand these artistic codes—served as a gatekeeper by carefully crafting societal rules to select those speakers. These rules always converted the speaker into the teller of truth, the holder of the ultimate aim of this capital. They followed the antebellum philologists, who were captivated by word histories, and traced that "truth" back in time. Their answer was simple: truth came from the speaker's race, strong "Anglo-Saxon" stock. Examining the questions of who may speak gives us a purchase on questions that Levine did not ask about the reordering of American culture in the second half of the nineteenth century: How did those excluded from the temples of culture respond? Did they believe they had a stake in the day's cultural capital? And does this cultural capital have something to tell us about the democratization of culture?[16]

These rules had an enormous impact on all writers marginalized as racial aliens. If antebellum blacks cast their lots with language reform but later found that reform defined as "white," postbellum writers had to position themselves against society's newly aestheticized construction of cultural capital. They crafted both their arguments and their forms of argument accordingly. We can examine the ways in which people said things to understand how they aimed to nudge society in their own direction. In other words, to possess these skills gave the writer of color much more than mere public acknowledgment. They offered the power to seize an audience's mind through pen or spoken word, to hijack their preconceptions as a way to gain social power. The black essayist Anna Julia Cooper and the self-fashioned Chinese American Edith Eaton, as we see in chapters 4 and 5, knew this well.[17]

Putting Up the Capital: Learning to Write with John Bascom

One avenue to understanding the use of cultural capital is to look at the writing manuals of the period and ask questions: What rules did these books embrace about who would speak? What social meaning did the act of speaking or writing carry? In other words, how did the very act of public discourse disrupt social boundaries around class, gender, and race? These questions drive us into the world of John Bascom and his rules about writing and speaking. Bascom helps us because he loved rules. As president at the University of Wisconsin, he curbed a host of rowdy students and brought down the hammer on a university regent who stole topsoil from campus grounds.[18] As a professor of rhetoric at Williams College, he published a series of books and journal articles in *The*

Atlantic and *North American Review* concerning what he called the "rules" governing beauty, or aesthetics, and those governing rhetoric. Bascom's book on rhetoric reigned as one of the most popular during the last quarter of the century.

Bascom believed that rhetoric revealed the laws of the universe, including the relationships among truth, beauty, and those who perceived these values. No one can know art or its power, he said, "without tracing its rules."[19] Here we see an example of what Levine says is the elite's interest in serving as the interpreter of "high" culture. Bascom claims that without an understanding of rules, people cannot even recognize beauty when it stares them in the face. "The beauties of the world can no more be understood without [their] recognition than those of the vegetable and animal kingdoms without a recognition of the living principles which rule therein," he said.[20] His books and articles, read in parlors and classrooms across the country, confront one central issue: how to give expression and form to beauty, language, and social responsibility. James H. Canfield, chancellor of University of Nebraska and a former Bascom student, referred to Bascom's work when he talked about "moral value" in a rhetoric text.

Bascom, a religious man of strict Puritan upbringing, not surprisingly traced his rules connecting the aesthetic and the social with a straightedge. He argued that beauty led to truth and language built society around that truth. "Beauty is often the door-keeper to those charmed precincts within which are truth and right," he said. The writer and language assumed a special role in this relationship. He created a world for "truth to be adduced and established or to be conveyed, feeling to be uttered, the purposes of men to be shaped." Language, he said, gives us the chance "to unite perfectly the inner force of truth to its outer form, the highest attainment in living as a fine art." Beauty, in his eyes, begat truth, and truth begat high culture, and high culture shaped the world. The conveyor belt was the writer and the writer's language. John Bascom, who as a young man left the ministry to devote his life to art and writing, meant to do some serious work.[21]

Bascom's work, however, did not accomplish what he expected. His ideas about aesthetics, like those of nearly every nineteenth-century thinker, did little to advance the field. Bascom's work retraced existing aesthetic ideas in concrete for mid-nineteenth-century America. Nevertheless, if his ideas by themselves do not help us, his work, as a cultural artifact that aimed to move in society and change its audience, does. Nearly every college considered it a field of study and placed great emphasis on it. Bascom was considered a pillar of the curriculum, and his contemporaries considered him a leading philosopher of education. The Wisconsin hiring committee said he enjoyed a "national reputation as an original thinker, able writer, and ripe scholar." A pupil at the University of Wisconsin said that Bascom was "among the prophets," a compliment that, bestowed on most teachers today, would make them feel like failures in creating independent thinkers.[22] Bascom's public acceptance and his determination to find "laws" for our "gut" feelings proves particularly useful in charting for us today the intersection of ideology, aesthetics, and language in the late nineteenth century.

As Bascom declared beauty to open the door of truth and right and to combine aesthetics and rhetoric, he and his contemporaries added a third term that helps our understanding of what glues ideology, aesthetics, and language together: race. Bascom fused three separate terms: language, nation, and race. He takes up where those antebellum philologists, probing the etymology of every word for its "Anglo-Saxon" roots, left off. He believed a nation draws its strength from its cultural production, and a unity of race helps make this possible. "National life springs from physical conditions, but has its fruitage in social and moral ones," he proclaimed. "Its starting point is usually unity in race. This carries with it unity in language."[23] This racial unity (what Bascom called the "progressive stages of civilization") causes "the lines of opinion" about aesthetics to converge on a common understanding of high culture.[24] Woe to a nation that fails to police these high aesthetic rules, for "animal appetites" soon send us "facing downward toward the brute."[25]

Indeed, racial diversity already had handicapped the nation in reaching its true potential, its "highest attainment in living as a fine art" or even in living out the nation's guiding principles. Only high culture can make a nation thrive, and only racial unity can generate high culture. America was troubled because two principal residents—black and white—differ enormously in aesthetic capacity. "The diverse capacity and attainment of blacks and whites," Bascom warned, makes it very difficult "to establish workable and bearable terms of liberty."[26] This thinking suggests that any marginalized writer resides outside Bascom's tight loop of aesthetics, language, and nation. Bascom's intellectual route tells us what the outsiders faced. How can blacks create the nation's guiding principles if they don't have the aesthetic capacity, as Bascom sees it, to understand them?

Bascom launched his prodigious writing career after completing seminary training and then joining the faculty of Williams College. In 1862, he published *Aesthetics; or, The Science of Beauty*; four years later he released *Philosophy of Rhetoric*; and in 1874, in *Philosophy of English Literature,* he sought the underlying laws "of causes, of controlling tendencies and leading minds, rather than a presentation of details." His approach guaranteed that his work made explicit the fusion of ideology and literature.[27]

Bascom's *Aesthetics; or, The Science of Beauty* explores the "distinct science" of "taste" and explains our perception of beauty.[28] It lays bare attitudes that some speakers and writers in the late nineteenth century held about aesthetics and aesthetic judgments. To Bascom's educated eye, action, power, and clarity evoke the beautiful. A person experiences beauty, says Bascom, at the sight of something "vigorous," in "perfect control" or "purifying" (24). Where the uneducated may miss the beauty in something, the educated see "a lively revelation" (23). His rules do not just tell us the relationship between characteristics and beauty. They even tell us when something becomes ugly. Take the pelican, for example. To Bascom, the pelican's beak was all wrong; he carried that "empty sack without vitality" (27) and doomed its aesthetic allure. Bascom's rules left little wiggle room.

Bascom aims to whet readers' appetites for his topic with an opening lecture called "Inducements." He demonstrates that aesthetics is at once a concept both fleeting in its nature and at the core of being. The perception of beauty, Bascom claimed, was "one of the constituents of our nature—a universal and most characteristic element of manhood" (1–2). But this sensibility is not the everyday part of our nature. Like many nineteenth-century thinkers, Bascom believed that the perception of beauty was hidden, to be cultivated and educated in the highest senses. "It does not belong to our animal nature," he said, "neither to the appetites nor passions, but, as a higher and or spiritual enjoyment, . . . and unite[s] its forces with those other perceptions which release us from the sensuous and passionate" (3). Our sense of beauty and art, said Bascom, has a place above everyday events.

So ennobled, the appreciation of beauty does more than form a key component of "manhood" or give pleasure. Beauty enters body and soul, helps make citizens virtuous, and becomes an important sign of morality. This idea that an aesthetic sense marks someone as moral is an important point that has been made for centuries. Aristotle's response to Plato, who wanted to ban all poets and painters from his Republic, looked to aesthetic arts as a foundation of moral education. Seventeenth-century writers and thinkers, who are credited with advancing aesthetics the furthest, followed Aristotle's lead—and imagined a tight relationship between morals and taste. Hugh Blair, the professor of rhetoric and belles lettres at the University of Edinburgh in the late eighteenth century, whose rhetoric text is credited with training half the English-speaking world's educated population, argued that mankind failed to develop its moral sense until it had a language that expressed the rules of beauty.[29] Bascom and other nineteenth-century writers merely adopted the form from Blair and his school. By the late nineteenth century, George P. Quackenbos, an editor, teacher, and textbook writer, argues that the rules governing "tastes" improve our moral being. "To examine what is beautiful and why it is so," he said, "can hardly fail to improve us in the most valuable department of philosophy, the philosophy of human nature. . . . They necessarily lead us to reflect on the operations of the judgment, the imagination and the heart." But then Quackenbos goes further. "The cultivation of taste has in all ages been regarded as an important aid in the enforcement of morality. Let the records of the world be canvassed, and we shall find that trespasses, robberies, and murders, are generally not the work of refined men."[30]

Bascom and others put great emphasis on aesthetics because they believed it served as an unerring gyroscope, a guide to "those charmed precincts" (3–4) of the true and the right. Aesthetics accomplishes this by drawing energies into the highest realms of the mind—or, that part of the mind devoted to the pursuit of beauty—and away from the merely physical. This centers men (no mention of women) on the moral and the enduring. Now right and beauty work hand in hand. Indeed, without "a most thorough knowledge and hearty appreciation of the great law of character,—the right," a person cannot even begin to understand beauty (5). This way, beauty leads to "best actions" (3). Without beauty and its appreciation, "no progress can be achieved" (6).

The aesthetic thus becomes Bascom's lever to move everything. If the aesthetic works from within, governs the sense of beauty, and even works with a sense of right, then the aesthetic, in turn, must influence all cultural work and even interpretations. Aesthetic judgment to Bascom at once generates "moral culture" and arises from it. "Art," Bascom declared, "not only prepares the way for moral culture, it itself is, and demands, as an indispensable antecedent, that culture" (6). No wonder University of Nebraska president Canfield believed Bascom's work on rhetoric had a "peculiar *moral* worth." To Bascom, ideas about art and society represented no ideology; rather, they sprang from an essential truth in humankind, a higher beauty, a higher calling. Contemporary "cultural production," to Bascom, amounted to a barometer of the person's inner character.

Bascom's ideas found receptive ears, and his argument about the core importance of aesthetics launched his message into unlikely places. The *New Englander and Yale Review* forecasted a "wide circulation" for *Aesthetics* and predicted the whole clan would take to it. It will be "an exceedingly popular one in the family as well as in the recitation room," it said.[31] Bascom was invited to deliver a series of lectures at the Lowell Institute where attendees sought "self-cultivation." Even *Manufacturer and Builder* magazine thought its readers had to know. It squeezed in a notice of Bascom's *Aesthetics* between columns about a new drill press and the cleaning of furnace boilers. The magazine instructed "every member of the profession" to read the book and promised to excerpt it in future issues.[32] At the end of his life, Bascom himself called the book "one of the most permanently successful of my ventures."[33]

Bascom carried the ideas of *Aesthetics* into his other work, including *The Philosophy of English Literature,* to link art and man's standing in creation and society:

> As man sinks in action, in emotion, in intuition, he loses high art; as he ascends he regains it, effecting a new entrance into that which is peculiar to himself, to a moral being with springs and laws of life hidden in its superiorly perceptive constitution. Even comedy cannot thrive on mere trifles. Unless its laugh has elation, election, taste, sense and sensibility in it, it sinks to low burlesque, in which the animal appetites so predominate, that we find ourselves in action and impulse facing downward toward the brute.[34]

Where Orson Fowler looked to a "vulgar body" to spy out a "vulgar mind," Bascom took the aesthetic angle. Low humor makes us brutelike, and brutes like low humor; conversely, high art reflects a higher nature. Indeed, when

Bascom states that high art, or the aesthetic sense, "effect[s] a new entrance" to man as a "moral being," he is, in effect, uniting the moral and aesthetic senses. Deflate the constituents of morality—action and emotion—and high art and the aesthetic sense withers too.

Bascom implies, unlike Fowler, that these aesthetic standards, which stave off the brutelike condition, develop from an internal monitor. No state apparatus imposes an external standard. The policeman of truth, right, and beauty is inside, "hidden in [our] superiorly perceptive constitution." Bascom not only makes the aesthetic dependent on our internal morality, but he also finds the control of that morality within.

Bascom's deployment of the aesthetic as a category, finding the control within, belongs to a longer history of that concept's use within a market-based economy. The aesthetic to Bascom and connoisseurs in the nineteenth century is a concrete, unswerving fact: a "high art" "standard" of taste built on "truth" resides in "morality." Of course this "fixed standard" is a cultural construction, as Terry Eagleton and others document, and as a standard it became a mechanism for social control during the Enlightenment. Eagleton historicizes the aesthetic, something Bascom claimed is essential to nature. In brief, Eagleton traces the process this way: a growing middle class, governed by the police state or a market economy, embraced the mechanism of the aesthetic as a way to change the site of societal control from the policeman's baton or the Exchange's pricing floor to inside the person who embraces the aesthetic standard. This standard supposedly resides outside either law or economy. Life becomes informed from within and gives the person a sense of autonomy. This purchase from within is just the beginning of the aesthetic's ability, as a socially constructed standard, to exert influence. Because the aesthetic manifests itself as a standard—a shared metric for assessing taste and beauty—it creates a "non-coercive consensus" about manners and definitions of how the world should work. That consensus of "aesthetic representation," says Eagleton, "is a society." Ultimately, aesthetics as social control "infiltrate the very textures of lived experience," says Eagleton.[35] With a gut feeling for what is and what is not beautiful, the individual probably has a stronger feeling of autonomy, but in fact plenty of others share the same gut feeling about beauty. Together, yet driven from within, they do the job of the state; others maintain a uniformity. The aesthetic sense—what Bascom called an internal, nearly divine sensibility that knows truth when it sees it—is, in Eagleton's mind, a mental implant designed to make one behave as society desires. We do not have to embrace a closed theoretical system to understand Eagleton's point that social, cultural, and economic factors drive society's aesthetic values.[36]

Aesthetic Competence: Taking a Man's Measure

Many nineteenth-century writers besides Bascom took a man's measure from his grasp of the aesthetic. In "A Plea for Culture" in 1867, Thomas

Wentworth Higginson declared that high culture called for "the training and finishing of the whole man." Latin and Greek, for example, "stand for a learning which . . . helps to make men." Higginson declared culture helps men to see "physical demands to be merely secondary, and [pursue] science and art as objects of intrinsic worth." Culture directs men's energy. "There are certain authors who are not only tests of taste but even of character," said an editor of *Harper's New Monthly Magazine*. "If a man gives himself . . . to Shakespeare, or Chaucer, or Jeremy Taylor—that also is enough; we have a clew to the man." Supposedly this aesthetic judgment is not a matter of personal whim. "Homer, Shakespeare, Dante, Raphael, Michael Angelo, Handel, Beethoven, Mozart, they are towering facts like the Alps or the Himalaya. They are the heaven-kissing peaks, and are universally acknowledged."[37] Anyone who wants to reach the heavens of humankind will have to worship society's consensus about culture, at the foot of its high cultural monuments.[38]

But not everyone can kiss the heavens and embrace the pinnacle of civilization. Some, evidently, could acquire high culture more easily than others. And often, class had much to do with who got what: "Some will show no capacity for receiving culture," said a columnist for *The Atlantic Monthly*. "Any wood may be varnished, but not every sort receives polish." Those working with their hands should expect difficulties, said Higginson. Culture "undoubtedly places the fine arts above the useful arts," he said, which held America back in producing the "fine arts": "Our brains as yet lie chiefly in our machine-shops." Suddenly, the aesthetic serves as the barometer of individual worth because, in this world view, not everyone has the same capacity to value beauty. The working class, or the focus on physical labor, blocks one's grasp of the aesthetic.[39]

How might one broadcast the coveted power one holds? Bascom's *Aesthetics; or The Science of Beauty* tells readers that they *ought to* admire moral art that elevates the senses. His next book offered readers a way to show off that power and offers a wonderful cultural example of how the aesthetic works as both a mechanism of social control and as a measuring stick of cultural capital, the sign of an exclusive model citizen. *Philosophy of Rhetoric,* also known as "Bascom's Rhetoric," appeared for the first time in 1866, stayed in print for nearly fifty years and reigned as a premier rhetoric text of the nineteenth century. In it, he argues, as do other well-known rhetoric text writers like Hugh Blair, John S. Hart, and David J. Hill, that truth and beauty—or the internal aesthetic sense of the speaker—drive any rhetorical practice.[40] Together, aesthetics and rhetoric highlight the tasks of the arbiters of good taste: who holds cultural capital and, thereby, who can speak, who can make the judgments that shape society, and who can raise their voices or put pen to paper to make themselves heard. Language "is preeminently their product, and accumulates for them its wealth. In turn, therefore, it renders itself into their hand, and from them receives its laws," says Bascom. "Those who most broadly and frequently make language the means of arousing the popular, the national, thought and feeling," he adds, "chiefly control it."[41]

Bascom's rhetoric text reappears when we examine Anna Julia Cooper, a writer who was schooled on Bascom but inverted his "laws" to give her voice power. For now, our purpose is to examine how Bascom gave his *Rhetoric* power to make such far-reaching claims: an almost religious belief in natural law and the internal control of the individual. Bascom begins by putting the validity of what he is saying beyond question. This is not a man making up conventions about language. This is someone laying bare the laws of nature—the a priori principles—that have always guided us. Bascom warns that the "foundation of a complete and broad control of Nature is laid in an extensive understanding of her forces," and no one can know art or its power "without tracing its rules to the laws on which they depend." In Bascom's world, of course, all parts of a presentation must fit into a perfectly rational order, embedded in natural law, for the speaker or writer to effectively reach the audience. "The mind is never satisfied till all its action becomes rational." And those who stick to a perfectly rational approach, following the laws of nature, speak truth and move all men to their purposes.[42]

Indeed, arriving at correct conclusions—and even having influence over an audience—has everything to do with what is *inside* the writer or speaker, the aesthetic sensibility of the individual. Bascom exhorts speakers to check their motivation: Is it socially sanctioned? Is it right? Speakers' "aims and methods are ever to be enclosed within those of virtue, lying in the same direction with them, always receiving their sanction, often enforced by their obligations" (56). Here, the internal *enforces* the outward speech. Speakers, he says in a section on the "The Laws of Influence," must accept "the law of virtue as the line and limit of influence" (56). Someone without the proper motives is a hollow person, and pretenders won't go far. "Illegitimate" ends, he warns, come from "ignorance," "misrepresentation," or someone who seeks to "excite or cherish excessive or unworthy emotion" (56–57). Anyone departing from the truth finds only temporary success. The process makes a man "weakened and wasted" and, in the long run, destroys his power to persuade (58). Bascom's book tells readers that the aesthetic—the inner dwelling and control of the individual—gives their speech power. Pretenders always fail because language arises from this exalted place—the truth and right within us.

Race Marks the Yardstick

This all appears straightforward until we realize that nineteenth-century Americans disagreed about the *internal nature* of African Americans and other marginalized racial and ethnic groups. Many commentators believed that race best marked what lies within us, and thus the roots of our cultural output. The South spent the century, one way or another, creating rules to make sure that someone with black skin controlled little cultural capital. Before Emancipation, southerners denied blacks training in skilled trades and tried to deny them literacy. We saw that in the antebellum North, many whites believed blacks could never master language as orators, and Major Noah believed blacks' supposed inferiority put both republicanism and Shakespeare beyond their reach. After blacks left the status of chattel property and federal troops tried to protect their political rights, the South still sought to justify a peonage system that exploited their labor.[43] Henry W. Grady, whom George Frederickson calls "the leading prophet" of the supposedly more enlightened New South ideology, claimed that white supremacy was "the right of character, intelligence, and property to rule." As Frederickson points out, this doctrine ran into trouble because, in the 1880s, it was not racialized *enough*. Whites without education or property found themselves further impoverished by a postwar system designed to exploit black labor and wanted to hoist further racial barriers.[44] Few then sought meaningful change. Even George Washington Cable, considered one of the most radical white critics of the New South ideology who favored giving blacks a limited kind of cultural capital did not imagine that his plan would change society's "necessary" power distinctions. In 1909, almost four decades past Reconstruction, Governor James K. Vardaman made the sham claim that "fabulous sums of money to educate [the negro's] head" succeeded only in "impairing his usefulness and efficiency as a laborer." "As a race," he said, "he is deteriorating morally every day."[45]

Indeed, race had always figured prominently in rhetoric instructors' view of who could assess beauty and control language. The venerated Hugh Blair asked in his 1833 text book, "Is there any one who will seriously maintain that the taste of a Hottentot or a Laplander is as delicate and as correct as that of a Longinus or an Addison?" George Quackenbos agreed so heartily with Blair that he made the very same comparison, in troublingly similar language, between the Hottentot, Addison, and Longinus; indeed, Quackenbos said that the African Hottentot embodied the very differences. "Examples of the vitiated Taste, whether we apply this term, literally, to the external sense, . . . meet us on all sides. The Hottentot smears his body with putrid oil."[46]

Quackenbos moved from the particulars of the body to the universals of taste and insisted that aesthetic "standards" themselves were racial. "When we speak of the concurrent Tastes of men, as the universal standard, it must be understood that we mean men placed in situations favorable to the proper development of this faculty," he said. "Rude and uncivilized nations carry with them no authority." Indeed, said Quackenbos, the standards of taste themselves "must not be dusky or muddy."[47]

Nature, morality, and tastes reinforced one another, and together they would keep blacks down. Listen to a late nineteenth-century scholar of rhetoric, who, apparently, forgot that slavery had ended nearly thirty years earlier: "From the dawn of our country's independence, free American orators have appealed, not to stupid, embruted slaves, but to American freemen who are able to fully appreciate and understand them; and so long as this continues, so long will endure

. . . the liberty of the people."[48] This scholar spells out the audience—not the stupid, embruted slaves—but the "freemen who are able to fully appreciate and understand them," and this exchange between the free and those with cultural capital generates citizens' liberties. To nineteenth-century whites, blacks so lacked elite cultural capital that they could never know universal truths or carry the persuasive power that goes with it. Cultural capital and aesthetic power marked a political divide.

Given that racial differences played an enormous explanatory role in the nineteenth century, the scholar's statement is not very surprising. But when race inserts itself in a causal chain connecting aesthetics, cultural capital, and persuasiveness, the collision of beauty, racial ideology, and power infuses any performance we take in. The audience cannot escape. Nineteenth-century commentators routinely linked aesthetic beauty and racial characteristics. One commentator noted that Americans did not love music in the way the French or the Germans did. A *Harper*'s writer observed that "as a national characteristic, to be song and music lovers belongs to the Irish and German races rather than to the Saxon." The "higher aesthetic civilization" of France, Italy, and Germany fostered music skill, said another commentator. "It is rare to find a German or an Irish girl without an ear for music." The German took to music because of "tradition and by the strong forces of heredity," said another.[49]

When the antebellum singing sensation Jenny Lind took her jubilant tour of the United States in the 1850s, periodical writers declared that her sweet warbling came from her Nordic roots. "The Northern Muse must sing her lesson to the world," enthused John Sullivan Dwight. "Her fresher, chaster, more intellectual, and . . . colder strains come in due season to recover our souls from the delicious languor of a music which . . . has degenerated into mere sensibility, and a very cheap kind of superficial, skin-deep excitability." After watching Lind perform, *The New York Herald*'s critic proclaimed that "the wand of civilization" had passed to the northern races. One publication called for trading racial capital for Lind's cultural capital. "Sell your old clothes, dispose of your antiquated boots . . . sell 'Tom' into perpetual slavery," exhorted *Holden's Magazine,* "whatever you must, to . . . hear Jenny Lind!" By contrast, Carla L. Peterson notes that the black singer Elizabeth Taylor Greenfield, who carried a wide range and style that rivaled Lind's virtuosity, had her tag transformed from the "Black Swan" to the "African Crow."[50]

For Jenny Lind's listeners, not just sweet warblings but language itself was racialized through the aesthetic. In this world, language has a direct link to the best of the human mind. "Of all the honors that Anglo-Saxon literature has won," wrote one editor of *Harper's New Monthly,* "this is its noblest—this only is immortal—that its language, growing slowly to perfection, has constantly struggled, and with memorable success, to give a voice to the deepest instincts and loftiest reasonings of the human mind and . . . the highest aspirations that our redeemed nature can experience." Now, not just language, but Anglo-Saxon language, embodies truth and beauty's fixed characteristics. Every word in this lexicon—even truth and beauty itself—is tinged with the Anglo-Saxon, or, the "whiteness" of the time.[51]

Likewise, the *Harper's New Monthly* editor smugly titled an essay "Anglo-Saxon Mind, and Its Great Thoughts" and argued that "Anglo-Saxon blood" itself stood behind the best of most cultural production. "Whether it utter itself in poetry or prose, whether it produce a scheme of political economy or invent steam-engines and huge ships, one inevitable characteristic stamps the creative act, and presents Anglo-Saxon intelligence and hope to the wonder of the world." The race "reaches out in all the manifestations of thought and activity . . . shaping its culture," the editor wrote, "conducting the whole movement of its restless, energetic, aspiring civilization."[52] The "unique" powers of whiteness shape all of culture and political systems and, thought *Harper's*, embodies the world's "hope."

Even those less sure of America's cultural domination believed that race determined all cultural production. T. W. Higginson bemoaned the dearth of American creativity. But he believed the "race," the American race, which implicitly for white intellectuals of the time was likewise white, held promise. "We, a younger and cruder race, yet need to go abroad for our standard of executions," he said. "But our ideal and our faith must be our own."[53] Frederick Nast claimed in 1881 that America would produce no worthy American music "until the present discordant elements are merged into a homogeneous people."[54] A few years later, Sidney Lanier pleaded that "our literature needs Anglo-Saxon iron; there is no ruddiness in its cheeks, and everywhere a clear lack of red corpuscles." The answer: get the blood flowing; get some of Jenny Lind's Nordic racial genes into the pool.

Reclaiming and Remapping the Yardstick

If race determined culture, were "other" ethnic and racial groups capable of producing works of high aesthetic quality? Could they see beauty and grasp aesthetic truth? If so, could they wield the tools of rhetoric to allow them to tap those wells of truth? Frederick Douglass knew this was a key question whites had about blacks. "We are literally the spectacle for man and for angels. The whole world, the civilized world, at least, appears to stand in doubt concerning us," he told a black audience. "It is asked by men of all nations, what manner of men are the descendants of Africa? Are they capable of the same educational advancement? Are they capable of rising to the same heights of civilization—of producing the same grand results produced by the great nations of the white race? . . . That's the question." Even at meetings with white supporters "the burden of nearly all the speeches is a confirmation of natural inferiority, perpetually hurled at the sable brows of the sons of Africa," he said. "It is a confession I blush to hear made."[55]

Scholars have thoroughly documented that most white citizens throughout the nineteenth century already had made up their minds about African Americans, just as they had prejudged Chinese Americans and Native Americans. As we recall from chapter 2, one observer of Native Americans stated that the "picturesque" Indian reveals himself on closer inspection to inspire "revulsion."[56] T. W. Higginson warned Americans not to become "as uninteresting as so many Chinese." All these races lacked the internal wherewithal to develop an aesthetic sensibility. Higginson and others suggested that training in science and art might help a particular individual. But this was a long shot.[57] Investing in cultural capital for any person belonging to these groups might not be worth the effort. The audience, then, had been biased. Clearly white Americans *expected* to hear the brutish and vulgar sounds issuing from the mouths of people of color.

In aesthetic matters, writers and orators outside the Anglo-Saxon fold were continually told that they came up short at the very core of their being. Many marginalized writers like Frederick Douglass strove to represent themselves as the "kind" of humans capable of understanding the aesthetic, of creating beauty, and of thus meeting the mark as human beings. They had to demonstrate, in other words, that they possessed the cultural capital associated with the white bourgeoisie or upper classes. For a black in the late nineteenth century, as we saw in the antebellum years, this meant to pretend a higher class position. Often this in turn meant wielding the elevated language of someone well steeped in learning (and thus privy to large amounts of linguistic capital). Their efforts created an ironic result: the very demonstration of meeting the "white" aesthetic standard implicitly announced to their audiences that they supported the status quo. Even if, in the end, marginalized writers revised that status quo, the form itself of their expression created yet another powerful expression of class and racial hierarchy. Thus more than one hundred years later, cultural studies students receive a perplexing and fascinating jumble of messages from the nineteenth century: people perform in accordance with an elite ideology that, on the surface, discounts what marginalized writers have to say and even who they are. Unless, in hindsight, scholars carefully consider the pas-de-deux that race and class perform in the cultural landscape, the obvious masking and role-playing escapes notice. Societal revisions remain cloaked in elevated language.

Belonging to a marginalized group in the nineteenth century produced a particularly awkward situation. The speaker had two choices when presenting to an audience: either act as the mainstream expected—without much elite cultural capital—and thereby play into the mainstream's preconception of racial inferiority; or act with elite cultural capital on full display by trotting out the Latin, the Greek, the sweep of history, and the long periodic sentences and appear, to those ideologically predisposed not to accept this, to be putting on airs. The first approach perpetuates racial ideology through stereotype. The second accentuates a profoundly uncomfortable part of the American story: the class divide.

It should hardly be surprising, then, that today, when college students read the following lines from W.E.B. Du Bois's *Souls of Black Folk,* they sometimes get annoyed at what they perceive as an enormous disparity—between the social and economic place that blacks occupied in the United States at the time Du Bois wrote and Du Bois's elevated language. Du Bois writes:

> I sit with Shakespeare and he winces not. Across the color line I move arm in arm with Balzac and Dumas, where smiling men and welcoming women glide in gilded halls. From out the caves of evening that swing between the strong-limbed earth and the tracery of the stars, I summon Aristotle and Aurelius and what soul I will, and they come all graciously with no scorn nor condescension. So, wed with Truth, I dwell above the Veil. Is this the life you grudge us, O knightly America? Is this the life you long to change into the dull red hideousness of Georgia? Are you so afraid lest peering from this high Pisgah, between Philistine and Amalekite, we sight the Promised Land?"[58]

Students ask, what does this arrogantly elevated language, this invocation of Aristotle and Balzac, have to do with African Americans in 1903, when a record number of lynchings beset the country? High-flown rhetoric does not repeal the law of gravity operating at the end of a rope. And to whom does Du Bois think he is talking? African Americans in the South struggled to get *any* education, much less glide arm and arm with literary greats. Today, in an age and place where racial inferiority is seldom consciously drawn on as an explanatory factor, W.E.B. Du Bois, through his erudite references to Shakespeare, looks like he is showing off.

He was, in part. He was showing that he knew the rules of cultural capital. But Du Bois also is doing something that John Bascom and many other members of his audience would not have expected but would have recognized. Du Bois summons the aesthetic, beauty, and, in a sleight of hand before an unsuspecting reader, "weds [himself] with truth." And this truth allows him to "dwell above the veil." There, those considered to be the greats of Western literature and thought—Shakespeare, Balzac, Dumas—"wince not" when they commune with Du Bois. He summons; they come. He controls; they enrich and elevate, and they transport Du Bois out of Georgia, where Du Bois taught and witnessed firsthand the brutal southern repression. Most important, Du Bois removed race from the aesthetic process by blurring the color line marking aesthetic creators. He inserts Dumas, the son of a Santo Domingo black, into a group that includes Balzac, a French intellectual, and Aristotle, the Greek anchor of what people like Bascom called Western Civilization. High culture in Du Bois's book ignores the color line.

Bascom, Du Bois, and even Aldridge all pose important questions that the final two chapters of this book seek to understand. Anna Julia Cooper, who studied Bascom's text as an Oberlin college coed, used the rules of rhetoric to remake women's role and race in America. Edith Eaton, who wrote under the pen name Sui Sin Far, pretended to a racial identity and a class position as a neurasthenic to remake her audience's conceptions of Asian Americans. These writers use the rules of high culture extolled by Bascom, those normally unspoken rules of writing and oratory, to remake people of color in their audiences' minds. In short, Cooper and Eaton used these rules to rewrite white.

CHAPTER 4

Anna Julia Cooper and the Black Orator

On an ideal day, Anna Julia Cooper might have risen before dawn in her Washington, D.C., house, brushed the hair from her soft-brown face, and meticulously dressed in a long, full prairie skirt and a high-necked Victorian blouse. She would glance over the newspaper, rue Calvin Coolidge's 1924 presidential landslide, and quickly turn to her doctoral dissertation for the Sorbonne. She would work on this treatise about the class structure of French-American colonies, file her work, feed and pack up her five adopted kids for school, and then begin her work day. She would teach a full day of Latin and Greek at the District of Columbia's M Street School by telling her black charges that Cicero and Virgil held secrets vital to them, return to her middle-class home, and polish an oration to the community about race and education. After she cooked dinner and put the kids to bed, the sixty-six-year-old's day still was not done. She would work on yet another project—plans for the school she was founding for black workers. Before she turned out the lights, she would say a prayer (she always said her prayers) for her mother, a North Carolina slave, and perhaps even for the eternal fate of her reputed father, her mother's owner.

Annie Cooper's extraordinary energy and long life filled with projects propelled her from the daughter of a bondwoman to among the most educated and articulate voices in America. She devoted her 105 years in North Carolina, Ohio, and Washington, D.C., to education, language, and social change. Putting her three areas of concern in a series hardly does her justice. For Cooper fit education, language, and social change all into the same day; indeed, she often shoehorned all three into the same activity. She used both education to prepare students for society's leadership roles and language to stake claims on society. She used her powers of language—the cultural capital she amassed as a life-long student and teacher—to rework the very foundations of race and gender in the United States. Cooper's eloquent words and remarkably long life help us answer a question about her: Was Cooper an "elitist" who stood over other blacks in the period? Or did she use her fancy language to change the ways race works in the country?[1]

Cooper worked these many years on a subterranean level, one that rarely if ever registered on the radar when literary bombs, lain by the likes of W.E.B. Du Bois and Ida B. Wells, detonated. Consider the World's Colombian Exposition in 1893, a year after Cooper published her collection of essays, *A Voice From the South*. Black women there neatly divided themselves into two categories—marginalized insiders standing within the fairgrounds and clearcut outsiders. Inside, speaking in the building that housed the Haitian exhibition, was a small group of women, including Cooper. Hers was a quick five-minute delivery, calling on women to "take our stand on the solidarity of humanity, the oneness of life." Outside the gate, distributing pamphlets about women's marginalization at the fair, stood the newspaper editor and activist Ida B. Wells, who delivered a protest much more direct than Cooper's. She called her pamphlet "a clear, plain statement of facts concerning the oppression put upon the colored people in this land of the free and home of the brave."[2] Her fiery work began with a history of slavery and included graphic descriptions of lynching in the United States. Common sense might suggest that Wells and those standing with her *outside* the fair's walls were the radicals, those fighting for the most dramatic changes for women.

But Cooper's style never had been to stand outside and project her voice into the inner sanctum. Cooper worked behind the scenes, using John Bascom's very tools: words. Annie Cooper, a teacher of Latin and Greek for forty years, reforged the masters' tools by using language itself in an attempt to change the rules and laws that governed women, African Americans, their rights in America, and even race itself. Her words and her manipulation of those words created an alternative social theory for the nation. These are big designs for someone born into slavery, and her alternative social theory was years in the making.

More Than a Floating Intention

Our fieldwork should begin in several places: Cooper's education in rhetoric at Saint Augustine's Normal and Collegiate Institute in Raleigh, North Carolina, and at Oberlin College and in her teaching of Latin in Washington, D.C. At these schools she learned the approach that would set her apart from other activists like Ida B. Wells and Mary Church Terrell. In her writing, Cooper's style of argument differed from either Wells or Terrell. Instead of firing facts machine-gun style until she overwhelmed her audience with evidence as Wells did, and instead of winding inductively from homey examples to the broader missions for women as Terrell did, Cooper built tight deductive arguments using the skills of classical rhetoric she learned in her youth. She quickly convinced her audience to agree with her on some point about general moral standards and, with a swift turn of phrase, hijacked their assumptions governing not only women's rights and women's right to education but also race itself.

Gaining the education to wage these battles was not easy for Cooper, and in these struggles she learned the value of both cultural capital and manual labor. This daughter of a slave woman came from a family of skilled tradesmen: her maternal grandfather was a carpenter, and her brothers Rufus and Andrew worked in skilled construction.[3] Cooper took to school immediately. She called her first school, Saint Augustine's Normal School, "my world during the formative period." The school had been founded as an outgrowth of the Freedmen's Bureaus, designed to teach citizenship to the freedmen and provide them with skills.[4]

Saint Augustine was no different than other schools for blacks at the time—it had to fight to provide blacks education, and Cooper had to fight, as a woman, to get her piece of it. In a report of the schools, one reviewer remarked that the teachers required "courage to face the opposition to the education of these freedmen."[5] The government closed the Freedmen's Bureaus in 1876 with the end of Reconstruction, when Cooper was just ten, but the school managed to continue. Cooper, however, struggled to get access to everything she wanted to learn. When the school organized its first Greek class, it excluded women by designating it only for ministry students. "A boy, however meager his equipment and shallow his pretensions, had only to declare a floating intention to study theology and he could get all the support, encouragement and stimulus he needed," she later complained in *A Voice* (77). But Cooper would not be kept down by a lack of support. She got into the Greek class, and, by the time she requested admission to Oberlin College as a twenty-three-year-old widow, she had read in Greek about three hundred pages of text, including Xenophon, Plato, Herodotus, and Thucydides, and in Latin, Caesar's seven books of commentaries, Cicero, and six books of Virgil's *Aeneid*.[6] Once at Oberlin in 1881, Cooper drank in the standard classical education of the era, which included a steady diet of rhetoric courses. She took the rhetoric course offered her sophomore year plus a logic course—then considered one of the ancillary fields of rhetoric—and three more courses in her junior year. In her senior year, Cooper took courses in Plato and two more terms of rhetoric.[7] After graduating from Oberlin, Cooper then taught Latin at the M Street School for most of the next forty years.[8]

Fashioning a White Rhetoric

Cooper's interest and training in rhetoric provides a springboard to ask what it meant to be a woman who used these skills to speak out. During the late nineteenth century, schools considered rhetoric a basic skills. Oberlin so prized students' speaking ability that four days a week juniors focused on the physical preparation for speech, including, "Position, Breathing, Flexibility and Looseness of Throat, Depth of Vibration or Chest Resonance, 'Touch' and Articulation," according to the *Oberlin College Catalogue, 1883–1884*. "A complete system of Vocal Exercises will be given," the catalogue said, "designed to secure strength, ease, and durability of Voice."[9]

Rhetorical training at the time did not consist simply of chest and breathing exercises. Rhetoric's strength lies in its ability to mold concepts. As with John Bascom and his cohort (discussed in chapter 3), nineteenth-century rhetoricians believed they rooted their practices in natural laws that gave writers and orators powerful ammunition. "Of one who assumes to instruct and direct a body of men in a matter connected with their common interests," Cooper read in her sophomore class rhetoric text, "we expect that he will realize the importance of that which he advocates and the seriousness of the occasion."[10] These skills allowed orators and writers in a democracy to shape minds and change society. Mastering the rhetorical form thus allowed the skilled rhetorician—always defined as a man[11]—to participate in the world's great issues, argued Bascom in his leading rhetorical treatise. "When as a writer and speaker he puts himself in a communion with men, in giving law to their thought," says Bascom, "he gives law, also, to the nation's language."[12] And, in a democracy, he can give law to the land.

As chapter 3 illustrates, common references to rhetorical practice and its rights should in reality read "white rhetorical practice and rights." In much the same way that antebellum philologists believed that blacks lacked the capacity to create meaning and move people with language, late nineteenth-century experts on rhetoric believed that blacks as orators and writers had nothing to contribute to shaping the public mind. By understanding how blacks were specifically excluded from the power of oratory and rhetoric, how they were considered people incapable of delivering useful information or shaping the public mind, we begin to grasp what Cooper faced from her audiences.

A writer in the magazine *The Galaxy* objected to frequently heard generalizations about black orators, but he followed with a few of his own. He complained of "a cheap school of humor" that had "become fashionable . . . which consists of fictitious reports of negro speeches made after some grotesque inventions in grammar and rhetoric." The writer even allowed that this racial scapegoating "wounds the negro, is a perpetual thorn in his side, a source of bad blood." But that writer, in his defense of blacks' potential as orators—as potential "forest-born Demosthenes"—cast serious doubt on any real potential for blacks at the moment. According to the scientific racism of the day, what blacks could contribute to oratory was not dispassionate reason, sound judgment, or the linguistic capital that showed a command of the culture; rather, they could contribute feeling, a sometimes dangerous commodity. Blacks had a "characteristic fondness for big words" that they did not understand, said *The Galaxy* writer. They enjoy a "tawdriness of rhetoric" that can evoke "the most weird and touching effects" in the audience. The "unheeded perspiration . . . the large, clumsy hands, trembling with emotion, and raining down from the air," explained one essayist, "attest that the negro speaker is feeling what he says, when he is in the full tide of exhortation, when, perchance, he sees his favorite religious phantasm, 'the old ship of Zion,' far away on the stormy waves, or sings, as of a longing spectator, the hymn of 'Swing low, sweet Chariot,' one of his characteristic visions of the sky."[13]

In 1870, philologist Maximilian Schele de Vere, imperceptibly humbled by the South's loss in the war, still reigned on the language scene, and he issued a warning about the black speaker. "The negro orator throws himself upon a tide of talk, without so much as a plank of political knowledge or literary reminiscence to sustain him, and goes on without coming to grief, for any distance or length of time," Schele de Vere warned. And this loquacity could be downright risky, he said. De Vere cited "episodes . . . when this natural gift of frenzied declamation has so wrought upon the negroes as to deprive them at once of reason and humanity." These race-bound views about language may be why Fannie Jackson Choppin, a black woman who took top honors in Greek at Oberlin just after the war, "could not," said a contemporary, "bring herself to rise and speak in class."[14]

Every day, Cooper saw the effects of these broader societal beliefs when she walked into her job at a black high school. In 1906, she found herself embroiled in a battle over what kind of education black children should have, and her stand may have resulted in her ouster from the M Street School. During these years Booker T. Washington pushed his program for industrial education. In his autobiography, Washington complained that some of his fellow Hampton College students "knew more about Latin and Greek when they left school, but they seemed to know less about life and its conditions as they would meet it at their homes."[15]

In a speech that the *Brooklyn Eagle* said contained something "rare among colored speakers, logic," Washington delivered an oddly self-serving reading of history.[16] He claimed that African Americans "forgot the industrial education that was given the Pilgram Fathers of New England."[17] The education of blacks in different skills, including the techniques of complex and abstract thinking, could nearly bring him to despair: "How often has my heart been made to sink as I have . . . found women who could converse intelligently on Grecian history, who had studied geometry, could analyze the most complex sentences, and yet could not analyze the poorly cooked and still more poorly served bread and fat meat that they and their families were eating."[18] Washington, unlike many whites at the time, is not saying that "complex sentences" are beyond the ken of blacks, but he places the priority for these skills so low that he and the stubbornly racist whites end up at the same place. What good can conjugating a Latin verb do you? He had little use for the classical education that teachers like Cooper delivered.[19]

Washington merely reflected much of the prevailing "wisdom" of the time. Neither Henry W. Grady nor George Washington Cable, who debated the rights of blacks to an education after the Civil War, believed that blacks made worthy recipients of society's valuable cultural capital. Grady, "the leading prophet" of the New South ideology, believed only whites had "the right of character, intelligence, and property" to hold thinking, governing jobs in society. One black leader recalled a professor of Greek searching for a job in Washington, D.C., who "was treated with bitter contempt, not even receiving a reply." "Damnable heresy" is what opponents called the application. "It was immodest and presumptuous for black men to aspire to such positions."[20] Where blacks were concerned, it was far better to stick with menial skills.

Cooper bemoaned this opposition to nurturing the black mind. Teaching Virgil in her classroom "caused a general raising of eyebrows," she said.[21] "It was once doubted if a Negro had a soul," she wrote. "After it was found that he [did] . . . there was still a question [of] whether he had a brain."[22] The ability of blacks "to learn Latin and construe Greek syntax needed to be proved to sneering critics," she said on another occasion.[23] And the policy did not end with education, of course. Those with the *verboten* skills found few places to ply the writer's trade. She lamented to her alma mater that publishers may not take her own work—a translation from French of the eleventh-century epic Pelerinage de Charlemagne—"solely on its merits" should they know that she was black, and she asked Oberlin not to reveal her race in a search for a publisher.[24]

In 1906 Cooper temporarily lost her job at the M Street school because she demanded mental training for her charges, and in the *Oberlin Alumni News* she bemoaned the national opposition to educating blacks: "The dominant forces of our country are not yet tolerant of the higher steps for colored youth; so that while our course of study was for the time being saved, my head was lost in the fray, and I moved west. Here I am teaching Latin and Greek eight hours to the day. . . . But if the industrializing wave that threatens, reaches us here too, it is likely to be another case of 'Move along, Joe!'"[25] These skills offered power that mainstream society did not want blacks to have, and Cooper paid with her job.

Black women faced an even more daunting challenge from this white rhetorical strategy. As Claudia Tate points out in *Domestic Allegories of Political Desire: The Black Heroine's Text at the Turn of the Century,* white women held "exalted cultural value" and were revered in "patriarchal society for producing heirs and regulating moral, spiritual, and emotional values." Society cast black women far below white women on the social hierarchy, stereotyped them as sluttish, and clung to an image of them as almost subhuman. "Black women had expendable value," Tate says, "as base items of consumption."[26] Many black women in the 1890s struggled to exercise their right to speak, including Cooper's Oberlin classmate Mary Church Terrell.[27] For years, Terrell had been eager to lecture on race in the United States. "When, however, my husband consented," she said, "some of his friends were so shocked and horrified that words simply failed them as they attempted to express their disapprobation."[28] Even among African Americans gender tripped her up.

Cooper faced hardships similar to Terrell's. In a letter to an old Oberlin professor, Cooper recalled that her commencement address evoked a faculty member's "infinite disgust" because she "delivered it mannishly, not pretending to read an 'essay' as a lady properly should."[29] In her introduction to *A Voice* Cooper writes that "the 'other side' has not been represented by one who 'lives there.'" The black woman deserved an opportunity to reliably represent the "long dull pain" of her experience (ii).[30] And in a speech before Episcopal ministers, she upbraided the clergy for their "phenomenally small" support for black women and their education.[31] Yet Cooper escaped the traps that sought to silence her. By embracing rhetorical practice, Cooper moved away from the race- and gender-based understanding of who can write. And by implicitly making herself, through her rhetorical skills and practices, a member of the government—a lawgiver—she upset the accepted order.

Responses to Cooper's *Voice* and her other writings and speeches show that her audiences felt her force and authority. The press uniformly praised the intellectual substrate of her work. One newspaper credited her argument as "keen," and another pronounced her work of "sound sense." Her work is "attracting wide attention," said another, "because of its originality and great literary strength." The intellectual integrity of Cooper's work and her command of language made a powerful statement to a reviewer at the *Boston Transcript*. "Indeed, the very fact of her criticism in excellent English and in welcome style and phrase," the reviewer cooed, "is a manifest of ability and cultivation of those she represents." The forbidden skills, artfully employed, proved her larger point.[32]

Cooper's power also moved her reading audiences. A contemporary said her essays in the *Voice* "make one of the strongest pleas for the race and sex of the writer that has ever appeared." The president of the Public Education Association of Washington called her "an inspiring lecturer and leader," and the *Asbury Journal* said that she had a "power of expression that held her audience spellbound." "She lays down boldly, clearly, and strikingly the great law that a race will finally be what its women are," said *Public Opinion*. Albion Tourgee claimed Cooper's book "would be a new sensation to many a white souled Christian woman of the 'superior race.'" And one reviewer said simply that Cooper's book was "impossible to shake off." Clearly, Cooper knew how to both give words power and touch her audience.[33]

Attacking One's Foes with a Feather

Cooper's "Woman vs. the Indian" challenges prejudice in the women's rights movement and offers an example of how she crafted this power with her rhetorical skills. Cooper wrote the last section as a peroration to direct readers' moral development. She urges them to a higher level, a level that she already has laid before them, and she calls on her readers to align their thinking with "the supremacy of the moral forces of reason and justice and love in the government of the nation" (126).

The shape of Cooper's argument made another statement: she would tackle head-on ideas about blacks as unintentionally comic orators and accept no compromise on her argument. Among the arguments whites made about blacks' ability to speak relied on a new spin from an old source: O. S. Fowler's fifty-year-old phrenological "conclusions." Cooper's contemporaries claimed that blacks lacked the ability to rigorously structure their orations and writings. Professor Schele de Vere lamented that blacks' "absurd misuse of words and confusion of ideas" rarely convince "an educated audience of white people."[34] The rhetoric critic in *The Galaxy* said that blacks' "favorite, almost exclusive figure [of speech] is the simplest one in the rhetorician's repertoire—allegory." This fondness overruns everything else in the talk. "So fond is he of this figure that often his whole speech on a given occasion is nothing more than one extended allegory," said the critic. "'Speaking in parables,' as he calls it, is his favorite rhetorical pastime. There is a great fondness for Biblical illustrations. But few instances of abstract ideas." Blacks, in other words, have the gift of gab, and they can ride the coattails of a biblical story, but they cannot load and launch a powerful argument.[35]

Cooper laid waste to this idea by drawing on the tools of classical rhetoric, which often uses two opposing sides to investigate issues.[36] In Cooper's introduction to *A Voice* she explains her task in terms of setting facts before a jury, and she presents her entire book as evidence in a trial (ii). The structure of individual essays reflect Cooper's approach. In "Woman vs. the Indian" Cooper casts the essay into an opposition: Cooper versus white women who want to exclude blacks from their clubs. She sets out the incontrovertible facts, defines the terms, refutes the racist women's arguments, and calls for a new moral and philosophical order on this topic. One can neither choose a middle ground nor deny that she's heading someplace of her own making.

Cooper's technique for building her arguments slayed preconceptions about black oratory, but it also sets her apart from other women of the period and illustrates how she manipulated male-dominated rhetorical styles for her own means. Bascom put much distance between feminine forms of expression and the necessary skills of a rhetorician. Strong rhetoricians considered memory the weakest way to marshal facts and only reluctantly used memory in a proof. Bascom identifies memory with the feminine by slipping into the feminine pronoun during his discussion.[37] Bascom also warned male readers away from forms that dwelt on the emotions, that lead the reader inductively from the specific to a broader point. Anecdote limited inductive reasoning's general applicability, he said, and its power.

Early feminists fashioned an inductive rhetorical style on purpose to avoid challenging the male order too forcefully. Aware that their power to speak was suspect, these women struck a more personal tone and relied on personal experience. In effect, they asked the audience to participate. "As a less authoritative and aggressive style," says Karlyn Kohrs Campbell, "it was a less confrontational violation of taboos against public speaking by women."[38]

Mary Church Terrell illustrates this feminine inductive approach in 1906. In "What It Means to Be Colored in the Capital of the United States," Terrell threads the reader through example after example of the indignities that she faced in Washington. "As a colored woman I might enter Washington any night, a stranger in a strange land, and walk miles without finding a place to lay my head," she writes.[39] Terrell struggles to find a restaurant that will serve her and a seat on mass transit to the Washington Monument. Only after Terrell recounts her personal trials and other ordeals endured by her acquaintances in Washington, D.C., does she make the overreaching statement of her essay, which comes in its last sentence: "The chasm between the principles upon which this Government was founded, in which it still professes to believe, and those which are daily practiced under the protection of the flag, yawns so wide and deep."[40] While Terrell effectively makes her point, she has not assumed the power of someone who can lay down principles or laws and then drag the audience by the collar through them. In those days, that would require a masculine hand.

Francis Willard, the head of the Woman's Christian Temperance Union, who wrote during Cooper's time, slightly modified this rhetorical pattern. Unlike earlier feminists, Willard uses deductive reasoning but conceals her arguments' premises by embowering them in flowery statements.[41] In 1890, for example, Willard wrote "A White Life for Two" and argues for a new role for women. Then she added: "To meet this new creation, how grandly men themselves are growing; how considerate and brotherly, how pure in word and deed!"[42] She clothed her assertion for women's power in flattery for men.

Contrast this with "The Higher Education of Women," Cooper's discussion of the new woman who gains the right to education:

> The question is not now with the woman "How shall I so cramp, stunt, simplify and nullify myself as to make me eligible to the honor of being swallowed up into some little man?" but the problem, I trow, now rests with the man as to how he can so develop his God-given powers as to reach the ideal of a generation of women who demand the noblest, grandest and best achievements of which he is capable; and this surely is the only fair and natural adjustment of the chances (70–71).

None of Willard's "grandly growing men" here. Cooper drops "the problem" at men's door. Moreover, instead of starting her essay with personal experience, as Terrell did, Cooper begins with an image of traditional white male power: a book produced in Paris. "The author declares that woman can use the alphabet only as Molière predicted they would," she razzes, "in spelling out the verb *amo*"

(48). Cooper takes the audience head on and invokes icons of high culture only to make fun of its provinciality.[43] Before our eyes have traveled halfway down the page, Cooper shows us that she can enter the Western tradition's dialogue *and* signify on it. By the time we reach the bottom of the page, Cooper's ironic voice has invoked Ovid, Penelope, Andromache, Lucretia, and Petrarch's Laura before the reader, and there can be no more questions about her right to speak. The essay proceeds from the premise that the "civilized world" needs women to keep it civilized and then develops Cooper's main point: Those civilizing women need to hone their skills with education. The small man in Cooper's prose just has to live with the new, more educated, woman, she says, and Cooper does not hesitate to point a finger at the group that needs to make a change. Thus, Cooper moves in the deductive fashion, from the general to the concrete, and she does it without flinching. She leads her audience to the source of their backward attitudes and demands that they change.

Cooper uses deductive reasoning again in "Woman vs. the Indian" to trounce southern white women's reasoning abilities. "Now the Southern woman," she taunts, "was never renowned for her reasoning powers, and it is not surprising that just a little picking will make her logic fall to pieces" (108–109). These women believe that "because her grandfather had slaves who were black, all the blacks in the world of every shade and tint were once in the position of her slaves" (109). First Cooper uses analogy to show how the argument fails in its entirety. "The black race constitutes one-seventh the known population of the globe," she says. "That [the white lady's] slaves were black and she despises her slaves, should no more argue antipathy to all dark people and peoples, than that Guiteau, an assassin, was white, and I hate assassins, should make me hate all persons more or less white" (109). Do not blithely reason from the particular to the general, Cooper warns here. Because President James Garfield's assassin was white, it does not follow logically that all white people are assassins.

Then Cooper draws on what Bascom called the "laws of influence" to represent their argument as a syllogism and to pinpoint the fallacy of thought: "Civility to the Negro implies social equality. I am opposed to *associating* with dark persons on terms of social equality. Therefore, I abrogate civility to the Negro" (109–110). She displays an analogous syllogism, spaced on the page as if it were appearing in a logic text:

> Light is opposed to darkness.
> Feathers are light.
> Ergo,
> Feathers are opposed to darkness.
> The "social equality" implied by civility to the Negro is a very different thing from forced association with him socially. (110)

In four short sentences, Cooper laid waste to the southern women's argument.

Despite her use of deductive logic, Cooper appeared less threatening to readers by anchoring her reasoning in safe and familiar waters: women's claim to the domestic sphere. Once Cooper had pulled readers into that sphere and assured them of the ground rules, she could play with the audience's assumptions about women's role in society. Readers continued their journey by believing that the timeworn truisms of domesticity, which denied women their rights, guided the argument. By the time readers finished the essay, they found that Cooper had inserted new definitions that created a new woman with the new power of expanded rights.

Although the notion of the domestic sphere appears backward to readers today, literary historian Claudia Tate shows us that we have to place ourselves in the historical context to understand those writers. At the time, the domestic ideal had a much different meaning to black women like Cooper than it did to whites like Willard. In the postreconstruction world, black women could not be expected to reject a notion that the woman's world was the domestic world. Because slavery had never allowed them to have a home and family, they first had to secure that right. "After all, such heroines could hardly reject what had not been broadly within their domain to embrace," argues Tate about the women in African American novels of the period. By clinging to the domestic purview, the black woman becomes a symbol of racial advancement.[44]

Consider first the tactics of Frances Willard, who stands on the more conservative side of Cooper. Willard wraps her demands in domestic values, but she softens them until they recede into much less radical aims and buttress traditional values. To change women's roles changes little in society, she says in "A White Life for Two." "Woman is becoming what God meant her to be . . . and Christ's Gospel necessitates her being, the companion and counselor not the incumbrance and toy of man."[45] She wants women to have a different position in society, but this position is not going to make us see our most closely held beliefs—something so basic as racism—anew.

Ida B. Wells's style stands on the other end of the spectrum from Willard and still shows us what Cooper does *not* do. As Hazel Carby explains, Wells focuses on a specific moral wrong: the ways white males manipulated black men and women's bodies for political ends.[46] She dwells less on redefining roles and race than she does in pinpointing morally reprehensible conduct and calling for its end. Unlike Cooper, Wells relies on an onslaught of facts drawn from white newspapers. "Out of their own mouths shall the murderers be condemned," she says in *A Red Record*.[47] Wells further pushes this aura of fact by quoting *herself* in *A Red Record,* making herself the authority, the source to which any writer, including Ida B. Wells in this case, would turn for the answer. And on this accretion of detail, Wells deliberately and relentlessly founds her case for change.

Cooper argues, however, that facts do not work. "It is absurd to quote statistics showing the Negro's bank account and rent rolls," she says in "Womanhood: A Vital Element in the Regeneration and Progress of a Race," "to point to the hundreds of newspapers edited by colored men and lists of lawyers [and] doctors" while society makes black women chattel. As long as women are property, African Americans get no respect (25). Cooper understood that hard figures poured into a biased mind go nowhere.[48] For deeper change, one needs to examine readers'—and society's—basic assumptions about women and race. Cooper must change readers' preconceptions so they can *see* the facts. Attack the problem at its root, at the basic cognitive level that whites use to understand African Americans, and redefine the notion of black women in the era.

Thus, if Cooper stands between both Wells and Willard in style, she surpasses them both in the changes she asks of the audience. Clothed in her learned rhetorical forms, Cooper remakes what it means to be both a woman and a black in America. As her audience agrees with her on the flag-waving issues of God and country, she hijacks notions of domesticity, of women's role in education, and of race.

Accordingly, Cooper uses the domestic sphere to establish more than the black woman's right to family and home. Cooper's writing turns the domestic sphere into leverage for building a more powerful and revisionary deductive argument. In "Woman vs. the Indian" for example, she leads readers into the peroration and rouses them to higher thoughts and exalted feelings. She culminates her charge in one stunning periodic sentence that illustrates reasoning central to her entire essay:

> Let her try to teach her country that every interest in this world is entitled at least to a respectful hearing, that every sentiency is worthy of its own gratification, that a helpless cause should not be trampled down, nor a bruised reed broken; and when the right of the individual is made sacred, when the image of God in human form, whether in marble or in clay, whether in alabaster or in ebony, is consecrated and inviolable, when men have been taught to look beneath the rags and grime, the pomp and pageantry of mere circumstance and have regard unto the celestial kernel uncontaminated at the core,—when race, color, sex, condition, are realized to be the accidents, not the substance of life, and consequently as not obscuring or modifying the inalienable title to life, liberty, and pursuit of happiness,—then is mastered the science of politeness, the art of courteous contact, which is naught but the practical application of the principle of benevolence, the back bone and marrow of all religion; then woman's lesson is taught and woman's cause is won—not the white woman nor the black woman nor the red woman, but the cause of every man or woman who has writhed silently under a mighty wrong. (124–125)

Here Cooper immediately frames the discussion as a trial: "every interest . . . is entitled at least to a respectful hearing." Thus, we know that there can be no compromise; one side must win. She uses two basic building blocks—her position as society's shaper granted by her rhetorical role and her notion of domesticity—to mold readers' approach to race, class, and gender. She calls on readers to reassess their own values and not let surface characteristics interfere with people's "life, liberty, and pursuit of happiness." She thus writes women and blacks back into the Declaration of Independence. Her deft handling of the male rhetorical form helps her insert African Americans into the most basic document of the Union and makes them part of her unstoppable sweep of history.[49]

Cooper further redefines the domestic sphere. First, she delivers the traditional take on women's roles to the audience—succor the trampled. She begins a sentence that appears to describe traditional jobs for women by forecasting a time "When the right of the individual is made sacred, when the image of God in human form . . . is consecrated and inviolable." But Cooper suspends the sentence between the first introductory clause and the subject and verb that we expect will follow. She inserts a series of modifiers to these truisms of women's labor, and she then reroutes the real point. She broadens our definition of who should receive help and thus broadens our definition of women's work.

She first establishes what women's sphere should include. By modifying "God in human form" with the phrase "whether in marble or in clay," she pairs two substances, marble and clay, that have the same constitution, for both come from God's earth; yet each stands apart because one is shiny and one is dull. Then by association, she presents two other substances, alabaster and ebony, in the same light and carries over the sense of kinship from the first pair to the second. Although the new pair consists of different colors, we group them with the first pair because they too are both natural substances. Cooper implicitly pulls white and black under the same godly banner and thereby groups alabaster and ebony in our minds with marble and clay. Cooper, who slew the southern woman's logic with a swift syllogism, here defies a simple logical progression. She shifts from a rock-soft rock comparison to a rock-wood comparison. Marble-clay gives way to alabaster-ebony, and she creates a new unit in our minds. At the time, Cooper's audience believed that blacks and whites arose from very different stocks. Her task was to unite them under the notion of "human being." With her new groupings, these substances can be different—one white, the other black—yet they are the same, all part of God's dominion. From here, she need only show that society denies a part of the whole, a portion of the "celestial kernel uncontaminated at the core," its proper rights to demand our action. Put this way, the task becomes clear. God's dominion is women's dominion, and their labor is redefined. Only when America bridges this gulf and finally slays the injustice of a white republic will women's work be done. For her part, the writer Cooper has finished her work before the reader reached the sentence's subject and verb.

After Cooper recasts what women's work means, she finishes the thought begun so long ago: "Then is mastered the science of politeness, the art of courteous contact." She has already won her point. Only when women stand up to claim proper rights for all of the whole, can the coveted domestic skills be claimed for one's own. Cooper here uses her rhetorical tools to find a niche within the dominant myth of domesticity. She carves out a new function for herself, for women, and for blacks. With such a large task before women, the women's movement needs all the soldiers it can muster, both white and black.[50]

Grabbing the Audience's Sympathy

Cooper's work here illustrates the change she is trying to bring to society despite her audience's expectations. The African American who perhaps drew the biggest crowds to talks at the time was Booker T. Washington. An examination of his reception and technique shows just how demanding Cooper was for her time and how cultural capital played a crucial role in her oratorical work. Washington dwells at length on the reception he received for his Atlanta Exposition speech, in which he said that blacks and whites in all things "social . . . can be as separate as the fingers, yet one as the hand in all things essential to mutual progress." In a *New York World* account, we understand the crowd's southern leanings when we learn that, as Washington walked to the podium, a band played "Dixie" and "the audience roared with shrill ki-yi's." As soon as the band moved onto "Yankee Doodle," "the clamor lessened." But when this group of southerners heard what Washington had to say, that blacks wanted to "serve" whites and "lay down their lives" for whites, the crowd went right back to their shrill ki-yi's. "The multitude was in an uproar of enthusiasm, handkerchiefs waved, canes flourished, hats tossed in the air," said the reporter. "The fairest women in Georgia stood up and cheered. It was as if the orator bewitched them."[51]

But a reader of even Washington's account wonders whether it was the polish of the oratory—or the obsequiousness of the language—that made the fair women of Georgia cheer. "No speech was ever before made by an American negro which won the admiration and concurrence of so many white people," claimed a writer at *Scribner's Magazine,* who then wholeheartedly expressed his approval of Washington's central idea: "It is better to teach the average negro boy to be a good shoemaker than to be a rascally politician or a farcical preacher."[52] The editor of the *Atlanta Constitution* wrote the *New York Herald* to call Washington's speech "epoch-making." Why? The praise centers not on the rousing language, the beautiful analogies, or the searing logic. The *Constitution* editor exalted that "the speech is a full vindication from the mouth of a representative Negro of the doctrine so eloquently advanced by Grady," and "the question of social equality is eliminated." The letter writer confided to readers that the Exposition's board of directors considered themselves bold in inviting a negro to participate in the opening exercises, and at first some opposed the invitation. But, he exclaimed, Washington came through for them. "There was not a line in the address which would have been changed by the most sensitive of those who thought the invitation to be imprudent." For southern white listeners, what's not to like? Washington promised the crowd that blacks would serve and obey, and not press for full social rights. Recent scholars have made a persuasive case that Washington's compromise was aimed at heading off the brutal repression blacks faced in the South. Nevertheless, even a parrot, delivering that kind of message, would have received a standing ovation.[53]

Perhaps most telling is Washington's own philosophy about oratory. Washington proudly reprinted accounts of his speeches and claimed that his favorite moment in any speech was when he and his audience "have gotten into full and complete sympathy with each other." Yet, Washington coyly said in his autobiography that he could never "understand why people come to hear me." And he said that oratory paled in importance compared with the former men who "reap the mighty harvest." Washington declared that he liked "to forget all about the rules for the proper use of the English language, and all about rhetoric and that sort of thing." He did not draw on logic or the powerful pull of argument. (Sometimes "I had left out of my address the main thing and the best thing that I had meant to say," he complained.) Rather, Washington drew on a technique that *The Galaxy* writer said all black orators were drawn to—the story—which he called "the most effective medicine" for the skeptic. Washington hoped to win his audience with his soft-serve philosophy dished up as the avuncular black man on the land.[54]

Washington knew what he liked in oratory, and his preferences, as much as his choice of rhetorical models, tells more about why he got those standing ovations. In his book, *My Larger Education,* Washington talked about a memorable commencement address by one of his Tuskegee students. This student did not stand before the Tuskegee directors, faculty, and family and say, as one student across the country did, that "we need more of the artistic instinct. It was through that instinct that the Greeks mastered their life, and it is through it, that we shall some day master ours."[55] He did not deliver "mannishly," as Cooper had, a tight, well-reasoned argument; instead, the student told a story about a vegetable. He described how he obtained cabbage seeds, prepared the soil, planted, and harvested the crop. The crowd loosed cheers when the graduate, "held up one of the largest cabbages on the platform for the audience to look at and admire," claimed Washington. Lest anyone miss Washington's lesson, he said, "there is just as much that is interesting, strange, mysterious, and wonderful; just as much to be learned that is edifying, broadening, and refining in a cabbage, as there is in a page of Latin."[56]

Cooper, presumably, enjoyed Latin more than cabbage, and her oratory and essays apply a redefining magic to ideas that her audience might at first find hard to take. Cooper called for more than industrial training in "The Higher Education of Women." She argues, as does Willard, that an educated woman can wisely choose a mate rather than run pell-mell into the arms of the first available man.[57] Once Cooper uses the domestic argument to demand education for women, she sets out to redefine what women are to do with it; in fact, she redefines the domestic sphere. In one long sentence in "The Higher Education of Women," Cooper pushes the narrative along, makes the audience *think* that its definition of woman has been reaffirmed, and then subverts the standard definition by redefining the notion of womanhood and redirecting what women can do with their education:

> To-day there are one hundred and ninety-eight colleges for women, and two hundred and seven coeducational colleges and universities in the United States alone offering the degree of B.A. to women, and sending out yearly into the arteries of this nation a warm, rich flood of strong, brave, active, energetic, well-equipped, thoughtful women—women quick to see and eager to help the needs of this needy world—women who can think as well as feel, and who feel none the less because they think—women who are none the less tender and true for the parchment scroll they bear in their hands—women who have given a deeper, richer, nobler and grander meaning to the word 'womanly' than any one-sided masculine definition could ever have suggested or inspired—women whom the world has long waited for in pain and anguish till there should be at last added to its forces and allowed to permeate its thought the complement of that masculine influence which has dominated it for fourteen centuries. (50–51)

Cooper gives no mention to Washington's popular model for educating black women at the time: training them as cooks or domestics. Instead, Cooper begins with well-established facts—the story told so far about colleges' growth. She recounts that colleges are sending out women with traits of which everyone can approve—strong, brave, energetic, well-equipped. In midsentence, Cooper uses parallel phrases that may not ratify ideas that black women can only provide grunt labor in the home, but the phrases do fit snugly with everyone's understanding of general womanhood; namely, women are "quick to see and eager to help the needs of this needy world." Who can deny Cooper here? Having built on these easy-to-swallow premises, Cooper's sentence has momentum. Then she hammers out the edges of what the audience considers feminine: "women who can *think* as well as feel." This is the contested territory. Cooper quickly buttresses her argument with a chiasmus which argues that this "thinking" strengthens the very traits that the audience is most comfortable accepting in women: "who feel none the less because they think." Cooper consolidates her ground with another defining clause, one that buttresses traditional beliefs—"none the less tender and true." So far, Cooper may not sound like Booker Washington, but she sounds almost like Frances Willard, only without the push of flowery phrasing.

But then Cooper works her cultural revision. Cooper suggests that these educated women are all the more women, in a "deeper, richer" sense, than "any one-sided masculine definition could ever have suggested or inspired." Cooper argues for a new definition of womanliness, one that men could never have concocted. She takes this new definition and gives it weight in her audience's eyes by arguing that the world *needs* the strength of these better-equipped women to do the work. She calls women a "complement of that masculine influence," thus not calling for an overthrow but suggesting that the world's intellectual, cultural, and political forces are not complete until women's ideas are added to them. Then she pushes her point further. In midphrase, Cooper tucks in her most revisionary concepts by demanding that women's ideas be "allowed to permeate" the world's thought. With "permeate" Cooper seeks to overturn the male conception of women *and* the male way of viewing the world and make women's thought part of the undivided whole. Cooper shows what this permeation means: "Religion, science, art, economics, have all needed the feminine flavor" (57). Men can close nothing off to women. And society, including Booker Washington, can close nothing off to black women.[58]

Cooper makes similar moves with the notion of race. Cooper, like other writers of the era, often speak of mulatto women and their plight. Claudia Tate persuasively argues that novelists in Cooper's time, like Pauline Hopkins, were creating a new racial stock from mulattos. This was a "transitional racial and class status," argues Tate, that after Emancipation created a new niche for African Americans in society. The slave becomes transformed from the chattel of the master to a new position "grounded in virtue, education, and hard work." In other words, writers like Hopkins used a fuzzy race background to move society's judgmental lens from skin color to individual accomplishment.[59]

Cooper also used light-skin heroines in her work, such as the "cream-colored applicant" in "Woman vs. the Indian" who ran into organizations, like Wimodaughsis, that fortified societal notions of "whiteness" (82). Like the novelists Tate writes about, Cooper is not lifting the mulatto above those with darker skins. In extolling women's abilities to reform in "The Status of Women in America," she talks about their fierce loyalty: "You do not find the colored woman selling her birthright for a mess of pottage" (139). But the mulatto becomes a weapon to show that skin color is an "accident, not the substance of life" (125). Cooper, in fact, mocks the whole notion of bloodlines or societal privilege based on whiteness in "Woman vs. The Indian." "If your own father was a pirate, a robber, a murderer, his hands are dyed in red blood, and you don't say very much about it. But if your great great great grandfather's grandfather stole and pillaged and slew, and you can prove it, your blood has become blue and you are at great pains to establish the relationship" (103). Blood—or, in this case, Anglo-Saxon blood—stands for little in the work that Cooper imagines for humankind, but she also questions whether it means anything by itself. The slave owner, for example, has created false divisions based on blood. "He sowed his blood broadcast among them, then pitted mulatto against black, bond against free, house slave against plantation slave, even the slave of one clan against like slave of another clan" (102). Cooper calls attention to whiteness and shows race to be the social distinction that it is rather than a biological one. She dismisses the "pure Anglo thought and tongue"; "purity" rests in the mind.

This revision of race's definition is precisely what Cooper sought to create in her audience. Artists "have wrought into their products, lovingly and impartially and reverently, every type, every tint, every tone that they felt or saw or heard" (176), she says in one *Voice* essay, and they integrate these colors into their work. The artist controls the ultimate meaning of the piece. "For each of us truth means merely the re-presentation of the sensations and experiences of our personal environment, colored and vivified, fused into consistency and crystallized into individuality in the crucible of our own feelings and imaginations" (176–177).

This is what Anna Julia Cooper accomplishes in *A Voice from the South*. She does use language to craft a new ideology about phenotype and social roles as the antebellum black editors do. She does not stage a retelling of American history as does William Apess. The ongoing struggles of African Americans in the 1890s were all too obvious. She commands society's governing tools for a black woman. She uses the rhetorical skills of the educated white man to package her own social criticism, a critique that fused the types, the tints, and the tones of the world into a consistent whole.

In her oratory and writing, she looked her audience in the eye and crafted an argument that rewrote whiteness. Later, in her defense of her dissertation at the Sorbonne, she challenged the assumptions of one member of her dissertation committee who claimed that only "Latin, German, and Anglo-Saxon races" had any inkling of democracy. Cooper characteristically demurred. "To assume that the ideas inherent in social progress descend by divine favor upon the Nordic people, a Superior Race chosen to dominate the Earth, assuredly pampers the pride of those believing themselves the Elect of God," she said. "But one may as well anticipate Surprises."[60] In a close reading of how Cooper crafts her new definitions, her own "surprises" for the audience, we see that she may be standing on the inside as she did at the World's Columbian Exposition, but, from this insider's place, Anna Cooper's language had crafted a new world order.

CHAPTER 5

Edith Eaton Plays the Chinese Water Lily

Look at one of San Francisco photographer Arnold Genthe's shots of Chinatown from the turn of the twentieth century and at first glance there is no room in the frame for someone who looks like Edith Maude Eaton. Eaton, to most eyes, appeared to be a blue blood. Her father, the son of a venerable British merchant, had raised her in England and Canada. She spoke no Chinese and was even laughed at by the residents of Chinatown when, because of her British-educated Chinese mother, she claimed Asian heritage. Yet Eaton identified so strongly with the Chinese that she eventually took up the pen name of Sui Sin Far, "the water fragrant flower," and spent her short life writing to advance the rights of Chinese Americans in Canada and the United States.[1]

Genthe, however, attempted to present in his photographs a "pure" China that thrived, transplanted, in San Francisco's Chinatown. In Genthe's "The Street Crossing," for example, two girls walk in embroidered Chinese outfits, the full cut of their tunics draping their frames and their sleeves extending over their hands (figure 5.1). They step off a corner at Dupont and Jackson streets, the heart of Chinatown, and, flanking them to each side, two Chinese men stand in dark clothes. Anchoring the photo's center in the background is a Chinese merchant's display case of vases. Genthe shows us a world foreign to most American eyes—distant, self-contained, and strange. These few blocks of San Francisco, Genthe later claimed, "throbbed [with] the pulse of China." It lay far from the "white" world around it. Text by Will Irwin that accompanied Genthe's photos made Chinatown seem stranger still. Irwin warns that behind the curio shop with elegant vases lurks a sinister underworld. "The Chinese has the most haughty contempt for our law," wrote Irwin. "He seldom appeals to it, and when he does, look out for some deeper plot."[2] Irwin and Genthe manage to make

FIGURE 5.1. Arnold Genthe, *The Street Crossing* [*At the Corner of Dupont Street*]. *Library of Congress, Prints and Photographs Division, Arnold Genthe Collection: Negatives and Transparencies, LC–G403–T01–0023.*

the Chinese so exotic that they invert the "maxim" delivered by Bascom that beauty only arises from some deeper truth. Here, the beauty is a front for an ugly scheme. The attractive costumes and curios of Chinatown were all part of a closed foreign presence to mask those schemes, Irwin and Genthe concluded. The strange beauty that tourists flocked to see merely masks the darkest workings on the earth.[3]

But a closer look at the photo and negative from which Genthe made his print reveals clues to something other than a closed, enigmatic, and dangerous Chinatown. Behind and to the left of the Chinese man is a white male in Western clothes—a three-piece suit and a bowler hat. The case in the background displays rows not just of Chinese vases but merchandise more popular with tourists at the time, Japanese vases. And the store lettering, cropped out of the book's image, is not in Chinese, exotic and illegible to the Western reader, but in English. It says, unapologetically, "Chinese and Japanese Curios." Old Chinatown suddenly appears less hermetically Chinese. The business offers what it purports to offer—"oriental" items for tourists to take home. Contrary to Genthe's claims, Chinatown's pulse quickened with a beat that originated in more places than simply China.[4]

But, of course, the tourists who poured into Chinatown at the turn of the century did not bother to parse Chinese from Japanese from bourgeois western United States. It was all "oriental" to them. They liked to believe that they had their finger on the true pulse of an exotic land. In 1905, carriages full of tourists clogged New York's Chinatown streets. Guides in San Francisco promised to carry citizens beneath the city to secret dens. Genthe and Irwin claimed to have captured the spirit of a "foreign country" within the California city. Yet, of course, what the tourists, the guides, and Genthe himself captured most were fabrications. What they saw were merely safe and obvious cues for their own submerged imaginations, an exotic routine that predictably promised beauty on the surface but sinister doings at its depths.[5]

Even as Genthe's photos and Irwin's stories of secret Chinese motives stoked Anglo curiosity, Edith Eaton tapped that prurient interest and inserted herself into the picture frame. Eaton had been raised in a home with exacting Victorian standards. Yet at age thirty she adopted a series of Chinese pen names to construct her identity as a Chinese insider. She promised with her news features and short stories an "authentic close-up" of the Chinese American way of life, and she used these close-ups to rewrite the aesthetic competence and the possibilities of citizenship for the Chinese. If Genthe doctored his photos to make Chinatown look especially exotic and picturesque, and if Genthe's writer, Will Irwin, doctored text to give that beautiful exotic a horrific and threatening gloss, then Eaton doctored herself to collapse the distance between her subjects and the viewer and to illuminate the beauty and the thoughtfulness within the racial alien. She intervenes in the culture of whiteness that constructs the Chinese as so foreign and internally ugly that they could never become part of a country whose citizens join in its leadership. Eaton's own construction—her work as a supplanter in white culture—allows her viewers to see the Chinese more fully and to appreciate them. As a supplanter, who effectively "reverse passes" from Anglo to Chinese, she shows that something new arises from the Chinese presence in America and illustrates that both the Chinese and mainstream Americans are better off for the boundary crossing.

Eaton used her "reverse passing" to tell her mostly middle-class readers that cultural transmission does not just run from a white mainstream to a "dark" minority. The mix between the two, a hybrid she called "Eurasian," combined the best from mainstream American culture and the ancient culture of China. In this way, she demonstrated that the Chinese were not the heathens, unable to assimilate, that Genthe and others presented in popular culture. Rather, they lived sophisticated full lives, with aesthetic sensibilities that ran well below the surface. Hybrid manners would create a stronger nation. The mainstream was no longer correct by default. For "Americanizing," she warned, "does not always mean improving or civilizing."[6] If Anna Julia Cooper constructed sentences that rewrote race and gender, then Edith Eaton constructed an identity as one of Genthe's exotic Chinese subjects to sway the racial formation of another group. She grabbed the edges of Genthe's photos, expanded the margins, brightened the darkened spaces, and refocused the "documentary" shots. She began to undo all the distancing that Arnold Genthe, Will Irwin, and others sought to put in place, to remake the image of the Chinese, and to dredge it from the sinister ugly to comfortingly beautiful. The cost for Eaton, of course, is that her form for this comfort and beauty reinforced middle-class bourgeois values. Nevertheless, within that middle-class world, she created a Chinese character with depth. And she smashed the constructed dichotomy between "Chinese" and "American."[7] If at first glance, she says, "the Chinese do not please our artistic taste," Eaton quickly adds, "there are signs that in the future we in this country may attain to the high degree of civilization which the Chinese have reached, but for the present we are far away behind them" (195). Eaton has turned the tables on Genthe, Irwin, and others. To understand just how she accomplishes this, we must examine Genthe's photographs, Irwin's text, and the stories constructing "the Chinese" at the time Eaton wrote.

A Nervous Sickness

Eaton began her campaign, appropriately, by looking within, and she fashioned the narrative of her life to help prove her point. Others have documented Eaton's upbringing, but a few key moments in her life reveal her aims in her writing.[8] The mixed heritage of her British merchant father and a Victorian England–raised Chinese mother and their surroundings confused Edith and created her sense of conflict in identity that lasted nearly all of her life. Her early years were filled with moments in which she does not recognize what is "Chinese" and in which the Chinese do not recognize her as one of their own. Edith's father was a failed merchant who longed for a life as an artist, and, before Edith turned seven, he moved the family to Montreal, where the family knew few other Chinese. Edith recalls seeing a Chinese man in New York as a child and exclaiming to her brother, "Oh Charlie. Are we like that?" Edith's own brothers and sisters managed to ignore their Chinese heritage—none of them married people of Chinese ancestry—and they left Edith alone to assert her Chinese makeup as an article of faith.[9] And Edith's sister, the writer Winifred Eaton, made herself famous by taking a more popular identity as a Japanese American, Onoto Watanna.[10]

What made Edith's chosen identity as Chinese more difficult is that she rarely received assurances that anyone else would recognize her as Chinese. As a youth, some local children who knew Edith's mother teased Edith about her heritage, but that did not last long. As Edith got older, one of the few Chinese women she met in Montreal questioned whether a Chinese man, despite the dearth of Chinese women in North America, would overlook Edith's "half-white" composition and marry her (223). When Edith worked in a midwestern town, she endured a dinnertime tirade from fellow employees who asserted that the Chinese were not "human like ourselves" and that "they always give me such a creepy feeling" (224). Only later did Eaton reveal her identity. When she took a job canvassing Chinatown for the *San Francisco Bulletin*, she knew only a few stock phrases of the Chinese language, and the residents did not trust her. "The Americanized Chinamen actually laugh in my face when I tell them that I am of their race," she complained (227).

Edith never really knew how to embrace the part of her that was supposed to be Chinese. Her first attempts meant diving into the library. She read everything she could get her hands on about China. As a newspaper solicitor in her thirties, she had her run of Chinatown, which allowed her to visit the noodle shops, the temples, and the grocers. Slowly, the Chinese women of San Francisco warmed to Eaton. They "discover that I have Chinese hair, color of eyes and complexion, also that I love rice and tea. This settles the matter for them" (227). And Edith's own resistance to the Chinese likewise began to dissolve. "I am no longer the little girl who shrunk against my brother at the first sight of a chinaman," she said (227). Her pursuit of Chinese customs gave her a provisional status as Chinese insider. Edith began to write with a series of pen names. She tried Sui Seen Far and then became Sui Sin Far as she tried to seal her new Chinese identity.

Learning about the Chinese also taught her some difficult truths: Most Americans considered the Chinese debased and unable to possess any depth of feeling. The people who had given her coworkers the creeps possessed qualities that would forever keep them distant. In an autobiographical essay, Eaton complained that she had "come from a race on my mother's side which is said to be the most stolid and insensible to feeling of all races." Eaton, however, meant to show that this was not so. Under the stillness, the Chinese "[possess] considerable inventive power," she said, "whatever may be said to the contrary by those who know him but superficially" (235). Eaton claimed to feel so acutely, she said, "that it is almost a pain to live" (221). And she used her own body as the way to demonstrate that feeling.

From an early age, Eaton suffered from physical ailments. A childhood doctor said that she had an "enlarged heart." Her move to Jamaica as a reporter at age thirty came in part as an effort to live in a more healthful climate. And Eaton's travels between the Caribbean, New York, Boston, Seattle, Vancouver, and Montreal often started as a means to find health. Eaton did not leave these ailments as merely physical matters. In her autobiographical essay for *The Independent,* in fact, she turned these sicknesses into a tool that reworked America's class and racial map. She described her internal trauma of growing up half-Chinese and half-white in physical terms, as nervous sickness, or neurasthenia. "I have no organic disease," she complained, "but the strength of my feelings seems to take from me the strength of my body. I am prostrated at times with attacks of nervous sickness."[11] With a "nervous sickness," or neurasthenia, Eaton, despite the disbelief of her midwestern coworkers, seized the social standing of a "sensitive" soul.

According to the experts' understanding of neurasthenia at the time, Eaton was not supposed to be so "fortunate" as to contract this disease. Neurasthenia traditionally served as the illness of choice not for working women like Eaton but for elite white women like Alice James or Charlotte Perkins Gilman. James, in her letters, describes finding a vocation in illness to compete with her brothers' more public fame; James thus established herself as a sensitive and perceptive soul despite her ingrown existence. The unnamed character in Gilman's story "The Yellow Wallpaper" illustrates how a woman of privileged class, educated but not allowed to work, could develop a nervousness of mind that accelerated to madness under the prescribed bedrest cure. Thus, neurasthenia signified the golden cage of the pampered woman. "What I say," wrote S. Weir Mitchell, one of neurasthenia's early promoters, "applies and must apply chiefly to the leisure class."[12] Eaton, however, came from a family of falling fortune. Eaton spent most of her childhood in poverty and sold lace door-to-door to help the family pay its bills. Weir Mitchell would have been surprised to see her on his list of patients. As an adult, Eaton finished her book *Mrs. Spring Fragrance,* only after friends paid her living expenses. Eaton used neurasthenia not to describe a malady stemming from elite women's truncated social role but to describe stress over a mixed racial heritage, what she called in retrospect, "the cross of Eurasia" (221).

Eaton's claim on neurasthenia crossed racial as well as class boundaries. Eaton knew that she was not the "pure" white stock of James or Gilman, despite her appearance; yet, only the pure and "advanced" Anglo-Saxon was supposed to feel the pain of nervous disorders. Anglo-Saxons' heightened states, according to the best medical minds of the time, freed them from the quotidian demands of finding food. This new leisure time, in turn, allowed their minds to turn in on themselves, become overly contemplative, and render the body ill. It arose not from ancient civilizations like Eaton's claimed China, but from "modern civilizations," according to George Beard, the grandfather of the disease and author of one of its key texts. True, British women were beginning to contract the disease in small numbers, but the Americans led the way and dominated the list of patients, he said. "No age, no country, and no form of civilization, not Greece, nor Rome, nor Spain, nor the Netherlands, in the days of their glory, possessed such maladies," enthused Beard, almost too happy about the arrival of the "disease." "Of all the facts of modern sociology, this rise and growth of functional nervous disease in the northern part of America is one of the most stupendous, complex, and suggestive."[13] Indulging in self-serving circular logic, Beard not only maintained that the disease was uniquely American, but he also claimed that the sheer number of neurasthenia cases in the United States proved that America was the highest civilization ever.[14] Accordingly, those who suffered from neurasthenia moved in the highest cultural circles. Other racial and ethnic groups were not supposed to be so sensitive. In *American Nervousness,* Beard specifically excluded Native Americans and Chinese from the effects of neurasthenia.

In 1902, railroad magnate Robert Baer dismissed immigrant workers by saying, "They don't suffer; they don't even speak English."[15]

As we shall see, the photographs of Arnold Genthe and text of Will Irwin maintained that the Chinese produced feeling only on the surface and, deeper down, harbored an ugly malice. Eaton, who wrote under a Chinese penname, toiled as a stenographer at low pay, and barely made ends meet, confronted this ideology head on. The work of transcribing another's thoughts as a stenographer proved too taxing for the woman who yearned to think and express deep thoughts. Only later in her life did she find the time to unleash "the passion to write all of [her] heart away" (295). She appropriated the elite's illness of neurasthenia to cross racial and class boundaries and make her acuity somatic. This Chinese woman *did* feel, and even wary readers saw that Eaton's incisiveness had a physical base.

What she felt most, she believed, was the pain of racial slight. Her body, like a thermometer, registered the heat caused by the internal friction between white and Chinese. Through neurasthenia, Eaton constructed her poor physical health as an aesthetic sensibility—the ability to feel deeply—which gave her a social status on par with the country's cultural elite. It also gave her the power to write. Her sensitive antennae would go into the Chinese world, record the most subtle workings of this supposedly enigmatic group, and report back with great fidelity to the mainstream reader. Though the Chinese were supposed to be "insensible to feeling," she felt "keenly alive to every shade of sorrow and suffering" (221). Eaton used her power acquired through a kind of racial neurasthenia to champion the rights of the Chinese, one group supposedly without nerve endings.[16]

As Sui Eaton tried to apply this insight to broader society: familiarity and information reduced prejudice. She embarked on a writing tour of the Chinese world in America to create her 1909 series on the Chinese in Chinatown for the Seattle-based magazine, *The Westerner*, and her 1912 book, *Mrs. Spring Fragrance*. But others—like Genthe, his writer Will Irwin, and Frank Norris—had already told the country what they thought whites needed to know about the Chinese in America. In photographs, text, and short stories, they created an image of the Chinese heathen, and the country formalized that image with laws designed to drive the Chinese out of jobs and into isolation.

"Say, How Did I Get That on Me?"

In the 1850s and 1860s, the same defensive white ideology that drove blacks into lower skilled jobs and thus into inferior positions in the republic also pushed the Chinese onto its list of enemies. White workers drove the Chinese from the gold mines and the factories into menial jobs in laundries and kitchens. In 1854, California extended to the Chinese the law that prohibited African Americans and Native Americans from testifying in court. In 1873, the city passed the "Queue Ordinance," which required any prisoner in the county jail to have hair no longer than one inch from the scalp. This guaranteed that any Chinese man put in jail would have his queue shorn and thus be disgraced among the other Chinese. And in 1882, the federal government passed The Chinese Exclusion Act, which barred the immigration of any Chinese, save middle-class immigrants like teachers, students, and merchants, to the United States and forbade the country to offer them citizenship.[17]

By the time Eaton arrived in San Francisco in 1898, the Chinese had become targets for roving youths who wanted to stone them and for tourists who wanted to bag them as another exotic sight. More than one hundred thousand tourists came to California each year, and most of them wanted to stop at the exotic city-within-the-city. "From the moment when you sailed between those brown-and-green headlands which guarded the Gate to San Francisco, you heard always of Chinatown," wrote Will Irwin in his text accompanying Arnold Genthe's photos of Chinatown. "It was the first thing which the tourist asked to see, the first thing which the guides offered to show." And the guides and other purveyors of culture sought to make Chinatown seem the most exotic land imaginable.[18] One guide promised sword fights over slave girls; another enticed young men to prostitutes with the promise that Chinese women have vaginas that run east and west instead of north and south. Travel writer Frank Morton Todd summarized the quarter as "unique and outlandish, a foreign country of ten city squares, supposed to be a part of Canton, or a part of Tartary, as you please; living its own customs, rites and practices."[19]

Most tourists made the same stops. They ducked into a restaurant for food or a cup of tea; they sought out the fortune teller at Stockton and Clay Streets for a mysterious look into the future; they watched for the sword man marching through the streets, long knives in each hand, scissoring as he high-stepped along. Then they descended into the basement of a building to witness a room full of men smoking opium. When they were lucky, they caught an ornate Chinese funeral. Genthe photographed all these figures and events.

As Genthe took his photos, Frank Norris published a short story in his magazine *The Wave* in 1897 that retraced the typical tourist visit and elaborated the gothic implications that tourists believed their travels discovered. Will Irwin called "The Third Circle" "the greatest of [Norris's] short stories" and borrowed Norris's framework of three circles for describing Chinatown in the text that accompanied Genthe's photos.[20] This is supposedly the city where Edith Eaton arrived. Genthe, Norris, and the tour books of the period show us more precisely what she was up against—a story about sexual and racial crossing that threatened society's foundation of domesticity. Norris introduces Chinatown by talking about what tourists see and what they can only imagine. "In reality there are three parts to Chinatown," he says. "The part the guides show you, the part the guides don't show you, and the section of town that no one ever hears of. It is with the latter part that this story has to do." Norris's story begins in the regular tourist haunts and then descends into a horror tale of blurred gender and racial boundaries, white slavery and saliva. He calls this terrifying part that no one hears of "The Third Circle."[21]

In the story, Tom and his fiancée Harriett stop on their tour through Chinatown for a cup of tea in a "quaint" restaurant. Harriett is of "unmixed American stock" and chic in her tailormade gown (16). "Might as well be China itself," says Tom. "Might?" retorts his fiancée. "We are in China, Tom—a little bit of China dug out and transplanted here. Fancy all America and the nineteenth century just around the corner!" Harriett and Tom meet a fortuneteller. At first the man does not look Chinese, but he shows his brown teeth, says that his father was Chinese, and explains that his mother "washum clothes for sailor peoples down Kaui way." Harriett and Tom immediately understand that he comes from the other side of the racial divide. The man offers Harriett a tattoo. The fair maiden is scandalized by the thought, but decides to be naughty and consents to a small butterfly on her left pinkie. Her glove comes off, exposing her bare flesh. The man wets an ink drawing with his mouth, presses the moist paper to her finger, and then traces it with his needles. The fair maiden has come into intimate contact with this inferior stock, mouth to skin; the bodily fluids and ink seep in, and the mark becomes permanent.[22]

The tea that Tom and Harriett ordered still has not shown up, and Tom leaves to hunt for it. When he returns, Harriett is gone. He searches long and hard. He even hires a private detective, who may have learned too much. The gumshoe meets his end in an alley at the hands of a Chinese sword expert. Tom "never saw her again," Norris informs us. "No white man ever did" (21).

Twenty years later, our narrator runs into a character who says "there are plenty of women living with Chinamen now" and implies that most were taken as white slaves (22). Our narrator's guide is addicted to opium, a freak who blows smoke through his ears and frequents Chinatown's underworld. He knows a white slave named Sadie who might give them information about Harriett. Sadie does not speak unless you ply her with gin, and then she speaks only haltingly. They find her in Chinatown, at work in a room under Ah Yee's parlor rolling the cleanings from opium pipes into pills for sale, "her fingers twinkling with a rapidity that was somehow horrible to see" (24).

Sadie makes our narrator sit back. Unlike Harriett, who had a "fresh, vigorous, healthful prettiness" (16), Sadie has crossed over into masculinity. She draws on a cigar "and from time to time spat through her teeth man-fashion" (24). This "dreadful-looking beast of a woman" has "hawk's claws" for fingers, but somehow she remains "a white woman beyond all doubt" (24–25). Once she gets a whiff of the gin, she guzzles it greedily. As smoke curls from the guide's ears, he plies her with questions. Sadie has crossed over racially to the "yellow peril." Why live with a Chinese man, the guide asks? "Like um China boy better." Why don't you make a run for it? "I been here so long I guess I'm kind of used to it. I've about got out of white people's ways by now" (26). Sadie can't remember how long she has been in Chinatown. In fact, Sadie doesn't remember much of her past at all. She drifts in and out of a gin- and opium-induced stupor and then, as if the questioning raises a conflict in her own mind, blurts out, "Say, how did I get that on me?" Sadie thrusts out her left hand. There is a butterfly tattooed on her little finger (27). Under the Chinese spell, lovely, "unmixed" Harriett has become manlike, racially suspect, and bestial. Chinatown has sucked in her beauty and deformed her.

Doctored Photos

Norris's story became documentary evidence to Arnold Genthe and Will Irwin. Norris's "The Third Circle" allowed all their disparate dealings with Chinatown to make sense. The German-born Genthe told readers of his autobiography that when he arrived in the United States, his Baedeker warned not "to visit the Chinese quarter unless one is accompanied by a guide."[23] The Chinese were up to no good, agreed Irwin, and they drew out the worst in whites by attracting "white tramps and soldiers of ill fortune who haunted that terminus of Caucasian civilization."[24] Arnold Genthe promised that his photographs, like the guides of Chinatown, allowed whites to see the "authentic" quarter, or, as Norris's Harriett said, "a little bit of China dug out and transplanted." But in fact, as Genthe's photo of the two girls crossing the street showed, many other forces found representation in the quarter. A close look at Genthe's photos and archival documents from the period show that Chinatown was far from the island transplanted in the West that Norris, Irwin, and Genthe want readers to believe. Indeed Genthe carefully chose his subjects, etched out unwanted images in the negatives, and cropped the finished photos all to make the Chinese look more remote to the mainstream American reader and create what he considered an aesthetically superior print—at the Chinese's expense. And Will Irwin's writing around the photos only accentuated the divide. Irwin's text takes pains to show that the beauty of the photos should not be confused with a beauty in the Chinese themselves. Rather, any beauty on the surface, upon closer inspection, he says, is merely a "grotesque grace" that bends toward the "debased."[25] The tool of the tourist, the camera, did not bring his readers closer to the Chinese. It distanced them.

That distancing made the Chinese look more akin to the freaks in Norris's story than to mainstream Americans. What nineteenth-century bourgeois American, for example, could in good conscience invite someone who blew smoke out his ears to become a citizen? The "assimilation" process, as Harriett's transformation into Sadie illustrated, dangerously might run in the wrong direction. Chinese may not become "American"; Americans may become exotic and debauched Chinese. Foreign-looking Chinatown moves like a virus that infects "respectable" whites, who, like Tom and Harriett, never see it coming. For, as Norris said in an essay about Chinatown in *The Wave,* "No two races the world round could be more opposite than the Mongolian and Anglo-Saxon. . . . In every Chinaman there is something of the snake and a good deal of the cat."[26] Norris's story and Genthe's photos helped craft an image of the Chinese as a knot of remote and threatening traits. This slithering and cunning tangle of associations—one unable to sense real beauty or uphold domestic relations, and one destined never to join "white Americans" in guiding a democracy—is just what Edith Eaton would have to untie in her readers' minds.[27]

Genthe wandered into Chinatown after coming to San Francisco to tutor the son of a wealthy resident. Between 1895 and 1906 he took the photographs that first drew public attention to his work and turned him into the subject of local gossip columnists. Genthe carefully crafted his image as a brilliant but footloose man-about-town. He presented his skills as endless, calling himself in his autobiography, *As I Remember,* "a Don Juan, a Hermit Monk, a Chinese Sage, a University Professor—all rolled into one."[28]

Genthe the storyteller maintained that his first subjects, the Chinese, resisted his efforts to make "art" of them. First, he ranged Chinatown to "look at things from a photographic point of view" (34). Then he walked the streets of Chinatown with his camera hidden and stalked his prey. He would "hide in doorways or peer out from an angle of a building at some street corner" and sometimes waited hours for one perfect candid shot.[29] But the Chinese, Genthe claimed, were superstitious about having their pictures taken. "To them the camera was a black devil box in which all the evils of the earth were bottled up, ready to pounce upon them."[30] They believed that their spirits would be stolen, he said. And Genthe wanted his readers to think that his photos uncovered the Chinese's "strange" and "inscrutable" faces.[31]

Years later, Genthe said his Chinese photos led him to a breakthrough in portrait photography. He sought photos that had "more relation to life and to art than the stiffly posed photographs" where "the soul of the subject was lost." He believed that candid shots, like those he took in Chinatown, offered the solution. "If they could be kept from knowing the exact moment the exposure was being made—then something more of their spirit might be brought out by the camera."[32] Genthe claimed to have captured "something of the soul, the individuality of the sitter." His fans believed Genthe had fused art and reality perfectly. "If the subject be a street scene, with its straggling group of quaintly garbed figures," exalted critic Porter Garnett, "they are treated as a motive in the picture in perfect harmony with the whole. . . . A hundred variations of the scene might not compose. Genthe fixed the one that does."[33] Genthe's stealthy photos painted the essence of the subject. The candid and heretofore unphotographed Chinese were colors on his palette.

But photos of the Chinese—the weird and exotic subjects—were not as candid and rare as Genthe wanted readers to believe. As John Kuo Wei Tchen points out, Chinese Americans had long been used to the camera. The Chinese used cameras in Hong Kong thirty years before Genthe's photos, virtually all

FIGURE 5.2. Arnold Genthe, *The Shoemaker. Library of Congress, Prints and Photographs Division, Arnold Genthe Collection: Negatives and Transparencies, LC–G403–T–0197–B.*

the immigrants had to have pictures taken for their identification papers, and many Chinese Americans took photographs to send back home.[34] Some Chinese subjects did cover their faces to Genthe's camera. But how did he think an immigrant, who faced persecution, would respond to a man who stared at them from a corner of a building? Genthe crafted an image of the Chinese before he bought his camera and then projected his own hopes for photography's reach onto those faces. He edited the shots before he put his eye to the viewfinder.[35]

Even Genthe's simple photos highlight the Chinatown that Frank Norris encouraged us to embrace. Contrast Genthe's shot of "The Shoe Maker" (figure 5.2) with other artists' photos of workers. A photo of a cobbler offered Genthe the chance to show a skilled workman, producing useful goods for the country—a hallowed symbol of republican ideology. But Genthe creates a photo for different purposes. Genthe's shoemaker posed with one foot on the step of a store. The man's forehead is shaved; he wears a bracelet on his right hand and holds the long stem of his Asian pipe. He stands at an oblique angle, and he does not look at the camera. A sign in Chinese over the shoemaker's shoulder stamps the photo with a Chinese "authenticity." Further, the stairs and dark light obscure part of his body, and the viewer's eye is drawn by the shoemaker's pointing finger down to what we presume is his workspace—a black hole. The Chinese may appear on the street, but their real lives are away from the white eye, subterranean and menacing.[36]

FIGURE 5.3. Chinese laundryman. *Courtesy of Moulin Archives.*

Another artist at the time, however, presented a laundryman with a different feeling (see figure 5.3). Laundry was by far the most common trade for the Chinese in San Francisco; they picked up and delivered their goods and thus spent much of their time out of Chinatown. This laundryman emerges not from some dark Chinese hole; rather, he stands in the street, in broad daylight, arms akimbo with his basket of linens in front of him. He wears a western hat and western slacks and looks straight into the camera. Over both shoulders, we see signs of the western city he lives in—the bay windows and picket fence of a Victorian house. And as if to stamp the photo with the familiar, the words "U.S. Mail" appear on the box behind him. As foreign as viewers believe this man is, the mailbox places him in their world. The photo's props and settings, unlike the pipe and sign in Chinese script in Genthe's photo, give the subject and the viewer something to share.[37]

Another photo of a seated Chinese laborer heightens the contrast with Genthe's shoemaker (see figure 5.4). The seated laborer wears a worker's baggy clothes and tufts of hair sprout from his unshaven forehead. His queue drapes over his left shoulder and falls into his hand. Adorning his jacket are etchings of Grover Cleveland and Allen G. Thurman—1888 candidates for president and vice president. This worker wears a queue showing respect for the ruling dynasty in China, but he also stakes a claim in U.S. elections. The work of this and other photographers underscores the extent to which Genthe showed only part of Chinatown's everyday life. When he snapped his shutter, his viewfinder purposely caught only the most exotic subject.

Indeed, as John Tchen has shown, Genthe's taste for the exotic led him past framing the "perfect" shot and into outright fakery. Genthe's *The Toy*

FIGURE 5.4. A Chinese laborer. *Courtesy of the California History Room, California State Library, Sacramento, Calif.*

FIGURE 5.5. Arnold Genthe, *The Toy Peddler. Library of Congress, Prints and Photographs Division, Arnold Genthe Collection: Negatives and Transparencies, LC–G4033–0199.*

Peddler (figure 5.5) shows a man pulling a Chinese toy down the street as two young women in ceremonial dress look on.[38] Behind the women stands an outdoor peddler next to a sign apparently written in Chinese. But the original glass negative reveals that the sign was not in Chinese, but in English. It read: "Chinese Candies 5 Cts. Per Bag." Genthe replaced the original sign of Western life

FIGURE 5.6. Arnold Genthe's *Etching* [*Washington Street, Chinatown, San Francisco*]. *Library of Congress, Prints and Photographs Division, Arnold Genthe Collection: Negatives and Transparencies, LC–G4033–0249.*

with a fake. In another example, Genthe's unreleased photo at 730 Washington Street intended to show four Chinese children in exotic costume on the street (figure 5.6). They wear embroidered outfits, felt slippers, and pillbox hats. Behind them in the original photo stands a white woman, peering out of the doorway of W. D. Hobro Plumbing. We see only her torso, however, because Genthe etched her legs out. The sloppy touch-up ruined the costumed world that Genthe sought to create and likely kept the photo from being released. The negative caught Genthe turning Chinatown into a falsely segregated world.[39]

Even when Genthe left the negatives alone, Will Irwin's accompanying text put a sinister spin on even the tamest Chinese subject, and he tried to train the viewer's eye to see a debased ugliness in that subject. Look, for comparison, at how Lewis Hine, another photographer of the period, handled photos of workers who seemed "foreign" to his middle-class viewers. Hine, of course, believed that he would bring about workplace reform if he documented workers' conditions. Despite his sympathy for the subject, his photos often presented an exotic-looking worker. Yet Maren Stange shows how the accompanying text of writer John Fitch pulls the viewer closer. Examine, for example, Hine's famous shot of Slavic laborers at Homestead (figure 5.7), published the year before Genthe's *Photos of Old Chinatown*. We see a phalanx of Hungarian workers, their faces darkened with factory soot, their clothes dirty and frayed from hard work; they stand shoulder to shoulder, apparently presenting a united front. A middle-class viewer might look at the dirty, foreign figure and see an ungrateful worker who makes more than he "deserves" and still threatens to strike, and white workers at the time might see immigrant competition for their labor. But in the text that ran with the photo, John Fitch explains that "the pay of over half the men in the Homestead mills in 1907 was that of common laborers" and that 85 percent of the Slavs received less than $12 a week. They scrimped on every expense except the bare necessities. One reason the Slavs dominated unskilled positions,

FIGURE 5.7. Lewis Hine, Slavic laborers, 1908. *Courtesy of George Eastman House, Rochester, N.Y.*

Fitch sympathetically suggests, is racism. "Many American boys fancy that they degrade themselves by entering into competition with a Slav for a job."[40] The text gives reasons for the apparent differences between viewer and viewed, and it thereby collapses the distance between the viewer and the subject of the photograph.

Contrast these photos with Genthe's shot of workers in *Old Chinatown,* such as *The Chinese Cook Grinning from the Doorway* (figure 5.8). The man stands in a simple traditional smock, his sleeves rolled up. His shorn forehead, part of the style worn by men with queues, separates him from almost any middle-class white viewer. He faces the camera and gives a grin. In the accompanying text, Will Irwin claims that these workers have found their way into the hearts of whites, but he supports the claim with odd reasoning; he links this most benign subject to the Chinese underworld. The Chinese men served loyally in white homes for years, he said. The servant may have "dropped his month's wages in the gambling houses of Ross Alley, perhaps he smoked a few pipes of opium, perhaps he knew more than the police would ever learn of the highbinder shooting," said Irwin. "He never troubled you with these things. To you, he was first the perfect servant."[41]

In other words, the cook may have put himself into an opium stupor, blown his earnings at the gambling house, and consorted with organized crime, but he still offered that simple grin to his master in the morning. "The Chinese had conquered our foolish hatred by patient service," Irwin claimed. As if to accent the point, another photo in the same section, *The Street of the Gamblers (By Night)*, illustrates the dark confines of gambler's alley. Men in dark clothes wander menacingly. In a middle-class view of the world, these men have idle hands, and they can only be up to no good (figure 5.9). The catlike Chinese man of Frank Norris appears docile and languid by day but quick and vicious by night. And in this same twisted way, by imagining the dark doings of even the most loyal and patient Chinese man he met, Irwin's text dredged viewers' unconscious for sinister connotations.[42] Irwin extended the "sinister intentions" of the Chinese to an inability to appreciate or produce beauty in America. Even as Irwin decried "race hatred" in his prologue of the photographs, he claimed that the Chinese had a "mental difference from us . . . oblique thinking as contrasted with our straight reasoning." Boys who played in the streets kicked the ball with "grotesque grace."[43]

Even Irwin's description of a Chinese fete tracks the pitiable denouement that inevitably follows from moving below the Chinese surface. At this fete, a dozen men, "very dignified" in "ravishing" tunics sat around a table. Behind them sat their wives, catering to every male whim in an elaborately choreographed formal dinner. But soon, the diners have too much drink, and they begin to play drinking games. At first, the laugher is "more subdued than ours" but soon enough breaks into convulsions. "And as they drank and played, and played and drank," Irwin tells us,

FIGURE 5.8. Arnold Genthe, *The Chinese Cook Grinning [from the Doorway]. Library of Congress, Prints and Photographs Division, Arnold Genthe Collection: Negatives and Transparencies, LC–G403–T–0031.*

FIGURE 5.9. Arnold Genthe, *The Street of the Gamblers* [*By Night*]. *Library of Congress, Prints and Photographs Division, Arnold Genthe Collection: Negatives and Transparencies, LC–G403–0035–A.*

> something deep below the surface came out in them. Their shouts became squalls; lips drew back from teeth, beady little eyes blazed; their very cheek bones seemed to rise higher on their faces. I thought, as I watched, of wars of the past[;] these . . . were those old yellow people with whom our fathers found before the Caucasus was set as a boundary between the dark race and the light; the hordes of Genghis Khan; the looters of Attila.[44]

A convivial dinner party, in the hands of Irwin, becomes an unmasking of the "true" Chinese character. The surface gentility gives way to marauding yellow hordes who need a boundary, Caucasus—or whiteness—to keep those yellows from the whites. Genthe's photos and Irwin's borrowed words only widened the divide between the Chinese and mainstream America that Eaton would try to collapse.

Yet even the period's tour books, which sought to make the Chinese as exotic as those found in Genthe's photographs, now betray evidence that Chinese and whites mixed. White Americans crafted an exotic and distant Chinese even as they blended cultures with them. Genthe and Irwin tried to pin the vice trade between whites and the Chinese on only the Chinese. Irwin implied that Chinese men coerced white women into prostitution for their sick pleasure. "These pretty and painted playthings of men," he intoned, "furnished a glimpse into Frank Norris's Third Circle, the underworld."[45] To let the reader know just how evil this circle was, he described how Chinese coercion blocked one woman from true domestic happiness. "Neither had she any education save in certain primitive arts of woman, any religion except a superstitious fear of her masters," Irwin reported. "'If you escape from us down to Hell,' they had told her, 'we will drag you up by the hair. If you escape to Heaven, we will drag you down by the feet.'"[46] In the social text of the printed page, the Chinese threatened the foundations of domestic relations, a foundation upon which American culture in part built its power relationships.

Not surprisingly, actual behavior departed from the script. Despite the imagined danger, whites looking to step outside of "respectable" Victorian behavior filled Chinatown's vice halls. Chinese lotteries drew whites to their twenty-four-hour operations. "Many a reputable citizen carried about in his waistcoat-pocket the squares of thin rough paper with their strange characters and red spots," said one observer on the scene.[47] Opium dens catered to not just Chinese workers but "thousands" of whites as well. "It is the curse of China," proclaimed one writer.[48] Police raids on the dens often netted both whites and Chinese. "Dark scandals resulted," reported one writer, "and the skeletons in the closets of various worthy and wealthy families rattled ominously."[49] An 1885 map of San Francisco's Chinatown, in fact, shows many white prostitution houses in Chinatown alongside the Chinese bordellos;[50] and whites looking for paid sex clogged Chinatown streets in their search. One Chinese family, in fact, posted a notice in English on their front door for those drunks who couldn't tell the difference between a house of prostitution and a residence: "CHINESE FAMILY—RESPECTABLE—PLEASE DO NOT RING BELL."[51]

But not all whites who visited Chinatown sought the illicit, and popular tourist guides recommended the town as a first stop for all those visiting the city.[52] Around 1900, Chinese restaurants, eager for the tourist trade, created a new dish, one that whites believed was authentically Chinese: chop suey.[53] Chinese funerals proved a big hit for the white tourists, with one article calling them "the most spectacular occasion in Chinatown."[54] At the burial of Little Pete, a merchant and leader of one of Chinatown's largest clans, more than two thousand whites showed up hours ahead of time. Frank Norris described the mayhem in an article for *The Wave* in 1897. At first Norris complained that the funeral did not match the tourist spectacle that he expected. Then he turned his eyes to what the tourists themselves were doing. "The women thronged about the raised platform and looted everything they got their hands on; China bowls, punk, tissue paper ornaments, even the cooked chickens and bottles of gin," wrote Norris. "This, mind you, before the procession had as much as arrived."[55] As the casket approached, the women in the crowd pressed forward to catch a glimpse of the corpse. They flattened mourners on a praying mat, and the press of the huge crowd forced the grieving family to go home early. Norris barely contained his sarcasm as he described what happened after the Chinese mourners left. "Then the civilized Americans, some thousand of them, descended upon the raised platform, where the funeral meats were placed—pigs and sheep roasted whole, and chickens and bowls of gin and rice. Four men seized a roast pig by either leg and made off with it." The crowd began throwing bowls full of gin at one another. "The roast chickens were hurled back and forth in the air," and women filched the remaining china bowls as souvenirs. Even Norris, the mythologizer of evil Chinatown, was disgusted.

Little Pete's funeral received another telling next to a Genthe funeral photo in *Old Chinatown*. Irwin first instructed the audience that Little Pete started as a "mere coolie" but with "the golden touch; he made everything pay." Then, of course, that gold took a sinister side. Little Pete lorded over Chinatown's gambling operations, rigged the horse races at California tracks, and was finally gunned down by his enemies, Irwin said. The funeral, said Irwin, "was the greatest public ceremonial that Chinatown ever saw." But Irwin makes Little Pete's burial sound like an affair only for Chinese criminals and the rest of the Chinatown community. He neglected one key detail that Norris explored at length: whites attended this spectacle, too, and the hungry white tourists turned Little Pete's funeral into a chicken-tossing farce.[56]

Underneath . . . a Wild Streak of Barbarism

White and Chinese relations went still further than the economic and voyeuristic tango of tourist and merchant, belying the supposedly unbridgeable gulf that separated Chinese and "white" Americans. The editor of a physicians' newsletter in San Francisco complained that too many whites frequented the Chinese doctors in town.[57] And economic ties laced the mainstream and Chinatown in surprising ways. In 1903, a miner named Hazen fell on hard times. A mine accident injured his leg, put him out of work, and he fell behind on his bills, so he wrote to his merchant at the Sun Sun Wo Company in Coulterville, California. Hazen explained how injury and weather made him broke and that he needed new supplies to resume work. He asked Sun Sun Wo to send a few supplies for a small cash payment to help him get back on his feet. An unpunctuated postscript adds, "I have every thing else I need I had grub left in the cabin."[58] Hazen's request attests to his experience of the Chinese not as someone in an opium fog or a conniving catlike pickpocket but as a thoughtful colleague. Hazen clearly explained his personal troubles and firmly expected the person on the other end to understand and extend sympathy; the business transaction quickly became a personal story of mutual understanding.

Another businessman, Woo Gen, exported the first flour from Washington

State to China. But when he visited the Pacific Northwest state, the hotel manager denied him a room, Woo reported. "Oh, no, this is joke," the manager said. "He can go into Chinese laundry." Woo Gen continued with his business, and the evening paper ran an article saying that a millionaire had arrived to buy all the town's flour, about twelve carloads full. Suddenly every Chinese man was not a laundryman to the manager. He saw Woo in a different light. "Hotel man treated me like the President," said Woo.[59] Economic ties acquired a social gloss.

Relationships like these forged countless links between the Chinese and the broader community. The links were so strong that in 1878, two years after the invention of the telephone, Quong Lee placed a telephone in his business.[60] Pacific Telephone and Telegraph later placed a public phone in the office of a Chinese American newspaper. Enough calls traveled through the office that in 1896—only one year after Genthe began taking his photos—Pacific Telephone installed an exchange in Chinatown with operators who spoke English and Chinese.[61] By 1910, more than one thousand two hundred Chinese had phones.[62] Because no one recognized that the Chinese sought ties to the country, in 1895 to prove their commitment to the United States in general and California in particular, Chinatown's Chinese Americans formed the Native Sons of the Golden State, a citizen's alliance to fight for Chinese-American rights. Their explicit purpose was "To fully enjoy and defend our American citizenship; to cultivate the mind through the exchange of knowledge; to effect a higher character among the members; and to fully observe and practice the principles of Brotherly Love and mutual help."[63]

Plenty of Chinese Americans living in Chinatown knew that Norris, Genthe, and Irwin were creating a straw man. Norris could claim, "Chinatown in San Francisco is as foreign to us—much more so—than a village in the interior of France or Spain. As a consequence Saxon visitors must be equally foreign in the eyes of the livers in Chinatown."[64] And Irwin claimed, "underneath their essential courtesy . . . runs a hard, wild streak of barbarism, an insensibility in cruelty, which, when roused, is as cold-blooded and unlovely a thing as we know."[65] An expedition into Chinese culture invariably ends far from the center of American culture in "the Third Circle," a place where its inhabitants turn anything beautiful and good into something sinister. Too bad that Irwin, the man the papers called a "famous interviewer," could not be bothered to do what the much less renowned Edith Eaton did—interview any Chinese for his text accompanying Genthe's photos. Too bad he could not show the many links that Chinese and mainstream Americans had forged despite the cultural differences and legal strictures. Will Irwin, ace reporter, should have picked up the phone.

Edith Eaton resented stock characterizations of Chinese Americans, and her stories show the Chinese as more complex people; they are not only able to recognize beauty, but they are also able to produce a depth of understanding that further enhances beauty. As part of this process, she shows, the Chinese create a hybrid of East and West by selecting the best of both. We can see how she reversed the formulae of Genthe, Norris, and others, in a series of ethnographies she wrote for *The Westerner* in 1909. Dominika Ferens has likened all of Eaton's work to ethnography and linked Eaton's writing to missionary texts, especially writing by the Reverend Justus Doolittle. Ferens argues that the "wily" label pinned on the Chinese flowed directly from the missionary writing into Eaton's fiction like *Mrs. Spring Fragrance*. Characterizations of the Japanese, however, came from tour guidebooks of Japan. Indeed, many of Eaton's stories, like the three-part series in *The Westerner*, "The Chinese in America," purported to be flat-out ethnography. Although Ferens does an excellent job of illustrating parallels between Eaton's texts and missionary texts, these nonfiction pieces most closely resemble tour guides themselves. Writing as Sui Sin Far, Eaton recruited her reportorial skills and storytelling talents to create the insider's view of the Chinese, a "counter-tour guide."

She strings together sixteen stories about individual men and women, their struggles in the United States, and their efforts to bridge the two cultures. In the introductions to these ethnographies she states as her goal the undoing of work that makes the Chinese appear distant, exotic, and insensate. She strives to create a Chinese inhabitant who can appreciate beauty, love without sinister intentions, and respect the bourgeois and gender boundaries so admired by middle-class American society. "You scarcely ever read about a Chinese person who is not a wooden peg," she complained a year after Irwin and Genthe released their book (234). "When with strangers, [they] hide the passions of their hearts under quiet and peaceful demeanors; but because a man is indisposed to show his feelings is no proof that he has none," she argues. "Under a quiet surface the Chinaman conceals a rapid comprehension and an almost morbid sensitiveness; he also possesses considerable inventive power and is more of an initiative spirit than an imitative one" (234). Eaton rewrites the Chinese.

Inverting Genthe and Unmasking the Chinese, This Time with Feeling

By showing the Chinese as inventive, sensitive, and aesthetically aware, Eaton is undoing the twist given to our understanding of the Chinese in America. Indeed, Eaton here follows the tenets succinctly articulated by John Bascom—that no beauty exists without some underlying truth—and uses these ideas to remake the Chinese in the readers' eyes. Eaton takes the issue head-on by asserting that China was "the birthplace of the arts" (208). She shows readers the same lovely clothing that Genthe pictured, but she recasts stories about an ugly substrate that these clothes hid in Irwin's text. And she shows us that the surface, that is, the outsider's take on the Chinese, misses the real beauty or depth of understanding that the Chinese in America have.

In her ethnography of Lu Seek, a *Bildungsroman,* Eaton plays with this relationship between beauty and truth and reverses the Norris story of Chinese enticing whites into a lair and then perverting them. Lu Seek is a young man searching to find his place in society. After collecting his inheritance, rejecting his elders' advice, and setting out on his own to follow "new ways," he runs into an uncle, a follower of the "old ways." The young man pines for the uncle's beautiful robes and, more important, all that those beautiful clothes represent. "As we talked together, he in his long silken robes, I in my exceedingly shabby American store clothes, I envied him his prosperity, his calm and affable manners, his pleasing reposeful face," says Lu. The clothes here show not just economic success but also inner qualities like calmness and affability. But Lu is not done with the significance of either these clothes or beauty in his uncle's life. His eye moves to his uncle's office and the significance of that space. "I knew that his elegantly furnished office was quite a resort for the perplexed of Chinatown's four hundred, and moreover, that many unsettled white people also surreptitiously visited him in the hope of having light thrown on certain difficult questions" (239). The elegance of the office parallels the wisdom of the man who provided solace to the Chinese population and, perhaps more interesting, to the white population, too. Unlike Irwin and Genthe's sinister sheen, beauty and elegance stand in for qualities valued by the community.

Eaton shows us this inversion of Genthe's photographs and Irwin's narrative by recasting the role of beauty and civilization in her own tale of a Chinese dinner party. Where Irwin described the Chinese as beginning the evening with perfect, if strange, comportment and then descending into beady-eyed drunken revelry, Eaton shows the opposite with the marriage ceremony story of Tin-a. Tin-a came to the United States as the arranged bride of a popular man in Chinatown. One celebratory party took place on the top floor of a Chinatown building, "elegantly furnished with black teak wood tables and carved chairs inlaid with mother of pearl" (242). Eaton, just as Genthe did, takes us through the rudiments of the dinner. The guests arrive in "gorgeous silk robes," with flowers in their hair. Chicken and bamboo shoot dishes load the table. But in this story, the party does not devolve into a drinking game unmasking an evil nature. Rather, one of the guests spots the bride crying off at the side of the room. We learn that Tin-a is not the woman originally contracted to marry the husband; the original woman is back in China, having fallen for a local man. The unattached Tin-a came in her place. Tin-a worries that her new husband will be furious with her and "falls to the ground at his feet." Will Eaton's story have a tragic end? Instead, we learn that the husband had never met his contracted proxy bride and had come to love Tin-a. "Instead of upbraiding her with hard words, [he] comforted her with loving ones" (243). The elegant dinner under Eaton's hands leads to tender feelings and a tender moment.

Eaton wastes no occasion to show that the Chinese in America have a depth of understanding that belies any depiction of the drunken or opium-stunned stock figures of the popular press. When Eaton's own autobiographical story recounts her neurasthenic episodes and concludes that "the spirit is more than the body," she hints at a deeper well of feeling and understanding that "longed for artistic expression."[66] One recurring figure in *The Westerner* series, Go Ek Jo, does what Irwin was unwilling to do: she researched Americans to understand their ways (236). In another story, a simple cook, one who might be standing, grinning, at the doorway, is working only to support his family back in China; his real vocation—and the vocation to which he intends to return—is as a scholar (237).

Indeed, getting past appearances, understanding oneself, and being true to that understanding is just the kind of depth Eaton shows us as meaningful. In Eaton's hands, the façade or mask for the Chinese is not the beautiful or romantic construction of Arnold Genthe's photographs. A trumped-up mask becomes the ugly thing in itself, which hides the deeper, more attractive qualities. In Eaton's autobiographical essay, she writes about meeting a "half Chinese, half white girl" whose "face is plastered with a thick white coat of paint." The woman's "eyebrows are blackened so that the shape of her eyes and the whole expression of her face is changed." In America, the woman had heard so much abuse of the Chinese that she tried to hide any features that identified her biological origins. The woman uses the encrusted makeup to pass as Spanish or Mexican, and this mask makes her life a living hell. She "lives in nervous dread of being 'discovered'" by her fiancé, Eaton tells us. An American "friend" insists that she reveal all to her intended. In the end, the girls comes clean to her fiancé, who "loves her enough well enough not to allow her nationality to stand, a bar sinister, between them" (227–228). Here the surface or mask perverts the person; the woman is unable to trust that her fiancé loves her for herself, and she lives in horror that he will reject her. The mask is a mistake.

The most powerful moment of *The Westerner* series in fact plumbs this issue with Eaton herself and her efforts to pass between whiteness and "Eurasian." In one story, Eaton inserts herself into the narrative and passes between "white" and "Chinese" several times. She writes a passage that simulated the guidebook experience of Chinatown, and she plays the white tourist. Her first stop is the Chinese temple, better known as the "Joss House." What happens in that temple humiliates her, but it also gives her a forum for her passing and, surprisingly, a way to combine the cultures. This occasion offered her a chance to highlight the Chinese's patient compassion with interfering tourists, and her changing roles allowed her to find answers beyond most mainstream readers' reach so that she could explode the mainstream myths. In the end, she compelled readers to leave their voyeuristic perspective and finish the passage with an understanding of Chinese Americans far different from the popular portrayal.

In the temple, Eaton acted as many tourists before her have and slipped a piece of ceremonial sandalwood up her sleeve. She was about to move away, she explains, "when a quiet voice just behind me said: 'If you like the wood you can take some more.'" The temple priest stood by the bowl and tipped it toward her. "Oh, I don't like to take any more. It is sacred, isn't it," she said.

"'Not at all,' he answered. Then, calmly, and I fancied sarcastically, 'Is it so to you?'" Eaton burned with shame.

She tried to engage him in conversation to cover her embarrassment, but the priest did not recognize her as Chinese and refused to talk. In his eyes, Sui Sin Far was Edith Eaton, thieving white tourist. The practiced eye of the Chinese priest would not buy Sui's reverse passing. When Eaton produced a letter of introduction from Chinese friends, however, he perked up. The letter bought her an interview and allowed her to take readers inside what she billed as the real Chinatown. She learned that the "heathen Chinese" were not praying to idols when they lay prostrate before an image. They worshiped "only the spirit that is supposed to dwell in the image, and not the image itself, which is nothing more to him than what it is—a piece of wood or stone" (248). A piece of wood to a bourgeois American was also a piece of wood to a "Chinaman." Abstract thinking about spirituality and divinity gives it intrinsic value, divorced from the simple value of the object itself. The tourist who coveted the object as a memento and pilfered it invested the object with more power than it deserved. The Chinese priest had the depth of understanding to patiently confront Eaton and ask her what the stolen trifle *meant to her*. The story neatly reversed just who held the high ground and who held the ability to think, reason, and act in a "civilized" way.

Edith Eaton as Sui passed twice in the story about the temple. First, she brought the story to her readers as the authority under her pen name Sui Sin Far. When she slipped into the temple, the priest took her as the white tourist, Edith Eaton. There Eaton acted like most tourists and tried to steal the sandalwood, a piece of that exotic place. The priest saw her for what she was at that moment—a white lady stealing from the temple, and Eaton tried to persuade him differently. Only when she produced a letter from Chinese friends did he change his mind. With the letter, Eaton passed back to Sui, the priest's trust grew, and they talked to each other. Here Sui gathered the information about what makes something divine. She illustrates the kind and open character of the "Joss House" priest, and she uses it to debunk mainstream thinking about the Chinese. As Eaton transformed herself, she hoped readers would feel transformed, too. She brought them into the "Joss House" as tourists and tried to send them out believers in the reasonableness of Chinese religion.

Eaton constructed an identity for herself by inverting the notion of passing, and then she constructed a Chinese character that confounded the stereotypes of Genthe and Norris. Eaton's passing proved to be a way to bring power to the Chinese with whom she so identified. And it gave her power as a self-styled Chinese writer by addressing a wide range of issues—from immigration to taxes to religion—who wanted to bring cultural change in the mainstream.[67] "My heart leaps for joy," she says, "when I read one day an article by a New York Chinese in which he declares, 'The Chinese in America owe an everlasting debt of gratitude to Sui Sin Far for the bold stand she has taken in their defense.'"[68]

Mixed Blessings

Eaton has the right to be proud of her work for the Chinese, but her narrative imposes its own limits on the Chinese themselves. Eaton's stories make much of the fact that the Chinese are "modernizing," and, despite claims that Americans can learn from the Chinese, she takes great pains to show that her characters toe the line of bourgeois values. "Although the scholars and students who come to our shores are properly conservative when pressing themselves concerning things American," she says, the Chinese "gladly acknowledge that many of the ways of the white man are better than the ways of the Chinese."[69]

Eaton's case for the ability of the Chinese to fit into American culture received a boost from political events in China itself. This complicates what the public had considered a monolithic nation and shows that there are diverse elements, but it also makes the Chinese, as themselves, less acceptable. The reform movement of Sun Yat-sen, which sought to overthrow the monarchy and the dowager empress, professed ideas about democracy and a republican government. Eaton did not miss an opportunity to point out how similar these ideas were to those ideas of republicanism professed in the United States. Eaton closes her *Westerner* series with a section devoted to Sun's party. Here she claims that the members of the party "are acutely conscious, and have been for many years, of the necessity of a new way of living for the Chinese" (258). Eaton herself calls for change in the community, but she does not stop there. She modifies her statement and extends it by demanding, "not only a new way of living—a new way of thinking" (258). The people "keenly alive" to the revolutionary movements in China are graduates of "American colleges," and "nothing causes their eyes to glisten more than to know that China is encouraging educational and industrial reforms" (258). The Chinese become more acceptable to Eaton as they "reform" and ally themselves with a political tradition more akin to that of the United States. Eaton uses the figure of Leung Ki Chu to deftly turn this story of incipient republicanism into the real interest of the Chinese. She points to Leung as the "hero" for the "enlightened Chinese people" and claims that "the Chinamen who by their hearing and intelligence reflect the most credit on their race, are those who believe in Leung Ki Chu and uphold his standard" (206). Eaton ends her story on Leung's efforts to topple monarchy and replace it with republicanism by quoting a third-century B.C.E. Chinese scholar who used Confucianism to develop a social contract philosophy, Meng Tzu, or Mencius. "The losing of empires comes through losing the people," Eaton quotes Mencius. "The government," she says, "has lost the hearts of the people. Who shall restore them?" (208). Leung, then, becomes the symbol for all Chinese—in both China *and* the United States, the great place of hope.

Those "reforms" toward a republicanism appear elsewhere in the ethnographies of individual characters. The story of Wah tells this story of reform, and Eaton stays true to the economic concept of republicanism from the days of the black press members: she puts this ideology in terms of commercial interests.

The best way for Wah to show that he is a modern man and ready to adhere to the reform ways is to be a merchant. "We do not think in China as we did in the old days," she quotes him. "In Canton we have as much esteem for the clever man of business as we have for the scholar." Wah came to the United States "to make money and to learn western ways quicker" (234). His economic success feeds his political reforms.

In other stories, too, Eaton concerns herself with the economic status of her characters and conflates these characteristics with their desirability as U.S. citizens. She strains to feature people with cultural capital and of "good breeding." In an article about the Chinese workingman, she claims that many Chinese laundrymen "are not laundry men only, but artists and poets," and then she quickly adds that they are "often the sons of good families" (232). Chinese workers, she says while currying favor with the bureaucrats in her audience, are "oftentimes cousins of government students" (232). She sympathetically quotes Lu Seek as someone with a "soul above domestic service" (239). In her article about the Los Angeles reformer Leung Ki Chu, she showers praise on the republican reformers by calling them "men of education" with "advanced ideas" (206).

But proper bourgeois etiquette to Eaton is just as important, a reflection of the "modern civilization" that the Chinese have attained. Her characters continually display not just the qualities of cultural capital that she believes her readers want to see but also the class-based values on comportment to which they warm. Lu Seek, the young man who set out to find his fortune with "American ways," ends up making his fortune by catering to the labor needs of the "society lady." "Maintaining a pleasant demeanor and an affable tongue," helped Lu get contracts (240). The narrative of the title story, *Mrs. Spring Fragrance,* turns on keeping the domestic stability of the household intact. Mr. Spring Fragrance worries that his wife is not in love with him and is seeing another man. Eaton here flirts with the societal notion that Chinese women are prostitutes who have no domestic allegiance. But Mrs. Spring Fragrance shows herself to be a stalwart devotee of her husband and writes to him in the most respectful tones. And we learn that despite the arranged marriage of the two, Mr. Spring Fragrance fell in love with Mrs. just by gazing at her photograph. When Mrs. Spring Fragrance returns from a round of matchmaking by uniting her neighbor in domestic bliss with the man she loves, she fawns over her husband, "You do not look well. You are not well. What is it?" (27). And she chats with him in the "wifeliest fashion possible" (27). Eaton restores domestic tranquility. Far from Frank Norris's story of Harriet turning into the "manlike" Sadie kept by a Chinese man, Eaton keeps the home a unit and the hierarchy of man over woman in place.

Two months after *The Westerner* series ran in 1909, Eaton continued her tales that defended domestic space and sent a letter to the editor of Chinatown's *The Chinese World*; she offered a story of how immigration officials rip young children from their mothers. She thanked him for his compliments on her previous work and offered him more articles. He would have to translate the stories, she told him, for she knew "very little" of the language. Then, without explanation as to why, Eaton acted as if she was unburdening herself before the editor as father-confessor. She gave the short history of the romance between her Chinese mother and British father. The woman who had been told a Chinese man would never have her and who had been laughed at when she claimed to be Chinese, finished her letter with an unflinching statement of identity: "My mother being Chinese, I am also." In the space of two paragraphs she both conceded her distance from Chinese language and culture and claimed its origins.[70] The neurasthenic conflict of race passed from a dual conflict written *on* the body and a sensibility *in* the body to a conflict written on the page as she admitted that her work drew compliments and yet needed translation. Eaton signed both names at the bottom of the page, placing "Sui Sin Far" in parentheses.

Eaton's construction of a Chinese American identity—teetering one way and then another on the fulcrum of a parenthesis—confounded the stereotypes of Genthe and Norris. She did not do this by trumpeting just how well immigrant Chinese aped the mainstream. Rather, she showed how a stronger stock grew from mixing the best of the two cultures, just as young Lu had. Indeed, mainstream Americans had best stop looking at the Chinese as willing servants with sinister and subterranean lives and start "find[ing] food for thought" (233). Chinese Americans *could* contribute to broader society. They were not as exotic, self-serving, or distant as the mainstream made them out to be. Eaton debunked the myth of whiteness that excluded Chinese Americans from participating in society.

Eaton wrote an essay for the *Boston Globe* three years after she wrote the *Chinese World* letter. In the essay, she described how she used introductions from Chinese merchants and financial assistance from friends to move East and garner time to write. "I came here with the intention of publishing a book," she said, "and planting a few Eurasian thoughts in Western literature" (288). And by passing as Sui Sin Far, by inserting herself in the frame of Arnold Genthe's photos that included evil fortune tellers, sword dancers, and wretched opium dens, and by showing herself to be a nervously sensitive woman who wrote about the Chinese Americans engaged in acts of generosity, kindness, and Franklinesque ambition, Edith Maude Eaton (Sui Sin Far) allowed her mainstream readers to see that East did meet West and that the West just might grow stronger for it.

Conclusion

In the 1998 novel *Causcasia,* Danzy Senna's heroine, Birdie, finally confronts a father whom she has not seen in nearly ten years, and she has an epiphany about her racial makeup. Birdie's white mother and black father had split under the pressure of the racial and political ferment of the early 1970s. Each followed different paths they felt were marked out for them by their race, and each took one of their two mixed-race daughters to live apart as "white" and "black." Birdie found her father only when she ran away from home, intent on establishing who she "really" was. Within minutes of reuniting with him, she launched into a confession:

> "Papa, do you even know where I've been? Do you even care? I've been living as a white girl, a Jewish girl. I've waited and waited . . . But you never came. . . . I passed as white, Papa."
>
> He was frowning at me, and I thought he was going to go into a tirade about the evils of passing. But he only shrugged and said, "Of course I care where you've been, Birdie. . . . I love you. . . . But baby, there's no such thing as passing. We're all just pretending. Race is a complete illusion, make-believe. It's a costume. We all wear one. You just switched yours at some point."[1]

While soothing her guilt about abandoning the imagined responsibilities of her racial heritage, Birdie's father nonetheless grew serious when he spoke about the burden she carried for the social construction of race. "Your whole life's work is going to have to be about correcting somebody else's four-hundred-year-old mistake. Now if that don't cause some existential angst, I don't know what will," he said. "I'm telling you, it's the myth of fucking Sisyphus."[2] Birdie's father knew that even if race were a costume, one that could be changed at will, its force in American society still carried enormous weight.

When Birdie "passed" as white in a rural New Hampshire town, she found herself divided over the racial segregation she witnessed. But she also found herself drawn to the ideas that she was white and whiteness offered her acceptance and power. She lived Roland Barthes's warning that social construction can look natural, make us believe that it's the way the world always was. Grasping how the social construction of race and whiteness affect American literature and culture changes all the rules for understanding a text. When we understand that a writer's hardest battle is how to make the natural, a "perfectly normal" construct like whiteness appear to be a prefabrication, then we better understand the construction writers of color have undertaken. The writers in this study—the antebellum black newspaper editors, William Apess, Anna Julia Cooper, and Edith Eaton—all cleverly sought to pitch an alternative social construction. They drew writing and speaking styles and ideologies from the mainstream, evinced an elite cultural capital that the mainstream thought belonged to whites only, enticed their audiences into the story they had to tell, and then slipped in concepts that deflated the power of whiteness over their lives. They used "white" language, they supplanted the dominant class, and they constructed their own social theories to rewrite the rights of free blacks, to recast the nation's history, to change societal definitions of African Americans, and even to change their own identities. In one form or another, they slipped on a new costume, as Birdie's father would say, to recast the white republic.

None of these writers or speakers hammered readers and listeners with information and points; instead, they worked subtly and tried to reach inside the minds of their audiences to rearrange the way audience members saw the world. Each used a different approach. The antebellum black editors of the 1830s and 1840s sought to combat the entrenched privilege of whiteness by appropriating the class-based discourse of language reform. They tried to overturn an antebellum system of privilege by remaking the idea of black capabilities. In their stories, contrary to popular lore, blacks exhibited a subtle command of words and displayed a mind as well as muscles. They could consider the rights of everyone and participate in a republican government as full citizens. Thus, reformers of the 1830s and 1840s reworked the mainstream version of cultural capital to break the links between black skin, menial jobs, and inferior political rights.

William Apess did not do his work on the level of ideology. He crafted his oration "A Eulogy on King Philip" as a carefully staged two-act performance designed specifically to change his audience's view of Native Americans and their place in the republic. As act 1, he chose a forum, a topic, and a mode of presentation that resonated with the audience, and then he artfully overturned their collective expectations, all designed to build a new foundation for Native American political rights. Apess's second act, his delivery of the eulogy, used the master himself, Founding Father George Washington, to make Native Americans the cornerstone of U.S. history. Apess's two-act performance bent signifiers of both mainstream and Native American culture and also brandished high and popular culture to forge a new republican history and tradition, a revisionist narration, for American Indians and EuroAmericans.

The efforts by Apess and the black press editors to show that they had the sensibilities to speak in the republican tradition worked less effectively as commerce appropriated republicanism, the public discourse of class hardened and an elite cultural capital signaling "inherent" aesthetic appreciation took its place. Actions that signify the ability to put the good of the whole above narrow interests give way to looking at the body to understand the competence a person has for aesthetic sensibilities. Emphasis on this competence allows those with access to elite cultural capital to stand out and, as Bascom says, "make the laws of the land." Furthermore, elite cultural capital becomes a code word for class, and, at a time when scientific racism rooted itself, cultural capital served as a code word for dominant race. Proper citizenship depended on class-bound and race-bound definitions as two examples have illustrated. Governor James Vardaman complained that Mississippi's expenditures to educate blacks not only wasted a lot of money but ruined some perfectly good laborers, and critic T. W. Higginson warned that investing in cultural capital for racial aliens like the Chinese doomed everyone to failure.

Anna Julia Cooper, Latin and Greek instructor and wordsmith, set out to put these cultural capital worries to rest. She chose as her field the very structure of language and aimed to uproot the ideology of whiteness that kept black women oppressed. Cooper drew on the formal rules of rhetoric to cast her discussions of race and women as a trial, and she positioned herself, despite social customs to the contrary, as the lawgiver. Cooper used this new position and her powerful command of language to create a new social theory that redefined white and black and confronted the treatment of black women. She implicitly *created* the audience she wanted to speak to and consequently *remade* the black woman. When Cooper was done, her audience had received a new understanding of the world and race relations that remapped white privileges such as education and the pursuit of cultural capital.

Edith Eaton began her change by focusing on herself. She tapped the prurient interest that Anglos had for the "exotic Oriental," and she used it to her advantage. In midlife, she adopted a Chinese pen name to pose as an insider of the culture. She claimed neurasthenia, a disease that doctors declared beyond the ken of Asians or anyone except elite whites, and she used that disease to rewrite the abilities of the Chinese. Her "reverse passing" allowed her to offer "authentic close-ups" of the Chinese-American way of life and present a Chinese figure with which mainstream culture could understand and sympathize. Her supplanter stories reroute popular ideas of cultural transmission. The exchanges run in both directions between a white mainstream and a "dark" minority. Her hybrid mix created stronger people by blending mainstream American culture and the ancient culture of China. The Chinese were sophisticated people with deep sensibilities, and a hybrid stock would create a stronger nation. Eaton refocused the societal lens on the Chinese and developed a new snapshot of American racial politics that defeated whiteness's ideology of privilege.

These writers teach lessons about reading, research, and the American literary canon. One lesson reaffirms that the tools the authors chose to use do not identify their aims. The writers sought to change the world in diverse ways: from ranting and complaining to telling an engaging, and apparently harmless, story. The antebellum black editors, for example, published prose by David Walker, but their own stories rarely declared that "white America" had better watch out for God's wrath as Walker had done: "O! coloured men!! O! coloured men!!! O! coloured men!!!! Look!! Look!!! at this!!!! And, tell me . . . how long, O! how long my colour shall we be dupes and dogs to the cruel whites?"[3] But the black editors nevertheless used language reform to rework the very foundation that kept antebellum free blacks oppressed. Anna Cooper likewise did not adopt the fiery tone of Walker, Frederick Douglass, or Ida B. Wells. But there is no mistaking that she aimed to present a new set of working assumptions about race that overturned her audience's ideology of whiteness.

Next, the authors show current readers that to understand their work, one must carefully set that work in a rich context including the social formation of race and class. If we aim to use race as a social construct, then the reader must avoid treating it as something fixed through time. We must carefully understand the construction of race operating at each moment, and how writers' visions diverged on the accepted definitions of their time. Further, rifts on accepted definitions are carried to listeners via class-coded ways of speaking and writing that depend on understanding the workings of those codes. William Apess's slim pamphlet publishing the text of his eulogy gives few hints at the spacial and rhetorical symbols on which his speech drew. Nowhere in the pamphlet do we find details of the blue-blood Federal Street Theater and its style. Nowhere does the pamphlet describe that the most popular theater production of the period made King Philip the hero or that the play made Philip look like a noble man unfit to live in the antebellum world and as such the "race" of Native Americans was extinct. Only by restoring this context through archival work—and considering the text as a dual object: the writer presents the text to the public, and the text assumes a life of its own as a piece of the popular culture—do we see the ambition of Apess.

Finally, the writers force readers to reconsider how we assemble the literary canon. They show us that we cannot segregate black, Native American, Chinese American, and "white" writers. They read each other, and they play off of one another's work. For the writers in this study did not live an American oedipal rebirth that the critic F. O. Matthiessen would recognize and applaud. Sure, the antebellum newspaper editors and Edith Eaton, like Matthiessen's Melville, were strong-minded individuals. Certainly, some made themselves independent and rootless by constant travel. Eaton, for example, crossed the country, roaming from New York through the Midwest to San Francisco. But the writers' relationships to the dominant culture or heritage worked differently than what Matthiessen would have us believe about rootless "American" writers who slayed their European forefathers. Matthiessen turned to Santayana and Malraux when he wanted to give heft to the cultural work of his writers in the American Renaissance—Melville, Whitman, Emerson, and Thoreau. Malraux, reported Matthiessen, said that "every civilization is like the Renaissance, and creates its own heritage out of everything in the past that helps it to surpass itself." Matthiessen allowed the French critic to continue with a clincher in italics: "*A heritage is not transmitted; it must be conquered.*"[4]

The writers of this study set out neither to conquer nor even appear to conquer their literary and cultural forebears. Instead, they sought to use America's forebears to change their relationship to the mainstream, and they supplanted whiteness, created revisionist narrations, and constructed new social theories to do it. Homi Bhabha argues that marginalized writers create a hybrid message formed from the dominant ideology and their own marginalized perspective. These writers emphasize "cultural difference" as opposed to "cultural diversity." Cultural diversity is about different worlds that remain completely separate; they are unsullied by each other. Its categories are fixed, like "comparative ethics, aesthetics or ethnology."[5] But cultural difference is a process that questions whether culture is something canned, "known," "authoritative," or "adequate." It knocks down balkanizations. It is not literary "multiculturalism"—a pluralism or collective of texts from subsets of society. In literary polyculturalism all texts combine into something new through their interaction. If cultural diversity is something that names and contains, then cultural difference eludes the grasp. It becomes more complex with every articulation.

The writers in this study used their complicated identities to prospect for the animating concepts of the period and then used this heritage, and their own marginalized experience, to deflate a corrosive ideology of whiteness and forge a new whole. If Matthiessen believed that the function of the artist was to give "full expression to [an age's] abundance, to its energetic desire to master history by repossessing all the resources of the hidden past in a timeless and heroic present," then the characters of this book broadened just what resources need to be reclaimed.[6] To these marginalized writers' minds—*pace* Matthiessen, Jefferson, and others who look for a narrow, homogeneous, and unified American legacy—the culture became stronger for the presence of marginalized peoples. The blending of diverse traditions, all made richer with an alternative American history, already had implanted itself in the culture, whether critics cared to recognize it or not.[7] Their newly constructed past handed them and their marginalized groups claims to a central role in guiding the nation, and their work should guide future thoughts about the American literary canon, too.

NOTES

INTRODUCTION *Recasting the Plot*

1. Advertisement in back matter in John Bascom, *The Growth of Nationality in the United States: A Social Study* (New York: G. P. Putnam's Sons, 1899).
2. Matthew Frye Jacobson, *Whiteness of a Different Color: European Immigrants and the Alchemy of Race* (Cambridge: Harvard University Press, 1998), 9.
3. David R. Roediger, *The Wages of Whiteness: Race and the Making of the American Working Class* (New York: Verso, 1991). Edwin Morgan argued that Virginia became the birthplace of the language of American freedom precisely because whites defined themselves against a black slave population. *American Slavery, American Freedom: The Ordeal of Colonial Virginia* (New York: W. W. Norton, 1975), and Alexander Saxton, *The Rise and Fall of the White Republic: Class Politics and Mass Culture in Nineteenth-Century America* (New York: Verso, 1990) discussed economic forces that led to the construction of white identity. Roediger begins to answer the call that whiteness studies pay attention to what people of color have to say about whiteness with *Black on White: Black Writers on What It Means to Be White* (New York: Schocken Books, 1998). I try hard in this study to avoid reifying whiteness, as Peter Kolchin warns in "Whiteness Studies: The New History of Race in America," *Journal of American History* 89:1 (June 2002): 154–174.
4. Frederick Douglass, "What to the Slave Is the Fourth of July?" 5 July 1852, rpt. James M. Gregory, *Frederick Douglass, the Orator* (New York, 1893), 103–106, online in the Douglass Public Archives, http://douglass.speech.nwu.edu/doug_a10.htm.
5. Michael Schudson, *The Good Citizen: A History of American Civic Life* (Cambridge: Harvard University Press, 1998).
6. Richard D. Brown, *Knowledge Is Power: The Diffusion of Information in Early America, 1700–1865* (New York: Oxford University Press, 1989). Cheryl Walker, *Indian Nation: Native American Literature and Nineteenth-Century Nationalisms* (Durham, N.C.: Duke University Press, 1997). Rafia Zafar, *We Wear the Mask: African Americans Write American Literature, 1760–1870* (New York: Columbia University Press, 1997).
7. See the essays in Henry B. Wonham, *Criticism and the Color Line: Desegregating American Literary Studies* (New Brunswick, N.J.: Rutgers University Press, 1996).
8. Ann duCille, *The Coupling Convention: Sex, Text, and Tradition in Black Women's Fiction* (New York: Oxford University Press, 1993), 68. For a brief but on-target

review of these questions, see Shelley Fisher Fishkin review of duCille's book, "Essentialism and Its Discontents" *American Quarterly* 48:1 (1996): 142–152. In addition to racial subject matter, institutional factors, including access to publishing, of course affected the placement of blacks in the canon. See, for just one example, Richard H. Brodhead, "Introduction," *The Journals of Charles W. Chesnutt*, ed. by Richard H. Brodhead (Durham, N.C.: Duke University Press, 1993). As Fisher Fishkin points out, an increasing number of critics, including Fisher Fishkin, Carla L. Peterson, Claudia Tate, and Eric Sundquist are working to change this bias. DuCille's book shows how black women used what critics had called the "white" marriage-plot. Quote from William J. Harris, "Black Aesthetic," in *The Oxford Companion to African American Literature*, edited by William L. Andrews, Frances Smith Foster, and Trudier Harris (New York: Oxford University Press, 1997), 67. One excellent exception is Shelley Fisher Fishkin and Carla L. Peterson, "We Hold These Truths to Be Self-Evident: The Rhetoric of Frederick Douglass's Journalism" (1990); rpt. *The Black Press: New Literary and Historical Essays*, edited by Todd Vogel (New Brunswick, N.J.: Rutgers University Press, 2001), 71–92.

9. "Major Noah's 'Negroes,'" *Freedom's Journal,* August 24, 1827.
10. James McCune Smith, "Citizenship," *The Anglo-African Magazine*, May 1859, 146; italics in the original.
11. I first heard Robin D. G. Kelley use the term "polycultural" in a lecture at the University of Texas. "People in Me: On the Polycultural Nature of Blackness" (lecture, University of Texas, Austin, December 4, 1997). He describes this theory in "People in Me," *ColorLines Magazine* 1:3 (Winter 1999). For an application of this polycultural idea, see Vijay Prashad, *Everybody Was Kung Fu Fighting: Afro-Asian Connections and the Myth of Cultural Purity* (Boston: Beacon Press, 2001), esp. chap. 2.
12. Gary Y. Okihiro, "Reflections of Self and Society," *Radical History Review* 79 (Winter 2001): 111–113.
13. "The Celestials at Home and Abroad," *Blackwood's Magazine* 77:441 (July 1852): 98–114.
14. "Shall We Talk Chinese?" *California China Mail and Flying Dragon,* January 1, 1867.
15. Samuel Gompers and Herman Gutstadt, *Meat vs. Rice: American Manhood Against Asiatic Cooliesm, Which Shall Survive?* (1902; repr., San Francisco: Asiatic Exclusion League, 1908), 4.
16. Of course, this bifurcation of high and low culture after the Civil War follows on and expands work done by Lawrence W. Levine, *Highbrow/Lowbrow: The Emergence of Cultural Hierarchy in America* (Cambridge: Harvard University Press, 1988).
17. Paul Lauter has long called for an inspection of class in the understanding of American cultural production. Most recently, see, *From Walden Pond to Jurassic Park: Activism, Culture, and American Studies* (Durham, N.C.: Duke University Press, 2001). Bourdieu makes his most extensive description of cultural capital in *Distinction: A Social Critique of the Judgment of Taste*, trans. by Richard Nice (Cambridge: Harvard University Press, 1984). See also Bourdieu's *The Field of Cultural Production: Essays on Art and Literature*, edited and introduced by Randal Johnson, edited by Lawrence D. Kritzman (New York: Columbia University Press, 1993). Scholars now argue that different kinds of cultural capital exist. For example, a teenage boy from

a family that preferred the auto shop to the library may not excel at standardized tests, creative writing, or scholarship—talents that would help him get into an elite college—but he may know very well how to work with his hands. If Harvard does not appreciate that form of cultural capital, the army, with its phalanx of Humvees, might well snap him up. Some critics charge that Bourdieu's conclusions apply only to the specific time and place of his study: France during the 1960s. But we do not have to marshal Bourdieu's detailed surveys and charts about consumer and class position to use the concept, if we properly contextualize it.

18. John Guillory, *Cultural Capital: The Problem of Literary Canon Formation* (Chicago: University of Chicago Press, 1993), 18. Several recent sociological studies bear out Guillory's conclusions. Annette Lareau and her colleagues track the impact of class and race on education in the United States. She finds that parents in the higher income brackets have more of the "cultural capital"—"linguistic structures, authority patterns, and types of curricula"—that help students with education. Working-class parents want their children to succeed just as much as the upper-class parents do, but they have a different view of the educational process and teacher. To them, school is a job for the student that ends when he leaves the building. The teacher's—not the parent's—job is to teach. Annette Lareau, "Social Class Differences in Family-School Relationships: The Importance of Cultural Capital," *Sociology of Education* 60 (April 1987): 73–85. In a study on race, she produces two findings that are important to our argument here: Lareau and her colleagues find that *whiteness* is a source of cultural capital that white parents of all classes benefit from; furthermore, she finds that the gatekeeping institutions—like schools—play a large role. Thus, we have to carefully historicize the relationships and those institutions. See Annette Lareau and Erin McNamara Horvat, "Moments of Social Inclusion and Exclusion: Race, Class, and Cultural Capital in Family-School Relationships," *Sociology of Education* 72 (January 1999): 37–53. Guillory points out that social identity becomes constructed through culture, a theory that nicely closes the loop. Institutional forces affect the means of cultural production. The culture produced, in turn, defines an identity. See *Cultural Capital,* passim and esp. chap. 1.
19. The paragraph is indebted to Ronald Takaki among others. Most specifically, see Takaki's *Iron Cages: Race and Culture in Nineteenth-Century America* (1979; rev. ed. New York: Oxford University Press, 2000). Franklin to Peter Collinson, May 9, 1753, in *The Writings of Benjamin Franklin, Philadelphia, 1726–1753,* Vol. 2, ed. Albert Henry Smyth (New York: Macmillan, 1907), 468–475.
20. Lewis Cass, "Removal of Indians," *North American Review* 30:66 (January 1830): 72, and Cass, "Policy and Practice of the United States and Great Britain in their Treatment of Indians," *North American Review* 24:55 (April 1827): 368.
21. Takaki, *Iron Cages*, 13.

CHAPTER 1 *Speaking to the Whiteness of the Brain*

1. Henry Box Brown, *Narrative of the Life of Henry Box Brown, Written by Himself,* First Eng. ed. (Manchester: Printed By Lee and Glynn, 8, Cannon Street, 1851), 60–61.
2. Ibid., pp. i–ii.
3. See, for example, Houston Baker, *The Journey Back: Issues in Black Literature and*

Criticism (Chicago: University of Chicago Press, 1980); Henry Louis Gates, Jr., *Figures in Black: Words, Signs, and the "Racial" Self* (New York: Oxford University Press, 1987); Leonard Cassuto, "Frederick Douglass and the Work of Freedom: Hegel's Master-Slave Dialectic in the Fugitive Slave Narrative," *Prospects: An Annual of American Cultural Studies* 21 (1996): 229–259; Eric J. Sundquist, *To Wake the Nations: Race in the Making of American Literature* (Cambridge, Mass.: Belknap Press of Harvard University Press, 1993); and Shelley Fisher Fishkin and Carla L. Peterson, "'We Hold These Truths to Be Self-Evident': The Rhetoric of Frederick Douglass's Journalism" (1990); rpt., *The Black Press: New Literary and Historical Essays*, edited by Todd Vogel (New Brunswick, N.J.: Rutgers University Press, 2001), 71–92. For more on the racial caste of labor and mental work in antebellum black writers, see Todd Vogel, "The New Face of Black Labor," in *The Black Press: New Literary and Historical Essays*, 37–54.

4. See, for example, the standard on the split between high and low culture, Lawrence W. Levine, *Highbrow/Lowbrow: The Emergence of Cultural Hierarchy in America* (Cambridge, Mass.: Harvard University Press, 1988).
5. John Ernest makes this argument nicely in "Liberation Historiography: African-American Historians before the Civil War," *American Literary History* 14:3 (Fall 2002): 413–443.
6. William Charvat, *The Origins of American Critical Thought, 1810–1835* (Philadelphia: University of Pennsylvania Press, 1936), esp. 7–26; for a more recent take that applies these questions to Frederick Douglass's oratory and his use of his body, see Robert Fanuzzi, "The Trouble with Douglass's Body: Nineteenth-Century Abolitionist Frederick Douglass," *American Transcendental Quarterly* 13:1 (March 1999): 27–49; see also Fishkin and Peterson, "We Hold These Truths to Be Self-Evident."
7. Ira Aldridge, *Memoir and Theatrical Career of Ira Aldridge, the African Roscius* (London: Onwhyn, Catharine St., Strand, 1848), 11.
8. Ibid. For a discussion of Aldridge and the complications surrounding the Matthews debate, see Marvin McAllister, *White People Do Not Know How to Behave at Entertainments Designed for Ladies & Gentlemen of Colour: William Brown's African and American Theater* (Chapel Hill: University of North Carolina Press, 2002), 160–161. This analysis suggests that high and low cultures were not as interchangeable as Lawrence Levine's work suggests. Lawrence Levine, *Highbrow/Lowbrow*.
9. David Damrosch, "The Semiotics of Conquest," *American Literary History* 8:3 (Fall 1996): 516–532, quote at 529.
10. For Noah's comments and the black press's response, see "Major Noah's 'Negroes,'" *Freedom's Journal*, August 24, 1827; Ohio, General Assembly, Senate, Select Committee on the Petitions of Sundry Citizens, Praying the Repeal of Certain Laws Restricting the Rights of Persons of Color and for Securing All Persons Within the Jurisdiction of the State the Right of Trial by Jury, *Report*, March 3, 1838, 11.
11. David Walker, *Walker's Appeal, in Four Articles; Together with a Preamble, to the Coloured Citizens of the World, but in Particular, and Very Expressly, to Those of the United States of America, Written in Boston, State of Massachusetts, September 28, 1829* (Boston: Revised and Published By David Walker, 1830), 12. For "hewers," see "African Free Schools in the United States," *Freedom's Journal*, June 1, 1827. On schools, see *The Colored American*, June 24, 1837; for subservience, see "A Mistaken Notion," *The Colored American*, April 8, 1837.

12. "Editorial Correspondence, No. 1, Philadelphia, July 31st, 1857," *Provincial Freeman, August 15, 1857.*
13. William Wells Brown, *The Black Man, His Antecedents, His Genius, and His Achievements* (New York: Thomas Hamilton, 48 Beekman Street, 1863), 213.
14. David S. Shields, *Civil Tongues and Polite Letters in British America*, published for the Institute of Early American History and Culture, Williamsburg, Virginia (Chapel Hill: University of North Carolina Press, 1997), 328.
15. Kenneth Cmiel, *Democratic Eloquence: The Fight over Popular Speech in Nineteenth-Century America* (New York: William Morrow, 1990), 12–13. I also rely on Cmiel's "'A Broad Fluid Language of Democracy': Discovering the American Idiom," *Journal of American History* 79:3 (December 1992): 913–936. Louis F. Klipstein, "A Grammar of the Anglo-Saxon Language," *The American Whig Review*, 10:23 (November 1849): 549. Phillip Hone, *The Diary of Philip Hone, 1828–1851*, Vol. 2, edited by Allan Nevins (New York: Dodd, Mead, 1927), 143.
16. "Colonel Davy Crockett Delivering His Celebrated Speech to Congress on the State of Finances, State officers, and State Affairs in General," http://www.towson.edu/~duncan/crockett.html (accessed June 23, 2003).
17. Maximilian Schele De Vere, *Americanisms; the English of the New World* (New York: Scribner and Company, 1872), 4.
18. Ibid., 249. Schele De Vere is writing in 1872, but, in context, he is talking about changes from Toqueville to his own moment.
19. James Parton, *The Life of Horace Greeley, Editor of the New York Tribune* (New York: Mason Brothers, 1855), 266. Cmiel, *Democratic Eloquence*, 64–66; Cmiel is quoted on 66. Cooper here is posing as a European visitor. James Fenimore Cooper, *Notions of the Americans*, 2 vols. (Philadelphia: Lea and Blanchard, 1840), 1:478; quoted in Cmiel, *Democratic Eloquence*, 66.
20. Pierre Bourdieu, *Language and Symbolic Power*, trans. by Gino Raymond, Matthew Adamson, and John B. Thompson (Cambridge: Harvard University Press, 1991), 51. For a discussion of Bourdieu and language, see Katharine W. Jones, "'I've Called 'em Tom-ah-toes All My Life and I'm Not Going to Change!': Maintaining Linguistic Control Over English Identity in the U.S.," *Social Forces* 79:3 (March 2001): 1061–1094.
21. Jill LePore, *A Is for American: Letters and Other Characters in the Newly United States* (New York: Alfred A. Knopf, 2002), 111–135.
22. "Colored Students," *The Colored American*, September 2, 1837. See also "Report of the Committee of the Manual Labor School," *Proceedings of the Colored National Convention*, Rochester: Printed at the Office of Frederick Douglass' Paper, 1853; rpt. Howard Bell, *Minutes of The Proceedings of the National Negro Conventions, 1830–1864* (New York: Arno Press, 1969), 31.
23. For an analysis of Christian millennial thinking and reform, including manual labor schools, see Robert H. Abzug, *Cosmos Crumbling: American Reform and the Religious Imagination* (New York: Oxford University Press, 1994). Patrick Rael analyzes education among antebellum free blacks in *Black Identity and Black Protest in the Antebellum North* (Chapel Hill: University of North Carolina Press, 2002). Also see the discussion of mental and manual work in Vogel, "The New Face of Black Labor." "Colored Students," *The Colored American*, September 2, 1837; "Report of the Committee of the Manual Labor School," 31. "African Free Schools in

The United States," *Freedom's Journal*, June 1, 1827. William Whipper, "EXTRACT. From An Address Delivered before the Colored Reading Society of Philadelphia Friends and Fellow Citizens," *Freedom's Journal*, December 26, 1828.

24. William Wells Brown, *The Black Man, His Antecedents, His Genius, and His Achievements* (New York: Thomas Hamilton, 1863), 28, 29, 52, 86–87, 149, 32, 91, 105, 257, 47.
25. "To The School!" *Christian Recorder*, March 29, 1862; "Lancaster City, Pa., Dec. 18, 1848," *The North Star*, January 5, 1849; Martin R. Delany, "Wilmington, Del., Nov. 30, 1848," *The North Star*, December 15, 1848.
26. Diary of Rev. James J. Griffing, http://www.griffingweb.com/i_will_keep_a_journal.htm# (accessed July 3, 2003); Brown, *The Colored Man*, 284.
27. William H. Robinson, *From Log Cabin to the Pulpit; or, Fifteen Years in Slavery*, 3d ed. (Eau Claire, Wis.: Rev. W. H. Robinson, 1913), 130.
28. "Literary Gossip: Correspondence," *The National Era* 1:21 (May 27, 1847): 3.
29. "Both Sides," *Provincial Freeman*, March 24, 1854.
30. "Popular Amusements in New York," *The National Era* 1:15 (April 15, 1847): 3.
31. "Meetings in New York," *The North Star*, June 8, 1849.
32. O. S. Fowler, *Hereditary Descent: Its Laws and Facts Illustrated and Applied to the Improvement of Mankind: With Hints to Woman: Including Directions for Forming Matrimonial Alliances So As to Produce in Offspring Whatever Physical, Mental, or Moral Qualities Are Desired: Together with Preventives of Hereditary Tendencies* (New York : O. S. & L. N. Fowler, 1843), 126.
33. O. S. and L. N. Fowler, *The Illustrated Self-Instructor in Phrenology and Physiology with One Hundred Engravings, and a Chart of the Character* (New York: Fowler and Wells, 1857), front matter. Hiram Powers used phrenology to pronounce on Michelangelo's work. The Powers and Audubon examples come from Charles Colbert, *A Measure of Perfection: Phrenology and the Fine Arts in America* (Chapel Hill: University of North Carolina Press, 1997), 11, 42–45, 52.
34. For the Jacksonian argument about phrenology and Boston physician survey statistics, see Colbert, *A Measure of Perfection*, xii, 20. Fowler and Fowler, *Illustrated Self-Instructor*, 57, 78. Woodbridge N. Ferris, *The Autobiography of Woodbridge N. Ferris* (Big Rapids, Mich.: Ferris State University, 1995), section 2. The autobiography was produced at http://www.ferris.edu/htmls/ferrisfaq/woodbridge/ (accessed June 23, 2003).
35. Fowler and Fowler, *Illustrated Self-Instructor*, 26–27.
36. George Combe, *Notes on the United States of North America during a Phrenological Visit in 1838/9–40,* 2 vols. (Philadelphia: Carey and Hart, 1841), 1:208–209, quoted in Colbert, *Measure of Perfection*, 233. John Neal, "Our Painters," *The Atlantic Monthly* 22:134 (December 1868): 641–651; quote at 644.
37. Fowler and Fowler, *Illustrated Self-Instructor*, 13–14.
38. "Daniel Webster," *The Colored American*, August 24, 1839. An editor's note claimed that this passage came from the New York correspondent for the *London Herald*.
39. "Remarks on the Eloquence of Debate," *The New-England Magazine* 7:2 (August 1834): 107, 106.
40. Fowler and Fowler, *Illustrated Self-Instructor*, 36–42.
41. Fowler, *Hereditary*, 126.
42. O. S. Fowler, *The Practical Phrenologist, and Recorder and Delineator of the Char-*

acter and Talents . . . A Compendium of Phreno-Organic Science (Boston: O. S. Fowler, 1869), 12. Fowler, *Hereditary*, 34–35; Fowler and Fowler, *Illustrated Self-Instructor*, 79; J.D.B. De Bow, *The Industrial Resources, Etc., of the Southern and Western States, Embracing a View of Their Commerce, Agriculture, Manufactures, Internal Improvements; Slave and Free Labor, Slavery Institutions, Products, Etc., of the South,* Vol. 2 (New Orleans: De Bow's Review, 1852), 328.

43. Fowler, *Hereditary*, 36.
44. "Anthony Burns a Freeman," *Provincial Freeman*, March 17, 1855; "Dagnerrian Gallery of the West," *Provincial Freeman*, June 3, 1854; "Communications: from Our Brooklyn Correspondent," *Frederick Douglass Paper*, February 12, 1852.
45. "Phrenology in the Pulpit: Testimony of Rev. Henry Ward Beecher," *Provincial Freeman*, June 23, 1855; for notices, see, for example, *Provincial Freeman*, July 15, 1854, and "Publications," *Provincial Freeman*, April 22, 1854. Quote in "Publications."
46. Brown, *The Colored Man*, 92, 110, 103. Interestingly, Frederick Douglass describes visiting the British phrenologist George Combe in England, but Douglass does not comment on Combe's phrenological ideas. Frederick Douglass, *The Life and Times of Frederick Douglass* (Hartford, Conn.: Park Publishing, 1881), 245.
47. For an overview of reform movements and perfectibility, see Abzug, *Cosmos Crumbling*. "Cingues," *Herald of Freedom*; rpt. in *The Colored American*, October 19, 1839.
48. Unattributed quote in Wells, *The Colored Man*, 254.
49. I draw biographical information on Smith from *The Colored American*, *The North Star*, and David W. Blight's thoughtful article, "In Search of Learning, Liberty, and Self Definition: James McCune Smith and the Ordeal of the Antebellum Black Intellectual," *Afro-Americans in New York Life and History*, 9:2 (July 1985): 7–25, and John Stauffer, *The Black Hearts of Men: Radical Abolitionists and the Transformation of Race* (Cambridge: Harvard University Press, 2002).
50. "Phrenology," *The Colored American*, September 23, 1837; "Dr. Smith," *The Commercial Advertiser*, rpt. in *The Colored American*, September 30, 1837; "Anti Phrenology," *The Colored American*, October 14, 1837. Smith became an editor of *The Colored American* in November 1837.
51. "Dr. Smith," *The Commercial Advertiser*.
52. George Frederickson, *The Black Image in the White Mind.*
53. Ralph Waldo Emerson, quoted in Cmiel, *Democratic Eloquence*, 95.
54. Cmiel, *Democratic Eloquence*, 95. The following paragraphs on language reform are heavily indebted to Cmiel's *Democratic Eloquence* and his "A Broad Fluid Language of Democracy.'"
55. Kenneth Cmiel, "A Broad Fluid Language of Democracy," 925.
56. Whitelaw Reid, *After the War: May 1, 1865, To May 1, 1866* (London: Sampson Low, Son, & Marston, 1866), 250.
57. Cmiel, "Broad Fluid Language of Democracy," 934.
58. "Editor's Table," *Harper's New Monthly Magazine*, 21, no. 124 (September 1860): 553.
59. Cmiel, *Democratic Eloquence*, discusses this at 51–52.
60. George Perkins Marsh, *Lectures on the English Language* (1859; rpt. New York: Charles Scribner's Sons, 1874), 86, 118–127; cited in Cmiel, *Democratic Eloquence*, 114–115. Find a report on Marsh's "findings" in "The English Language," *The Christian Recorder*, May 18, 1861.

61. Henry Reed, *Lectures on English Literature* (Philadelphia: Parry & Macmillan, 1855), 120.
62. Anonymous, "Anglo-Saxons, and Anglo-Africans," *The Anglo-African Magazine* 1:8 (August 1859); rpt. (New York: Arno Press and The New York Times, 1968), 247.
63. "Prospectus," *Anglo-Saxon* 1:1(December 5, 1846), 3.
64. "The Anglo Saxon," *Anglo-Saxon* 1:3 (February 6, 1847); 4, emphases in the original.
65. "The Anglo-Saxon," *The North Star*, July 14, 1848.
66. "From the Editor of the Zanesville Gazette," *Anglo-Saxon* 1:2 (January 23, 1847), 1.
67. "The Anglo-Saxon," *The National Era* 1:10 (March 11, 1847), 2.
68. "A Card, from the Proprietors of the 'Anglo-Saxon,' to Their Patrons," *The North Star*, April 7, 1848.
69. "A Report upon Phonotypy," *Anglo-Saxon* 1:3 (February 6, 1847), 3.
70. The paper says that it supports the "brotherhood of man." One reason it may have adopted the name is that the reformer's detractors claimed that Americans would lose the etymology if they got hooked on phonics. This may be, then, an example of using the name to head off some of that criticism. However, the overall point still stands. The reformers sought to set the language in concrete, and the concrete they used is found in the foundations of whiteness in antebellum America.
71. John Stauffer's *The Black Hearts of Men* nicely shows a remarkably equal friendship among Douglass, Gerrit Smith, John Brown, and James McCune Smith. But, as Stauffer points out, this kind of relationship at the time was the exception, not the rule.
72. Harriet Beecher Stowe, "Sketches of Modern Reforms and Reformers, in Great Britain and Ireland: No. 1.—Introductory—The 'Condition of England' Question," *The National Era* 2:66 (April 6, 1848), 53; Harriet Beecher Stowe, "Selections from the National Era: Sketches of Modern Reforms and Reformers in Great Britain and Ireland," *The North Star*, June 9, 1848.
73. "Development of the English Language," *The Christian Recorder*, October 12, 1861.
74. "From the Syracuse Chronicle: Liberty Party State Convention," *Frederick Douglass' Paper*, October 13, 1854.
75. "Selections from the Pennsylvania Freeman, Speech of Wendell Phillips, Delivered on Saturday Afternoon the 14th inst. at the Assembly Buildings, Philadelphia," *The North Star*, June 9, 1848.
76. "Speech of Wendell Phillips at the Adjourned Meeting of the American Anti-Slavery Society," *The North Star*, June 8, 1849.
77. Smith, "Citizenship," 149.
78. *The Life of William J. Brown* (Providence, 1883); rpt., *The Black Worker: A Documentary History from Colonial Times to the Present*, Vol. 1*: The Black Worker to 1869*, edited by Philip Foner and Ronald L. Lewis (Philadelphia: Temple University Press, 1978), 56.
79. James McCune Smith, "Communications, 'Heads of the Colored People,' Done with a Whitewash Brush," *Frederick Douglass' Paper*, March 25, 1852.

CHAPTER 2 *William Apess's Theater and a "Native" American History*

1. On Jackson and the Cherokees, see Michael Paul Rogin, *Fathers and Children: Andrew Jackson and the Subjugation of the American Indian* (New York: Alfred A.

Knopf, 1975), esp. 206–248. See also the connections Rosemary K. Bank makes in "Staging the 'Native': Making History in American Theatre Culture, 1828–1838," *Theatre Journal* 45:4 (December 1993): 461–487.

2. For the Mashpee incident, see Barry O'Connell's introduction in *On Our Own Ground: The Complete Writings of William Apess*, edited by Barry O'Connell (Amherst: University of Massachusetts Press, 1992). For a postcolonial reading of Apess that relies heavily on the Mashpee incident, see Maureen Konkle, "Indian Literacy, U.S. Colonialism, and Literary Criticism," *American Literature* 69:3 (September 1997): 457–486.
3. William Apess, "Eulogy on King Philip, as Pronounced at the Odeon in Federal Street, Boston" (Boston: Published by the Author, 1836); rpt. *On Our Own Ground*, 296. Apess used Apes and Apess as surnames. I follow O'Connell in sticking with the one the writer used in his last works, Apess.
4. Jay Fliegelman, *Declaring Independence: Jefferson, Natural Language, and the Culture of Performance* (Stanford: Stanford University Press, 1993), 45.
5. The volume of work on Apess is slight, but recent writing about him has been scrappy. O'Connell, in *On Our Own Ground*, recovered Apess and placed him in a rich historical context. For a Bakhtinian reading that makes Apess an example of a text that speaks with only one voice and is overrun with "salvationism," see Arnold Krupat, *The Voice in the Margin: Native American Literature and the Canon* (Berkeley: University of California Press, 1989), 144–148. For a take on Apess that makes him a "reverse ventriloquist"—that is, mimicking a white voice to destabilize it—see Larry Murray, *Forked Tongues: Speech, Writing, and Representation in North American Indian Texts* (London: Pinter Publishers, 1991), esp. 57–60. Cheryl Walker, *Indian Nation: Native American Literature and Nineteenth-Century Nationalisms* (Durham, N.C.: Duke University Press, 1997), argues that Apess offers a sophisticated text that uses what she calls a subjugational and transpositional or egalitarian relationship. Apess uses these discourses to open up new roles for Native Americans. She is troubled, however, by how much he both seems to want to join with the mainstream and mimics the Methodists. Konkle, "Indian Literacy, U.S. Colonialism" takes on all these readings as not sufficiently concerned with nationhood.
6. Cotton Mather, *Magnalia Christi Americana; or, The Ecclesiastical History of New-England, from Its First Planting in the Year 1620 Unto the Year of Our Lord, 1698* (1702; rpt. Hartford, S. Andrus and Son, 1855), 566. See Jill Lepore's discussion of Philip in *The Name of War: King Philip's War and the Origins of American Identity* (New York: Alfred A. Knopf, 1998). Lepore shows how the victor's story silenced all others. The best traditional history of the war is forty years old, Douglas Edward Leach's *Flintlock and Tomahawk: New England in King Philip's War* (New York: Macmillan, 1958).
7. Apess himself referred to Indians as one of the lost tribes of Israel. Sandra Gustafson argues that Apess used the Lost Tribes concept to staunch evangelical talk of Indians as heathens and to create a common Indian community. See her "Nations of Israelites: Prophecy and Cultural Autonomy in the Writings of William Apess," *Religion and Literature* 26:1 (Spring 1994): 31–53.
8. Roy Harvey Pearce, *The Savages of America: A Study of the Indian and the Idea of Civilization* (1953; rev. ed. Baltimore: Johns Hopkins University Press, 1965); and Robert F. Berkhofer, Jr., *The White Man's Indian: Images of the American Indian*

from Columbus to the Present (New York: Vintage Books, 1979). Timothy Dwight, *Travels in New York and New England* (1821–1822; rpt. Cambridge: Belknap Press of Harvard University Press, 1969), 3:14. In her early article, "William Apes, Pequot: An Indian Reformer in the Jackson Era," *New England Quarterly* 50 (December 1977): 605–625, Kim McQuaid describes Apess's background and some views of Indians at the time. For a discussion of how America's movement toward a representation of self as a means to self-understanding followed a parallel shift from fighting wilderness and Indians to representing wilderness and Indians, see Larzer Ziff, *Writing in the New Nation: Prose, Print, and Politics in the Early United States* (New Haven: Yale University Press, 1991).

9. William Apess, *A Son of the Forest* (1829); rpt., as *A Son of the Forest and Other Writings*, edited by Barry O'Connell (Amherst: University of Massachusetts Press, 1992), 10.
10. Apess, *A Son of the Forest*, 12.
11. Apess lays out the vicissitudes of his life in *Son of the Forest* and his complaints at the Mashpee revolt in *Indian Nullification of the Unconstitutional Laws of Massachusetts Relative to the Marshpee Tribe; or, The Pretended Riot Explained* (1835); both are reprinted in Barry O'Connell, *On Our Own Ground.* O'Connell's introduction provides an excellent summary of Apess's life along with research that fills in some of the gaps. For more on Apess's Methodism and how the religious rhetoric in his writing challenges the period's power structure, see Karim M. Tiro, "Denominated 'SAVAGE': Methodism, Writing, and Identity in the Works of William Apess, A Pequot," *American Quarterly* 48:4 (1996): 653–679, and Carolyn Haynes, "'A mark for them all to . . . hiss at': The Formation of Methodist and Pequot Identity in the Conversion Narrative of William Apess," *Early American Literature* 31:1 (1996): 25–44.
12. Major Mordecai Noah, *She Would Be a Soldier; or, The Plains of Chippewa* (1819); rpt. in *Dramas from the American Theatre, 1762–1919*, edited by Richard Moody (New York: World Publishing Company, 1966), 123–142. For the box office draw, see page 124. For surveys of American Indians on stage, see Don B. Wilmeth, "Noble or Ruthless Savage?: The America Indian on Stage and in the Drama," *Journal of American Drama and Theater* 1 (1989): 38–78; Marilyn J. Anderson, "The Image of the Indian in American Drama during the Jacksonian Era, 1829–1845," *Journal of American Culture* 1:4 (1978): 800–810; and Richard E. Amacher, "Behind the Curtain with the Noble Savage: Stage Management of Indian Plays, 1825–1860," *Theater Survey* 7 (1965): 101–114.
13. *The Fire Warrior*, Warren Theatre playbill, written by J. S. Jones, performed on April 1, 1834, *Warren Theatre Playbills*, Boston Public Library, Rare Books Division, T 10.15, np.
14. "The Indian's Lament," in *Songs of the Hutchinson Family*. Words and music by J. M. Hutchinson, arranged with symphonies and accompaniments by E. L. White (Boston: Stephen W. Marsh, c1846); see esp. 5–6. Dartmouth College Library, Archives.
15. William Rounseville Alger, *Life of Edwin Forrest, the American Tragedian*, 2 vols. (Philadelphia: J. B. Lippincott, 1877), 1:168.
16. John Augustus Stone, *Metamora*, in *Metamora and Other Plays*, edited by Eugene R. Page (Princeton: Princeton University Press, 1941), 25. All other citations are noted parenthetically in the text.

17. Reviewer quoted in Alger, *Life of Edwin Forrest*, 476–477.
18. Noah quoted in Sally Leilani Jones, *The Original Characters of Edwin Forrest and His American Style* (Ph.D. diss., University of Toronto, 1992), 111. Jones argues here that the characters of Forrest are products of American nationalism during the Jacksonian period.
19. Alger, *Life of Edwin Forrest*, 477.
20. Jones, *Original Characters of Edwin Forrest,* 111.
21. *The Evening Gazette*, February 20, 1830, 2, col. 7, quoted in Jones, *Original Characters of Edwin Forrest*, 6 n, 112. The distance between the theaters is shown in the *Boston City Directory, 1829*.
22. Alger, *Life of Edwin Forrest*, 124.
23. Gabriel Harrison, *Edwin Forrest: The Actor and the Man: Critical and Reminiscent* (Brooklyn: n.p., 1889), 37–38.
24. Forrest's trip coincided with Margaret Fuller's trip, which elicited the same response to the Macinaw Indians during her *Summer on the Lakes in 1843* (1844; rpt. Urbana: University of Illinois Press, 1991).
25. For how the nation looked toward a more civilized history after the revolution and thus turned Indians and nature into romantic items to be contemplated and commemorated, see Philip J. Deloria, *Playing Indian* (New Haven: Yale University Press, 1998), 5. Gerald Vizenor in *Manifest Manners: Post Indian Warriors of Survivance* (Hanover, N.H.: Wesleyan University Press, 1994) uses Baudrillard as a framework to investigate what is "real" and what is "simulation" about American Indians. He argues that "manifest manners"—the imperialism of manifest destiny—eradicated American Indians. But because the conquerors wanted to pretend at least to have a conversation, they invented, or simulated, Indian customs and discourse. Vizenor's method knocks at the same door as Deloria, but it lacks the suppleness of Deloria's more complicated appropriation, exchange, and reappropriation.
26. Details about the Federal Street Theatre and the Odeon come from the theater's archives, Boston Public Library, Rare Books Division. The theater was rebuilt in the same year by Bulfinch. Frank Chouteau Brown argues that the theater's interior was refurbished like the original structure. See Brown, "The First Boston Theatre, on Federal Street," *Old-Time New England* 36:1 (July 1945): 1–7, esp. 6. This is supported by Bulfinch's granddaughter in *The Life and Letters of Charles Bulfinch, Architect, with Other Family Papers*, edited by Ellen Susan Bulfinch (Boston: Houghton Mifflin, 1896). She says that the reconstruction project allocated most of its money to restoring the interior (see p. 96). Other details and history of the theater come from William T. W. Ball, "The Old Federal Street Theatre: A Paper Read before the Bostonian Society, Council Chamber, Old State House, June 11, 1889," in *The Bostonian Society Publications* (Boston: Old State House, 1911), 8:51, and from William W. Clapp, Jr., *A Record of the Boston Stage* (1853; rpt. New York: Greenwood Press, 1969). The most thorough rendering of the first theater can be found in Richard Stoddard, "A Reconstruction of Charles Bulfinch's First Federal Street Theatre, Boston," *Winterthur Portfolio* 6 (1970): 185–208. Finally, compare the Federal Theatre to E. L. Boulle's 1781 design for an opera house in Paris in Nikolaus Pevsner, *A History of Building Types* (Princeton, N.J.: Princeton University Press, 1976), 81.
27. Clapp, *A Record of the Boston Stage*, 19.
28. Early owners found in Federal Street Theatre, Box D, Item 20. Adams quitclaims

his stake in the theater on November 7, 1804, Box D, Ms.Th.D52. Harold and James Kirker, *Bulfinch's Boston, 1787–1817* (New York: Oxford University Press, 1964), and Charles Place, *Charles Bulfinch: Architect and Citizen* (Boston: Houghton Mifflin, 1925), discuss the repeal of the Boston law.

29. *Boston Daily Evening Transcript*, January 6, 1836.
30. For the role of history teller as shaper of the nation, see Nina Baym, *American Women Writers and the Work of History, 1790–1860* (New Brunswick, N.J.: Rutgers University Press, 1995).
31. For a discussion of environmentalism, oratory, and Indians, see Helen Carr, *Inventing the American Primitive: Politics, Gender and the Representation of Native American Literary Traditions, 1789–1936* (Cork, Ireland: Cork University Press, 1996).
32. *North American Review* 46 (1838): 11.
33. Apess outlines white travesties in William Apess, "Eulogy on King Philip," in O'Connell, ed., *On Our Own Ground*, 279–288, quote at 281. Future citations noted parenthetically in the text. On Native Americans helping white settlers with food, see William Cronin, *Changes in the Land* (New York: Hill & Wang, 1983).
34. See esp. O'Connell, "Introduction," *On Our Own Ground*, xxi–xxii and lxxii–lxxiii. Apess quote at "Eulogy," 310. I expand on O'Connell's analysis by showing how Apess fuses Philip with republican rhetoric and further uses performance and the figure of Washington to rewrite American history toward creating a more useable history.
35. Apess, "Eulogy on King Philip," 277.
36. See, for example, *The Life of Washington and History of the American Revolution* (New York: J. Slater, 1825). William Alfred Bryan, *George Washington in American Literature, 1775–1865* (New York: Columbia University Press, 1952), 15–16. For Washington's own shaping of his image, see Garry Wills, *Cincinnatus: George Washington and the Enlightenment* (New York: Doubleday, 1984). For the shaping of Washington's image in the early years, see Barry Schwartz, *George Washington: The Making of an American Symbol* (New York: Free Press, 1987). George B. Forgie, *Patricide in a House Divided: A Psychological Interpretation of Lincoln and His Age* (New York: W. W. Norton, 1979) shows how the Civil War generation used the Founding Fathers in their conflict. Also, see the following statistics in the text about the number of books and articles written.
37. Information about classical allusions comes from Carol Eaton Hevner, "The Paintings of Rembrandt Peale: Character and Conventions," in *In Pursuit of Fame: Rembrandt Peale, 1778–1860* (Washington, D.C.: Smithsonian Institution Press, 1992), 245–282, 277–278. Hevner tracks the mythological allusions from an early nineteenth-century text, *A History of Heathen Mythology*, trans. H. North from the French of M. L'Abbe De Tressan (London, 1806). Peale followed phrenology and believed that he had captured the essence of Washington with the shape of his head. See his tract on the Washington painting, Rembrandt Peale, *Portrait of Washington* (Philadelphia, 1824). See also William T. Oedel, "The Rewards of Virtue: Rembrandt Peale and Social Reform," in *The Peale Family: Creation of a Legacy, 1770–1870*, edited by Lillian B. Miller (New York: Abbeville Press in association with the Trust for Museum Exhibitions and the National Portrait Gallery, Smithsonian Institution, 1996), 151–167. Oedel argues that Peale created the George Washington portraits as homage to the old order, and he sought to fix Washington's characteristics in the public mind forever. For an overview of paintings of Washington, see Mark Edward

Thistlewaite, *The Image of George Washington: Studies in Mid-Nineteenth-Century American History Painting* (New York: Garland, 1979).

38. *Speeches and Other Proceedings at the Public Dinner in Honor of the Centennial Anniversary of Washington* (Washington, D.C., 1832). American Antiquarian Society Holdings (hereafter, AAS). Reports on the gathering from the *National Intelligencer* (Washington, D.C.), February 25, 1832. *Speeches* also appended a copy of Washington's farewell address.
39. Numbers detailing the writing about Washington are compiled from W. S. Baker, *Bibliotheca Washingtoniana: A Descriptive List of the Biographies and Biographical Sketches of George Washington* (Philadelphia: Robert M. Lindsay, 1889). The texts published about Washington from 1810 to 1820 number 61, from 1820 to 1830, 32, and from 1830 to 1840, 62. For a brief discussion of this revival, see Barbara J. Mitnick, *The Changing Image of George Washington* (New York: Fraunces Tavern Museum, 1989), 11. Horatio Hastings, *Life of George Washington; Embracing Anecdotes Illustrative of His Character. The Young American's Library* (Philadelphia: Lindsay and Blakiston, 1845), iii–iv.
40. Jacob Flint, *An Address on the Character and Services of George Washington, Delivered to the People of Cohassest, at Their Request, in the House of Worship of the First Church and Society, February 22, 1832* (Boston: Leonard C. Bowles, 1832), 12, AAS. Paul F. Boller, Jr., finds that Washington was a Christian, "in the most nominal sense." See Boller, *George Washington and Religion* (Dallas: Southern Methodist University Press, 1963), 90.
41. Thomas B. Fox, *Oration, Delivered at the Request of the Washington Light Infantry Company, in Newburyport, Feb. 22, 1832, at the Centennial Celebration of the Birthday of Washington* (Newburyport: T. B. and E. L. White, 1832), 14, AAS.
42. *National Gazette* (Philadelphia), February 23, 1832, 2, AAS.
43. Broadside, *Grand Civic and Military Procession in Philadelphia, February 22d, 1832, Being the 100th Anniversary of the Birth of George Washington, the Soldier and Statesman—The Brave and Good* (Philadelphia, 1832), AAS BDSDS 1832, PF Drawer 351. A writer later complained that Washington had been hijacked: "He will be engaged, like a symbolical figure of some Hindoo Deity, in doing one thing with one hand and something else with the other; he will point to heaven with one finger, and to his sword or the earth with the other; so that we wish him provided with several more of those graceful organs, to perform as many symbolical actions." "Hints to Art Union Critics," *The American Review: A Whig Journal of Politics, Literature, Art, and Science* 4 (December 1846): 608.
44. American Sunday School Union, *The Life of George Washington* (Philadelphia: American Sunday School Union, 1832), 38. The Braddock story was remarkably popular in Washington lore during the 1830s, as if the Indians—not the British—were Washington's chief foe. For other uses, see John Pitman, *Judge Pitman's Oration on the Centennial Birth-Day of Washington* (Providence: Weeden and Knowles, Printers, 1832), AAS; Hastings, *Life of George Washington*; and Solomon Lincoln, *An Oration Pronounced at Plymouth, at the Request of the Young Men of that Town on the Centennial Anniversary of the Birth Day of George Washington* (Plymouth, 1832), 8, AAS.
45. American Sunday School Union, *The Life of George Washington*, 39.
46. Charlotte M. S. Barnes, *The Forest Princess; or, Two Centuries Ago*, in *Plays, Prose, and Poetry* (Philadelphia: E. H. Butler, 1848), 262–263.

47. The centennial of Washington's birth also brought out the links between Columbia, Washington, and Indian removal. See, for example, the broadside *Songs for the Centennial Celebration of the Birth-day of Washington*, February 22, 1832, AAS, BDSDS 1832, and Charles Caldwell, MD, *A Discourse on the First Centennial Celebration of the Birth-Day of Washington, Delivered by Request, to the Citizens of Lexington on the 22nd of February 1832* (Lexington, Ky.: N. L. Finnell and J. F. Herndon, 1832), AAS.
48. Stone size at Horatio Greenough (hereafter HG) to Charles Sumner, July 12, 1840, in *Letters of Horatio Greenough, American Sculptor*, edited by Nathalia Wright (Madison: University of Wisconsin Press, 1972), 285–286, quote on 285; length of work at HG to Charles Sumner, July 12, 1840, in *Letters of Horatio Greenough*, 286. For a discussion of the classical underpinnings of the statue, see Wills, *Cincinnatus*, 67–79.
49. Wills, *Cincinnatus*, 67–79.
50. HG to Charles Sumner, July 12, 1840, in *Letters of Horatio Greenough*, 285–286, quote on 285.
51. HG to Washington Allston, December 8, 1833, Dana Papers, Massachusetts Historical Society, reprinted in *Letters of Horatio Greenough*, 170.
52. HG to Lady Rosina Wheeler Bulwer-Lytoon, before May 8, 1841, Misc. Manuscript Collection, Library of Congress, reprinted in *Letters of Horatio Greenough*, 309.
53. HG to Samuel F. B. Morse, May 24, 1834, *New York American*, August 4, 1834, reprinted in *Letters of Horatio Greenough*, 176–178, quote on 176.
54. HG to John Forsyth, November 15, 1837, RG 59, General Records of the Department of State, Accession 161, Item 135, NA, reprinted in *Letters of Horatio Greenough*, 221–222, quote on 221.
55. "Greenough the Sculptor, and His Last Production," *Bulletin of the American Art-Union* (September 1851): 971.
56. Fliegelman, *Declaring Independence*.
57. Frontispiece, William Apes, "Eulogy on King Philip, as Pronounced at the Odeon in Federal Street, Boston" (Boston: Published by the Author, 1836), AAS.

CHAPTER 3 ***Sharpening the Pen: Racial and Aesthetic Transformation***

1. Hay, 1994, 7–8. *National Advocate*, quoted in William Over, "New York's African Theatre: Shakespeare Reinterpreted," in *Shakespeare Without Class: Misappropriations of Cultural Capital*, edited by Donald Hedrick and Bryan Reynolds (New York: Palgrave, 2000), 67.
2. "African Amusements," *National Advocate*, September 25, 1821, 2. "Blacks," *National Advocate*, September 26, 1821.
3. *National Advocate*, August 3, 1821, 2, quoted in Over, "New York's African Theatre," 71.
4. *National Advocate*, August 3, 1821, 2, quoted in Over, "New York's African Theatre," 75.
5. *New York Evening Post*, January 10, 1822, 2, quoted in Over, "New York's African Theatre," 70. *National Advocate*, September 21, 1821.
6. Lawrence W. Levine, *Highbrow/Lowbrow* (Cambridge: Harvard University Press, 1988), 230.

7. *The Herald of Freedom*, March 25, 1837, Black Abolitionist Papers, Reel 22, Frame 26.
8. Gordon S. Wood, *The Radicalism of the American Revolution* (New York: Vintage Books, 1991); Charles Sellers, *The Market Revolution: Jacksonian America, 1815–1846* (New York: Oxford University Press, 1991); Karen Halttunen, *Confidence Men and Painted Women: A Study of Middle Class Culture, 1830–1870* (New Haven: Yale University Press, 1982); Kenneth Cmiel, *Democratic Eloquence* (New York: William Morrow & Co., 1990), 55–93.
9. This discussion of virtue and Republicanism draws heavily on Bernard Bailyn, *The Ideological Origins of the American Revolution* (Cambridge: Harvard University Press, 1967); Gordon S. Wood, *The Creation of the American Republic, 1776–1787* (New York: W. W. Norton, 1972); Gordon S. Wood, *The Radicalism of the American Revolution* (New York: Vintage Books, 1991); and Drew R. McCoy, *The Elusive Republic: Political Economy in Jeffersonian America* (Chapel Hill: University of North Carolina Press, 1980). The terms "Republican" and "virtue" can be fraught with multiple meanings in historical study, as Daniel T. Rodgers shows in "Republicanism: The Career of a Concept," *Journal of American History* 79:1 (June 1992): 11–38. I use the terms here in the tradition of Wood in *Creation* and *Radicalism*, and Stanley Elkins and Eric McKitrick, *The Age of Federalism* (New York: Oxford University Press, 1993); these concepts do not organize all of revolutionary life, but they explain important social reforms that the Founding Fathers believed they accomplished by writing the Constitution.
10. The best treatment bringing Franklin's ideas forward into self-help thinking is in John Cawelti, *Apostles of the Self-Made Man* (Chicago: University of Chicago Press, 1965). On Franklin's notion of virtue, see Donald Meyer, *The Democratic Enlightenment* (New York: Capricorn Books, 1976), 61–81, and Joseph Fichtelberg, *The Complex Image: Faith and Method in American Autobiography* (Philadelphia: University of Pennsylvania Press, 1989), 83–115.
11. Washington to James Warren, October 7, 1785, in *Writings of Washington*, edited by Fitzpatrick, 28:291. Quoted in Wood, *Radicalism*, 252–253. Aiding commerce in replacing virtue, argues Ann Fairfax Wirthington, was a new definition of sovereignty, which distributed power among countervailing groups in society. This distinction has little bearing on our argument here because with either method, African Americans wind up on the margin. See Wirthington, *Toward a More Perfect Union: Virtue and the Formation of American Republics* (New York: Oxford University Press, 1991).
12. Elkins and McKitrick, *The Age of Federalism*, 739–740; quote on 739.
13. R. W. Pomeroy (supposed author), *The Young Merchant* (Philadelphia: Published by R.W. Pomeroy, No. 3, Minor Street, 1839), 279. For a strong examination of self-help, see Leonard N. Neufeldt, *The Economist: Henry Thoreau and Enterprise* (New York: Oxford University Press, 1989). Neufeldt finds this self-help exclusively conservative when he says the books "invoke conservative republican values and lament the degeneracy of the times" (144). Yet chapters 1 and 2 show that these "conservative republican values" can play another role, too.
14. Roediger, *The Wages of Whiteness* (New York: Verso, 1991).
15. See Eric Foner, *Reconstruction: America's Unfinished Business, 1863–1877* (New York: Harper & Row, 1988), 564–601. For a terrific capitulation and analysis of

the change in rights talk in the United States, see William E. Forbath, "Caste, Class, and Equal Citizenship," *Michigan Law Review* 98:1 (October 1999): 1–92. I benefited immensely from conversations with Forbath on this point.

16. Levine, *Highbrow/Lowbrow*, 202, 211. Levine does not use the term "cultural capital" for discussion of the "ability" to understand high art, but the term is consistent with his discussion of the phenomenon. Roland Marchand raises some of these questions in a review of Levine's *Highbrow/Lowbrow* in *Journal of American History* 76:2 (September 1989): 565–566.
17. This cultural capital is not a story about the "literary" as Richard Brodhead would define it. Broadhead argues that racial aliens might aspire to the literary, but they find a market only by resorting to a form of regionalism—deploying dialect and other markers of the "primitive." (See Brodhead, ed., *Journals of Charles W. Chesnutt* (Durham, N.C.: Duke University Press, 1993), 131–137. Regionalism created a velvet coffin that Charles Chesnutt, among others, fell into. (See Brodhead's discussion of Chesnutt in chapter 6, 182–210.) However, black writers were as likely to write for a white audience as a black audience, more likely to place their stories in a newspaper than a national magazine, and often only found the racial press willing to reprint their pieces. These writers had to draw on an authority reliable for myriad, not just the literary, audiences. And as we shall see, Edith Eaton's portrait of Chinese Americans confuses any sense of regionalism by placing her story where we would least expect and by showing the broad reach of the Chinese in America. Eaton identifies herself as "Eurasian," and held writing jobs in places as diverse as Seattle and Kingston, Jamaica.

    Michael Warner's *The Letters of the Republic* demonstrates that print does its work in multiple public spheres. Whites used print to define themselves as white, and they imagined their audiences as white, too. Warner, *Letters of the Republic: Publications and the Public Sphere in Eighteenth-Century America* (Cambridge: Harvard University Press, 1990), 11–13. But racial aliens, after all, had no monolithic public to address. Anna Julia Cooper sought to address African Americans as well as those who considered themselves white Americans, and her work sought a different kind of "literary" sphere than a "high literary" writer like Henry James sought with *The Turn of the Screw*. Cooper never published in *The Atlantic*, for example, and apparently never aimed to do so. Nevertheless, for writers of color to demonstrate their rights to address a diverse audience, from those who read *The Atlantic* to readers of less high-brow publications, they had to demonstrate the necessary cultural capital.
18. Details for Bascom's life come from his posthumously published autobiography, John Bascom, *Things Learned by Living* (New York: G. P. Putnam's Sons, 1913). University of Wisconsin history comes from Merle Curti and Vernon Carstensen, *The University of Wisconsin: A History, 1848–1925* (1949; rpt. Madison: University of Wisconsin Press, 1974), esp. vol. 1, chaps. 10 and 11.
19. John Bascom, *Philosophy of Rhetoric* (1866; rpt. New York: Woolworth, Ainsworth & Co., 1872), 12.
20. John Bascom, *Aesthetics; or, The Science of Beauty* (1862; rev. ed. New York: G. P. Putnam's Sons, 1886), 5–6.
21. Bascom, *Aesthetics*, 3; Bascom, *Rhetoric*, 22; Bascom, *Things Learned by Living*, xi. See also Bascom, *Rhetoric*, 10.

22. Charles R. Van Hise, *Memorial Service in Honor of John Bascom* (Madison, 1911), 9, quoted in Curti and Carstensen, *The University of Wisconsin,* 280–281.
23. John Bascom, *The Growth of Nationality in the United States: A Social Study* (New York: G. P. Putnam's Sons, 1899), 1.
24. Bascom, *Aesthetics*, 101.
25. Bascom, *Philosophy of English Literature*, (1874; rpt. New York: G. P. Putnam's Sons, 1895), 7.
26. Bascom, *The Growth of Nationality*, 92.
27. Bascom, *Philosophy of Literature*, iv, 1.
28. Bascom, *Aesthetics*, vol. 3. I note future citations parenthetically in the text.
29. Monroe C. Beardsley, *Aesthetics from Classical Greece to the Present* (New York: Macmillan, 1966). Hugh Blair, "Lecture VI, The Rise and Progress of Language," in *Lectures on Rhetoric and Belles Lettres* (1833; rpt. Philadelphia: Hayes & Zell, 1856), 58–68. William Charvat, *The Origins of American Critical Thought, 1810–1835* (Philadelphia: University of Pennsylvania Press, 1936), 44–45.
30. G. P. Quackenbos, *Advanced Course of Composition and Rhetoric: A Series of Practical Lessons on the Origin, History, and Peculiarities of the English Language* (New York: American Book, 1885), 167. Nan Johnson, *Nineteenth-Century Rhetoric in North America* (Carbondale: Southern Illinois University Press, 1991), gives a brief history of the use of "moral" terms in aesthetics and rhetoric.
31. "Aesthetics; or The Science of Beauty," *New Englander and Yale Review* 22, no. 83 (April 1863): 361.
32. "Literary," *Manufacturer and Builder* 4, no. 1 (Jan. 1872): 17. I found no evidence that the magazine later actually reprinted parts of Bascom's treatise.
33. Bascom, *Things Learned by Living*, 158.
34. Bascom, *Philosophy of English Literature*, 7.
35. Terry Eagleton, *The Ideology of the Aesthetic* (Oxford: Blackwell, 1990), 77. See also Eagleton's compact, "The Ideology of the Aesthetic," in *The Rhetoric of Interpretation and the Interpretation of Rhetoric*, edited by Paul Hernadi (Durham, N.C.: Duke University Press, 1989), 75–86, 99.
36. Eagleton also shows how this internalization gives the bourgeoisie, or some of the bourgeoisie, some power to resist. But that comes later in the story.
37. "Editor's Easy Chair," *Harper's New Monthly Magazine* 34 (January 1867): 261–268; quote at 261.
38. T. W. Higginson, "A Plea for Culture," *The Atlantic Monthly* 19:111 (January 1867): 30–31. See Lawrence Levine's discussion of Higginson in *Highbrow/Lowbrow*, 213–214.
39. Higginson, "A Plea for Culture," 30, 33; "The Contributors' Club," *The Atlantic Monthly*, November 1877, 625. Lawrence Levine gives a wonderful taxonomy of the bifurcation of culture in *Highbrow/Lowbrow*.
40. Hugh Blair, *Lectures on Rhetoric and Belles Lettres* (1783; rpt. London: Charles Daly, 1839); David J. Hill, *The Elements of Rhetoric and Composition* (New York: Sheldon and Co., 1878); John S. Hart, *A Manual of Composition and Rhetoric* (Philadelphia: Eldredge and Brother, 1870). Hill says: "It is as reasonable to discuss the nature of *truth* or of *right* in a text-book on Rhetoric, as to admit the discussion of Taste, Beauty and Sublimity." Hill, *The Science of Rhetoric, An Introduction to the Law of Effective Discourse* (New York: Sheldon and Company, 1877), 5 (emphasis

in original). For a brief discussion of this subject, see Albert R. Kitzhaber, *Rhetoric in American Colleges, 1850–1900* (Dallas: Southern Methodist University Press, 1990), 87–92.

41. Bascom, *Rhetoric*, 135.
42. Ibid., 10–13. Future references appear parenthetically in the text.
43. For a discussion of blacks' role in the postreconstruction economic system in the South, see Gerald David Jaynes, *Branches without Roots: Genesis of Black Working Class in the American South, 1862–1882* (New York: Oxford University Press, 1986).
44. George M. Frederickson, *Black Image in the White Mind: The Debate on Afro-American Character and Destiny, 1817–1914* (Hanover, N.H.: Wesleyan University Press, 1971), 203.
45. "Message of James K. Vardaman, Governor of Mississippi, to the House and Senate of Mississippi, Thursday, January 9, 1909," *Journal of the House* (Nashville: Brandon Printing Co., 1910), quoted in Horace Mann Bond, *The Education of the Negro in the American Social Order* (1934; rpt. New York: Octagon Books, 1966), 101–103.
46. Blair, *Lectures on Rhetoric*, 22; Quackenbos, *Advanced Course in Rhetoric*, 176–177.
47. Quackenbos, *Advanced Course in Rhetoric*, 216.
48. William Schuyler, "The Orator's Training in America," in *The World's Best Orations: From the Earliest Period to the Present Time*, official ed., edited by David J. Brewer (St. Louis: Ferd. P. Kaiser, 1899), 9:3267.
49. "A Lenten Bit," *The Atlantic Monthly,* April 1887, 568; "Music," *The Atlantic Monthly*, January 1875, 122; EllisGray, "The Mission of Music," *Harper's New Monthly Magazine*, October 1875, 739; for an overview of racial ideology and music, see Joseph A. Mussulman, *Music in the Cultured Generation: A Social History of Music in America, 1870–1900* (Evanston, Ill.: Northwestern University Press, 1971), esp. 106–107.
50. Quoted in Levine, *Highbrow/Lowbrow*, 219. *New York Herald* and *Holden's Magazine* quoted in Gladys Denny Shultz, *Jenny Lind: The Swedish Nightingale* (New York: J. B. Lippincott, 1962), 200–201. Carla L. Peterson, *Doers of the Word*, 122–124.
51. "Editor's Table," *Harper's New Monthly Magazine*, September 1860, 553.
52. Ibid., 547.
53. T. W. Higginson, "Literature as Art," *The Atlantic Monthly*, December 1867, 754.
54. Levine, *Highbrow/Lowbrow*, 221.
55. Frederick Douglass, "These Questions Cannot Be Answered by the White Race: An Address Delivered in New York, New York on 11 May 1855," *New York Evening Express*, May 12, 1855, and *New York Herald*, May 12, 1855. Reprinted in *Frederick Douglass Papers: Speeches, Debates, Interviews*, edited by John Blassingame (New Haven: Yale University Press, 1979), 3:85–90.
56. William Rounseville Alger, *Life of Edwin Forrest, The American Tragedian*, 2 vols. (Philadelphia: J. B. Lippincott, 1877), 1:127. For more information on racial theory about African Americans, see Winthrop D. Jordan, *White Over Black: American Attitudes Toward the Negro, 1550–1812* (New York: Penguin Books, 1969), and George Frederickson, *The Black Image in the White Mind.* For more about Native Ameri-

cans, see Robert F. Berkhofer, Jr., *The White Man's Indian: Images of the American Indian from Columbus to the Present* (New York: Vintage Books, 1979), and Rosemarie K. Bank, "Staging The 'Native': Making History in American Theatre Culture, 1828–1838 (Disciplinary Disruptions)," *Theatre Journal* 45:4 (December 1993): 461–486; for more about Chinese Americans, see Anthony W. Lee, *Picturing Chinatown: Art and Orientalism in San Francisco* (Berkeley: University of California Press, 2001), and Robert G. Lee, *Orientals: Asian Americans in Popular Culture* (Philadelphia: Temple University Press, 1999).

57. Higginson, "Literature as Art," 745.
58. W.E.B. Du Bois, *The Souls of Black Folk* (1903); Norton critical edition, edited by Henry Louis Gates, Jr., and Terri Hume Oliver (New York: W. W. Norton, 1999), 74.

CHAPTER 4 *Anna Julia Cooper and the Black Orator*

1. See Anne DuCille, *The Coupling Convention: Sex, Text, and Tradition in Black Women's Fiction* (New York: Oxford University Press, 1993); Hazel V. Carby, *Reconstructing Womanhood: The Emergence of the Afro-American Woman Novelist* (New York: Oxford University Press, 1987), 96–97; and Mary Helen Washington, "Introduction," in Anna Julia Cooper, *A Voice from the South* (Xenia, Ohio: Aldine Press, 1892; reprinted with introduction by Mary Helen Washington, New York: Oxford University Press, 1988), xxvii–liv. Charles Lemert's essay, "Anna Julia Cooper: The Colored Woman's Office" reviews many opposing views on Cooper, and it calls her at once an elitist and someone who worked for the neglected; see 26–34. This essay introduces some of Cooper's archival material and collected writing in *The Voice of Anna Julia Cooper*, edited by Charles Lemert and Esme Bhan (New York: Rowman & Littlefield, 1998), 1–43.
2. Anna Julia Cooper, "The Intellectual Progress of the Colored Women in the United States since the Emancipation Proclamation: A Response to Fannie Barrier Williams" (1893); reprinted in *The Voice of Anna Julia Cooper*, 204. Ida B. Wells-Barnett, *Crusade for Justice: The Autobiography of Ida B. Wells*, edited by Alfreda M. Duster (Chicago: University of Chicago Press, 1970), 117. For description of the Fair scene, see Jeanne Madeline Weimann, *The Fair Women* (Chicago: Academy Chicago, 1981), 123.
3. Karen A. Johnson, *Uplifting the Women and the Race: The Educational Philosophies and Social Activism of Anna Julia Cooper and Nannie Helen Burroughs* (New York: Garland Publishing, 2000), 34.
4. The Freedmen's Bureau contributed $6,243, about 20 percent of the founding budget, for Saint Augustine. See document from Moorland-Spingarn Research Center, Howard University, reproduced in Louise Daniel Hutchinson, *Anna Julia Cooper: A Voice from the South* (Washington, D.C.: Smithsonian Institution Press, 1981), 20. For the role of Freedmen's Bureaus, see Foner, *Reconstruction*, and W.E.B. Du Bois, *Black Reconstruction* (1935; reprinted, New York: Russell & Russell, 1956), and *Souls of Black Folk*, chapter 2, his essay on the bureaus.
5. H. C. Vogell, Eighth Semi-Annual Report of Schools, 1868, reproduced in Hutchinson, *Anna Julia Cooper*, 25.
6. Handwritten letter of John E. C. Smedes, reproduced in Hutchinson, *Anna Julia Cooper*, 35.

7. Course listing, Anna Julia Cooper file, Oberlin College Archives, 392.
8. Hutchinson, *Anna Julia Cooper*, 148. Cooper shifted her duties through her career at the high school, but she never moved far from teaching Latin.
9. Oberlin College Catalogue, 1883–1884, 60.
10. Ibid., 65, lists "Hepburn's Manual" as the text for the second term, second semester rhetoric course. I believe this refers to A. D. Hepburn, *Manual of English Rhetoric* (Cincinnati: Wilson, Kinkle, 1875), quote on 255.
11. Nan Johnson, *Nineteenth-Century Rhetoric in North America* (Carbondale: Southern Illinois University Press, 1991), 246. Johnson also drew my attention to Bascom's *Philosophy* as a leading rhetoric text of the era. Kenneth Cmiel in *Democratic Eloquence: The Fight over Popular Speech in Nineteenth-Century America* (New York: William Morrow, 1990) wonderfully illustrates the contested terrain of language and power in the nineteenth century. Yet while he notes that women were excluded from public speaking, he does not analyze how the very shaping of arguments and teaching of rhetoric sought to exclude women and African Americans; see 15, 44, and 130. For a discussion of manliness and the study and teaching of rhetoric, see Miriam Brody, *Manly Writing: Gender, Rhetoric, and the Rise of Composition* (Carbondale: Southern Illinois University Press, 1993). Brody discusses Bascom on 135 to 140.
12. John Bascom, *Philosophy of Rhetoric* (New York: Woolworth, Ainsworth, 1872), 135.
13. For the scientific racism of the day, see George Frederickson, *The Black Image in the White Mind* (Hanover, N.H.: Wesleyan University Press, 1971). For expectations of how blacks should write in the 1890s, see Richard H. Brodhead, "Introduction," *The Journals of Charles W. Chesnutt*, edited by Richard H. Brodhead (Durham, N.C.: Duke University Press, 1993); Edward A. Pollard, "The Romance of the Negro," *The Galaxy* 12:4 (October 1871): 470–478; quotes at 476, 477, and 478.
14. Professor Schele de Vere, "A Rare Work," *Appletons' Journal: A Magazine of General Literature* 4:69 (July 23, 1870): 110–112; quote at 109–110. Hallie Q. Brown, ed., *Homespun Heroines and Other Women of Distinction* (Xenia, Ohio: Aldine Publishing Company, 1926), 122.
15. Booker T. Washington, *Up From Slavery* (1901; reprinted, *The Booker T. Washington Papers*, Vol. 1: *The Autobiographical Writings,* edited by Louis R. Harlan (Champagne: University of Illinois Press, 1972), 260.
16. *Brooklyn Eagle*, October 1, 1896, 4, quoted in *The Booker T. Washington Papers,* Vol. 4: *1895–1898*, edited by Louis R. Harlan (Champagne: University of Illinois Press, 1975), 222–223, n1.
17. Booker T. Washington, "Democracy and Education: A Speech at the Institute of Arts and Sciences," September 30, 1896, Brooklyn, N.Y.; rpt. *The Booker T. Washington Papers,* Vol. 4: *1895–1898*, 211–223; quote at 215.
18. Washington, "Democracy and Education," 215.
19. Cooper, for her part, did not deny that an industrial education was right for some. "I believe in industrial education with all my heart," said the woman who numbered skilled craftsmen as part of her family. "We can't all be professional people." But at the same time, she fiercely defended blacks' right to perform mental work. See her comments, in "Proceedings of the Second Hampton Negro Conference," May 25, 1894; reprinted, *Booker T. Washington Papers,* Vol. 3: *1889–1895*, 427–447, quote at 444.
20. Mrs. N. F. Mosell, *The Work of Afro-American Women*, 2d ed. (Philadelphia: Geo. S. Ferguson Co., 1908), 136–137.

21. Anna J. Cooper, "The Third Step (Autobiographical)," mimeograph, Anna J. Cooper Papers, Moorland Spingarn Collection, Howard University, 3.
22. Cooper text quoted in Hutchinson, *Anna Julia Cooper*, 61.
23. Cooper, "What Are We Worth," in *A Voice*, 228–285, quote on 260.
24. Anna J. Cooper to George M. Jones, August 21, 1926. Oberlin College Archives. This letter is reprinted as part of a web project by Oberlin's Katherine Shilton, "'This Scholarly and Colored Alumna': Anna Julia Cooper's Troubled Relationship with Oberlin College," http://www.oberlin.edu/external/EOG/History322/AnnaJuliaCooper/AnnaJuliaCooper.htm (accessed July 14, 2003).
25. Cooper in "Class Letters '84," Oberlin College, 1909, reproduced in Hutchinson, *Anna Julia Cooper*, 83. At least part of the reason for Cooper's dismissal comes from her opposition to the forces of Booker T. Washington. Cooper's experience with education and her goals as an educator almost foreordained her opposition to the Washington forces. Hutchinson and Lemert, "Introduction," discuss the circumstances of her firing.
26. Claudia Tate, *Domestic Allegories of Political Desire: The Black Heroine's Text at the Turn of the Century* (New York: Oxford University Press, 1992), 25.
27. Karlyn Kohrs Campbell, *Man Can Not Speak for Her,* Vol. 1: *A Critical Study of Early Feminist Rhetoric*, Contributions in Women's Studies, No. 101 (New York: Greenwood Press, 1989), 151.
28. Mary Church Terrell, *A Colored Woman in a White World* (Washington D.C.: Ransdell, 1940), 158. Quoted in Campbell, Vol. 1: *Critical Study*, 151.
29. Anna Julia Cooper to Alfred V. Churchill, January 21, 1941, Oberlin Archives; http://www.oberlin.edu/external/EOG/History322/AnnaJuliaCooper/AnnaJuliaCooper.htm.
30. Cooper may exaggerate somewhat. Condit and Lucaites argue that National Negro Conventions beginning in 1830 started a debate about equality that sometimes sought to extend the definition of freedom beyond gender. See Celeste Michelle Condit and John Louis Lucaites, *Crafting Equality: America's Anglo-African Word* (Chicago: University of Chicago Press, 1993), 77–80. In short, other black women had spoken. But this doesn't cancel Cooper's general point that black women rarely were included in public debate.
31. Cooper, "Womanhood: A Vital Element," *A Voice*, 44.
32. These reviews from the New York *Independent*, Philadelphia *Public Ledger,* Chicago *Inter-Ocean,* Boston *Transcript, Public Opinion,* Detroit *Plaindealer*, and Kingsley (Iowa) *Times*, and from Albion Winegar Tourgee are compiled in M. A. Majors, *Noted Negro Women: Their Triumphs and Activities* (Chicago: Donohue & Henneberry, 1893), 284–287.
33. Mrs. N. F. Mosell, *The Work of Afro-American Women*, 61. Public Education Association and *Asbury Journal* quotes from a January 1, 1909, handbill for a Cooper speech; reprinted in Hutchinson, *Anna J. Cooper*, 82. Other quotes from reviews in Majors, *Noted Negro Women*, 284–287.
34. Schele de Vere, *A Rare Work*, 110.
35. Edward A. Pollard, "The Romance of the Negro," 477.
36. See Richard A. Lanham's discussion of "Dissoi logoi," 57–59, and of "Arrangement: The Parts of an Oration," 171–174, in *A Handlist of Rhetorical Terms*, 2d ed. (Berkeley: University of California Press, 1991).
37. Bascom, *Philosophy of Rhetoric*, 66. It is our good fortune that this writer of one

of the nineteenth century's most popular writing texts hated rhetoric. Bascom's *Philosophy* dwells as much on what it *means* to speak as how one ought to speak. See his posthumously published autobiography, *Things Learned by Living* (New York: G. P. Putnam's Sons, 1913). Bascom makes concrete the material construct that language becomes to Mikhail Bakhtin. Language, to Bakhtin, is a material construct that reflects the ideology of the period in which it is used. It registers a war of ideologies taking place in society and thus becomes a fine barometer for scholars. See V. N. Volosinov (Mikhail Bakhtin), *Marxism and the Philosophy of Language*, translated by Ladislav Matejka and I. R. Titunik (New York: Seminar Press, 1973), 11.

38. Campbell, Vol. 1: *Critical Study*, 2–15, quote on 14.
39. Mary Church Terrell, "What It Means to Be Colored in the Capital of the United States" (1906); rpt. in *Man Can Not Speak for Her,* Vol. 2: *Key Texts of the Early Feminists*, compiled by Karlyn Kohrs Campbell, Contributions in Women's Studies, No. 102 (New York: Greenwood Press, 1989), 422.
40. Campbell, *Vol. 2: Key Texts*, 432.
41. Campbell, *Vol. 1: Critical Study*, 129.
42. Frances E. Willard, "A White Life for Two" (1890); rpt. in Campbell, Vol. 2: *Key Texts*, 325.
43. Cooper's use of the icons of high culture reassured her audience even as it sought to subvert it. Cmiel, in *Democratic Eloquence*, shows that at this time, insecure members of the elite still had a white-knuckled grasp on the idea of refinement and the right to lead and they still believed that they must have these refined discriminations to build a civilized order; see 203–204.
44. Tate, *Domestic Allegories*, 138. Ann du Cille makes a similar point in *The Coupling Convention,* 50. Nina Baym also has argued that critics must begin to see the domestic story as part of an allegory of black people taking a role on the national stage. See Nina Baym, "A Refusal to Be Other," *American Quarterly* 46:3 (September 1994): 434–440, esp. 439.
45. Willard, "A White Life," 325.
46. Carby, *Reconstructing Womanhood*, 111–115.
47. Ida B. Wells, *A Red Record* (Chicago: Donohue & Henneberry, 1894); reprinted in Ida B. Wells-Barnett, *On Lynchings: Southern Horrors, A Red Record, Mob Rule in New Orleans* (Salem, N.H.: Ayer, 1991), 15.
48. This is not to say that neither Wells nor Terrell enjoyed success. Both did succeed with segments of the population. But for a stunning example of a writer missing the point of Wells's cold, hard facts, see Thomas Nelson Page, "The Lynching of Negroes—Its Cause and Its Prevention," *North American Review* 178 (January 1904): 33–48. Page uses the same figures as Wells does in *The Red Record*, and he, incredibly, still draws the conclusion that lynchings result from black men raping white women. After a southern mob lynched Sam Hose, W.E.B. Du Bois decided that hard facts would not sway the country. He then turned his efforts from data-intensive sociology to persuasive journalism. See W.E.B. Du Bois, *Dusk of Dawn: An Essay toward an Autobiography of a Race Concept* (1940); rpt. in *Writings* (New York: Library of America, 1986), 602–603.
49. Cooper used nearly the same phrasing of this passage to the same effect in Cooper, "The Intellectual Progress of the Colored Women," in Cooper, *The Voice of Anna Julia Cooper*, 205. Compare to Frederick Douglass's use of the Declaration. See

Shelley Fisher Fishkin and Carla Peterson, "We Hold These Truths," in *Frederick Douglass*, edited by Eric Sundquist (Cambridge: Cambridge University Press, 1990).

50. Cooper's facility with definitions in this sentence mimics what she does in the essay as a whole. She draws on her audience's universal disdain for bullies, shows that bullies treat African American women badly, and reminds readers that women are responsible for taming these bullies. By grouping bullies in the same group with racism, Cooper makes both the target for women's civilizing influence. See esp. 85–90.
51. *The New York World*, quoted in Booker T. Washington, *The Story of My Life and Work* (Atlanta, Ga.: J. L. Nichols, 1901), 147–148.
52. "About The World," *Scribner's Magazine,* 19:1 (January 1896): 129–134, quote on 132.
53. Booker T. Washington, *The Story of My Life and Work*, 149–151. For Washington and the Compromise, see David Levering Lewis's balanced treatment of the issue in *W.E.B. Du Bois: Biography of a Race, 1868–1919* (New York: Henry Holt, 1993).
54. Washington, *Up from Slavery*, 343–344; Washington, *The Story of My Life and Work*, 122.
55. Henry R. Gledhill, "Harvard Commencement Essays, I: The Harvard Senior," *The New England Magazine* 10:6 (August 1891): 734–736, quote at 734.
56. Booker T. Washington, *My Larger Education* (New York: Doubleday, Page, 1911), 142–143.
57. Compare with Willard, "A White Life," 334–335.
58. Cooper makes this argument explicitly in her prospectus for the Women's Page of *The Southland*. As editor she wrote a column to readers, "All will admit that the modern idea of the 'sphere,' by broadening, widening, and deepening the range of women's activities, has rendered very complex the definition of a Woman's Department." Mrs. A. J. Cooper, "Prospectus to Our Woman's Department," *The Southland* 1:3 (May 1890): 159–162, quote at 159.
59. Tate, *Domestic Allegories*, 147.
60. Anna J. Cooper, "Equality of Races and the Democratic Movement: Question Proposed by Monsieur C. Bouglé at Soutenance of Thesis," The Sorbonne University of Paris, March 23, 1925; rpt. in Cooper, *The Third Step* mimeograph.

CHAPTER 5 *Edith Eaton Plays the Chinese Water Lily*

1. Sui Sin Far, "Leaves from the Mental Portfolio of an Eurasian," *The Independent*, January 21, 1909; rpt. in *Mrs. Spring Fragrance and Other Writings*, edited by Amy Ling and Annette White-Parks (Urbana: University of Illinois Press, 1995), 218–230, quotes at 218–219. I make future citations to this article parenthetically in the text. Details of Sui's life come from this article and from "Sui Sin Far, the Half Chinese Writer, Tells of Her Career," *Boston Globe*, May 5, 1912; rpt. in Sui Sin Far, *Mrs. Spring Fragrance*, 288–296. Annette White-Parks's literary biography of Sui, *Sui Sin Far/Edith Maude Eaton: A Literary Biography* (Urbana: University of Illinois Press, 1995) is the best secondary source on Sui's life. White-Parks and Amy Ling have done the best detective work on Eaton. See also Amy Ling, "Edith Eaton: Pioneer Chinamerican Writer and Feminist," *American Literary Realism* 16 (1983): 287–298, and Ling, "Writers with a Cause: Sui Sin Far and Han Suyin," *Women's*

Studies International Forum 9:4 (1986): 411–419. I use Amy Ling's translation of the name "Sui Sin Far" in *Between Worlds: Women Writers of Chinese Ancestry* (New York: Pergamon Press, 1990), 41.

2. Arnold Genthe, *Pictures of Old Chinatown, with text by Will Irwin* (New York: Moffat, Yard and Company, 1908), 37.
3. Arnold Genthe, *As I Remember* (New York: Reynal & Hitchcock, 1936), 32, and Genthe, *Old Chinatown with text by Will Irwin* (New York: Mitchell Kennerley, 1912), following 11. Genthe and Irwin's first edition of *Pictures of Old Chinatown with text by Will Irwin* (New York: Moffat, Yard and Company, 1908), carries only one-half the photos of the second. Genthe's photo can be seen in John Kuo Wei Tchen, *Genthe's Photographs of San Francisco's Chinatown* (New York: Dover, 1984), 53. Tchen's book unfortunately does not also carry Will Irwin's original text.
4. Whites valued "Japanese" over the "Chinese" in this period, and the merchants picked up on consumer tastes. But many customers could not tell the difference. Chinese proprietor Andrew Kan, did not bother to change the merchandise when he set up a "Japanese Bazaar" in 1880. "At that time, everybody cares buy Japanese goods—Chinese goods not amount to much. You have to sell as Japanese goods instead of Chinese goods," he said. *Life History and Social Document of Andrew Kan*, Seattle, Washington, August 22, 1924, Survey of Race Relations Collection, Hoover Institution of War, Revolution, and Peace Archives, Stanford University, Box 27, Folder 178.
5. As I discuss below, Genthe reports that his Baedeker warned him not to go to Chinatown without a guide. A short note in one railroad-sponsored guide serves as an example of the tone that the tour guides struck: "A trip to Chinatown is an experience which no traveler should miss, and which on no account should he repeat." John Sebastian, *The Golden State, California: A Gratuitous Guide* (Chicago: Passenger Dept. Rock Island System, 1903), 61.
6. Sui Sin Far, "The Chinese in America, Part IV," *The Westerner* (August 1909); reprinted in *Mrs. Spring Fragrance*, 257. Sui's stories ran in publications that included the *Boston Globe*, the *Chautauquan*, *The Westerner* (devoted to development of the West), *Good Housekeeping*, and *The Independent*.
7. Amy Ling looks at Eaton's autobiography and fiction to argue that she sought to bridge "two worlds"—Asian and Caucasian. See Ling, *Between Worlds*. Annette White-Parks argues that Eaton made whites the "other" in her writing. See "A Reversal of American Concepts of 'Other-ness' in the Fiction of Sui Sin Far," *MELUS* 20:1 (Spring 1995): 17–36. Lisa Lowe takes on the all-too-current notion that Asian Americans are a homogeneous lot in "Heterogeneity, Hybridity, Multiplicity: Marking Asian American Differences," *Diaspora* 1:1 (Spring 1990): 24–44.

    I use "documentary" here to refer to the representational quality Genthe and his reviewers believed that the photos captured. As explained below, Genthe, as an artist, can be considered a pictorialist. For a discussion of how Genthe fits into the photography tradition, see Anthony W. Lee, *Picturing Chinatown: Art and Orientalism in San Francisco* (Berkeley: University of California Press, 2001), esp. 153–177.

    We can think of Eaton as effecting a "reverse passing" here. Eaton, as Sui, moved from the comfort of a white bourgeois culture to the identity of one of the most maligned groups in the country at the time. This makes her particularly useful for our analysis, as critic Elaine Ginsberg notes, "passing has the potential to create a space for creative self-determination." For a discussion of this, see Elaine K. Ginsberg, "Introduction," in *Passing and the Fictions of Identity* (Durham, N.C.: Duke University Press, 1996), 4.

8. For biographical information about Eaton, see Amy Ling, *Between Worlds*, Annette White-Parks, *Sui Sin Far/Edith Maude Eaton*, Dominika Ferens, *Edith and Winnifred Eaton: Chinatown Missions and Japanese Romances* (Urbana: University of Illinois Press, 2002). Diana Birchall's biography of Edith's sister (and Birchall's grandmother), Winifred, also contains helpful background about the family. See Birchall, *Onoto Watanna: The Story of Winnifred Eaton* (Urbana: University of Illinois Press, 2001).
9. White-Parks, *Edith Maude Eaton/Sui Sin Far*, 30.
10. For more information on Watanna, see Ferens, *Edith and Winnifred Eaton*, and especially Birchall's *Onoto Watanna*. See also Amy Ling, "Revelation and Mask: Autobiographies of the Eaton Sisters," *Auto/Biography Studies* 3:2 (1987): 46. Winifred went on to enormous success in writing best-selling novels and Hollywood screenplays. But this "passing" as Japanese exacted a cost. See Amy Ling. "Winifred Eaton: Ethnic Chameleon and Popular Success," *MELUS* 11:3 (Fall 1984): 5–15.
11. Sui Sin Far, "Leaves from the Mental Portfolio of an Eurasian," *The Independent*, January 21, 1909; reprinted in *Mrs. Spring Fragrance*, 218–230.
12. Charlotte Perkins Gilman, *The Charlotte Perkins Gilman Reader: The Yellow Wallpaper, and Other Fiction*, edited and introduced by Ann J. Lane (New York: Pantheon Books, 1980). S. Weir Mitchell, *Doctor and Patient*, 142–143. Tom Lutz notes that other women of the period, including the anarchist Emma Goldman, appropriated neurasthenia to describe their own ailments. See Lutz, *American Nervousness, 1903: An Anecdotal History* (Ithaca, N.Y.: Cornell University Press, 1991), 34–35. Indeed, Lutz argues that when the middle class began to invoke neurasthenia, too, the elite became less enamored with it as a metaphor for their ailments. Of course, men could also have neurasthenia, but they were only those men who worked with their minds, not their hands. See Lutz, *American Nervousness*, 6.
13. George M. Beard, *American Nervousness: Its Causes and Consequences* (New York: G. P. Putnam's Sons, 1881), vii–viii.
14. Ibid. Beard believed that "nervousness" was particularly frequent in the "Northern and Eastern portions of the United States" because "modern civilization" was more advanced in these regions (vi).
15. Baer is quoted in Anthracite Coal Commission, *Report to the President on the Anthracite Coal Strike of May-October, 1902* (Washington, D.C., 1903), 35, quoted in Lutz, *American Nervousness*, 7. For Beard's racial exclusions, see *American Nervousness*, xv–xvi. Gale Bederman in *Manliness and Civilization: A Cultural History of Gender and Race in the United States, 1880–1917* (Chicago: University of Chicago Press, 1995) argues that Gilman turned neurasthenia into a racial disease, too. Neurasthenia showed an imbalance between men and women. As differences between the sexes expand, women become oversexed, and the man a primitive rapist. Only by keeping differences between the sexes to a minimum, she argued, could the white race keep their minds fit for advancing the race. See 124–169, esp. 135–142.
16. See Sui's discussion of her health in "Leaves," 221.
17. The mainstream did not always rebuff the Chinese. Nearly twenty years before Sui's birth in 1865, railroads and other industries welcomed the Chinese to America with open arms. They needed the labor. One San Francisco newspaper called for the city

to establish a college devoted to teaching the Chinese language. The Chinese reciprocated the warmth (and the interest in promoting trade). In an act that would have made Native American William Apess proud, they celebrated George Washington's birthday in the early 1850s. No oxen passed with portraits of the first president dangling from the horns, and no bakers tossed their bread into the crowds. But more than two hundred Chinese marched in full ceremonial dress under the banner "China boys of San Francisco." The group towed a wagon seating six musicians, who played Chinese ceremonial music. Residents, who benefited from cheap supply of labor, hailed their Chinese neighbors.

Later, the United States modified the Exclusion Act in 1892, 1902, and 1904 to extend its life and to broaden the exceptions to ten categories, including newspaper editors and government officials. See Thomas W. Chinn, H. Mark Lai, and Philip P. Choy, *A History of the Chinese in California: A Syllabus* (San Francisco: Chinese Historical Society of America, 1969), 26–27. For a copy of the special tax levied on Chinese gold miners, see "An Act to Provide for the Protection of Foreigners, and to Define Their Liabilities and Privileges," March 30, 1853, California Statutes, 1853; reprinted in Cheng-Tsu Wu, ed., *"Chink!" A Documentary History of Anti-Chinese Prejudice in America* (New York: World Publishing, 1972), 20–25. The strongest discussion of the Chinese and labor is still Alexander Saxton's *The Indispensable Enemy: Labor and the Anti-Chinese Movement in California* (Berkeley: University of California Press, 1971). For a survey of Western views of China and an argument that places European Americans as the colonizers, see Gary Y. Okihiro, *Margins and Mainstreams: Asians in American History and Culture* (Seattle: University of Washington Press, 1994), 3–30.

18. Statistics on tourism from *California: The Golden State, a Gratuitous Guide*, 5. Irwin quotes from Genthe, *Old Chinatown*, 1.
19. For descriptions of the swordfights and east/west running vaginas, see Ivan Light's study of vice and Chinatown merchants in "From Vice District to Tourist Attraction: The Moral Career of American Chinatowns, 1880–1940," *Pacific Historical Review* 43:3 (August 1974): 367–394. Find Todd's comments at Frank Morton Todd, *The Chamber of Commerce Handbook for San Francisco—Historical and Descriptive: A Guide for Visitors* (San Francisco: San Francisco Chamber of Commerce, 1914), 67. Todd continues by conflating foreignness and lawlessness in his description of the quarter: Chinatown Chinese "modified by the white man's laws as far as the United States Marshal's office and the 'Chinatown Squad' from the Hall of Justice are able to put them into effect" (66–67). See also James Cameron, *Guide to San Francisco and Map, 1908* (San Francisco, 1908); William Bode, *Lights and Shadows of Chinatown* (San Francisco: H. S. Crocker, 1896); William Doxey, *Doxey's Guide to San Francisco and the Pleasure Resorts of California* (San Francisco: W. Doxey, 1897), 116; and Frederic M. De Witt, *An Illustrated and Descriptive Souvenir and Guide to San Francisco: A New Handbook for Strangers and Tourists: With a Short Historical Sketch and a Bird's-Eye View of the Business Center of the City*, 2d ed. (San Francisco: M. DeWitt, 1898), 30.
20. Genthe, *Old Chinatown*, 61. Genthe claimed to know the exact spot for "Third Circle." He does not say exactly what this means, but Genthe clearly means for the claim to add to his aura of knowing Chinatown's underbelly. See Genthe, *As I Remember*, 38–39. K. Scott Wong argues that Chinatown's has always proved contested terrain in American culture. The Chinese there had to define themselves by what

they are not rather than by what they really are. See Wong, "Chinatown: Conflicting Images, Contested Terrain," *MELUS* 20:1 (Spring 1995): 3–15. My analysis of Eaton deepens our understanding of defining oneself within a master narrative.

21. Frank Norris, "The Third Circle," in *Works, Vol. 4: The Third Circle*, introduction by Will Irwin (New York: John Lane Company, 1909), 13–27. Future references are made parenthetically in the text. This piece originally appeared in *The Wave*, August 28, 1897, 5. See Joseph R. McElrath, Jr., *Frank Norris and the Wave: A Bibliography* (New York: Garland, 1988), 50.
22. Saliva and gloves play interesting roles in Norris's novel, *Vandover and the Brute* (1914; reprinted, Lincoln: University of Nebraska Press, 1978). People who die or find themselves in abject circumstances drool or froth at the mouth; witness Vandover's mother's death (5), another dying woman's frothing at the mouth (136), and the man beaten as he tried to get into the Steamer's lifeboat (140). Further, when Vandover's illicit lover, Flossie, "removed her veil and gloves it was as though she were partially undressed, and her uncovered face and hands seemed to be only portions of her nudity" (52).
23. Genthe, *As I Remember*, 29; quote on 32.
24. Irwin, *Old Chinatown*, 61–62. Irwin evokes Norris from his first page of *Old Chinatown*. Irwin also wrote the introduction to the short story volume of Norris's works, called *The Third Circle*. Genthe draws on Norris in his autobiography. See, *As I Remember*, 38–39. Irwin quotes Genthe, *Old Chinatown*, 62.
25. Irwin, *Old Chinatown*, 64, 62, respectively.
26. Frank Norris, "Cosmopolitan San Francisco: The Remarkable Confusion of Races in the City's Quarter," *The Wave*, Christmas edition, 1897, 4.
27. Irwin said in his preface, framed as a letter to Genthe, "I but write as a frame for your pictures; I am illustrating you." Genthe, *Old Chinatown*, 5.
28. Genthe credits his Baedecker with sending him into the quarter in his autobiography, *As I Remember*, 32. Genthe also recounted his brave exploits to the local gossip columnists and stocked the stories with details. One piece recounted his steely courage before a wild beast's charge. The bear's "eyes shone like big black beads; his open red mouth flecked with foam," Genthe said. The doctor looked around him at the dogs who had already been "dispatched by a blow from one of those knife-armed paws." He raised his rifle. "I looked into those defiant eyes, into the cruel, red mouth. Then I saw his chest swelling where his heart was beating." But the German gentleman knew how to go for the kill: "I stung him there with a Mannlicher bullet." The wounded bear flung himself toward the renowned photographer, "fall[ing] dead so near I could feel his fetid breath." "Wounded Bear Falls Dead at Feet of Dr. Genthe," newspaper clipping, nd, np, *Genthe Scrapbook*, Bancroft Library Collection, University of California, Berkeley. The *Genthe Scrapbook* is filled with gossip columns about Genthe, his amours, and his travels on horseback. Don Juan quote in Genthe, *As I Remember*, 280.
29. Genthe, *As I Remember*, 35.
30. Ibid., 34–35.
31. Ibid., 33.
32. Ibid., 41.
33. Arnold Genthe, "Rebellion in Photography," *Overland Monthly* 43:2 (August 1901): 92–102, quote at 96. Porter Garnett, "Camera Pictures Rival Paintings," Genthe Scrapbook, Bancroft Library. Some later scholars accepted that the Chinese feared

Genthe's ability to capture their souls. They "indeed understood instinctively the power of this mysterious art form . . . to permanently distill the essence of experiences," said Barry Leo Delaney, in his foreword to *Arnold Genthe, 1869–1942: Photographs and Memorabilia from the Collection of James F. Carr, A Survey Exhibition*, September 28–November 2, 1975 (Staten Island, N.Y.: Staten Island Museum, 1975). For a wonderful essay about viewing Genthe's Chinatown photos as a Chinese woman growing up in America and how the absence of whites in the photos distanced the Chinese, see Maxine Hong Kingston, "San Francisco's Chinatown," *American Heritage* 30:1 (1978): 36–47.

34. Tchen, *Genthe's Photographs*, 11. The Genthe section is indebted to his work.
35. Genthe also selectively chose his subjects. For example, few children lived in Chinatown because immigration laws restricted Chinese women's entry into the United States and thus restricted the number of heterosexual families that formed. Yet nearly two-thirds of his photographs showed children. Furthermore, more than half of Genthe's shots were of people in their ceremonial costumes, exotic clothing they wore only a few days out of the year. See Tchen, *Genthe's Photographs*, 13–14. Cf. Toby Quitslund, "Arnold Genthe: A Pictorial Photographer in San Francisco, 1895–1911" (Ph.D. diss., George Washington University, 1988).
36. Genthe, *Old Chinatown*, 197; (1908 ed.), 13.
37. Chinese Laundryman (Gabriel Moulin Studios); reprinted in Laverne Mau Dicker, *The Chinese in San Francisco: A Pictorial History* (New York: Dover, 1979), 35.
38. Genthe, *Old Chinatown*, following 10.
39. See Tchen's discussion of the "Toy Peddler" in *Genthe's Photographs*, 14. See the 730 Washington Street photo at Tchen, *Genthe's Photographs*, 41, plate 25.
40. John A. Fitch, *The Steel Workers* (New York: Russell Sage Foundation, 1910), 17–18. Maren Stange, *Symbols of Ideal Life: Social Documentary Photography in America, 1890–1950* (Cambridge: Cambridge University Press, 1989), 83–84, discusses Fitch and the photo. I am indebted to Stange for the reading of this photograph.
41. Genthe, *Old Chinatown*, 29. The photo appears in the 1908 edition following page 22. (It runs opposite a discussion of the secret Tong organizations and just before the photo of the knife-dancer.)
42. For two examples, see Genthe, *Old Chinatown*, 29, 113. Irwin repeatedly invokes Norris's "Third Circle." For examples, see *Old Chinatown*, 113, 153, 168.
43. Irwin, *Old Chinatown*, 89, 64, respectively.
44. Ibid., 109–112, quote on 112.
45. Genthe, *Pictures of Old Chinatown*, 32.
46. Ibid., 53. For tour books, see, for example, *California for the Tourist: The Charm of the Land of Sunshine by Summit Sea and Shore* (San Francisco: Southern Pacific, 1910); Doxey, *Doxey's Guide to San Francisco*; J. Torrey Conner, "A Western View of the Chinese in the United States," *Chautauquan* 32 (January 1901): 373–378; and Todd, *The Chamber of Commerce Handbook for San Francisco*.
47. Herman Scheffaner, "The Old Chinese Quarter," *Living Age* 254 (August 10, 1907): 359–366, quotes at 361.
48. Washington M. Ryer, "The Spread of Opium Smoking, Leprosy and Other Imported Evils," in *The Conflict of Races: The Migration of the Manufacturing Industries of the United States and Europe to the Eastern Shores of Asia* (San Francisco: P. J. Thomas, Printer and Publisher, 1886), 48.

49. Scheffaner, "The Old Chinese Quarter," 362.
50. W. B. Farwell, John E. Kunkler, and E. B. Pond, "Official Map of 'Chinatown' in San Francisco," in "Report, Special Committee on Chinatown," 1885. Bancroft Library, University of California, Berkeley. Chinese prostitution declined precipitously after 1870. In 1885, 567 professional prostitutes worked in Chinatown. See Luci Cheng Hirata, "Free, Indentured, Enslaved: Chinese Prostitutes in Nineteenth-Century America," *Signs: Journal of Women and Culture in Society* 5:1 (1979): 3–29.
51. East-to-west material in Judy Yung, *Unbound Feet: A Social History of Chinese Women in San Francisco* (Berkeley: University of California Press, 1995), 28. Sign quote from Pardee Lowe, *Father and Glorious Descendant* (New York: Council On Books in War-Time, 1943), 38.
52. See, for example, *California for the Tourist*, 17; Doxey, *Doxey's Guide to San Francisco*, 122–124; Conner, "A Western View of the Chinese," 373–378, and Todd, *The Chamber of Commerce Handbook for San Francisco*.
53. Ivan Light, "From Vice District to Tourist Attraction: The Moral Career of American Chinatowns, 1880–1940," *Pacific Historical Review* 43:3 (August 1974): 367–394.
54. See, for example, Sophie E. Gardiner, "A Chinese Colony in San Francisco," *California Ladies' Magazine* 4:4 (April 1903): 4–6, quote at 6, in Chinese Historical Society/San Francisco Collection, Box #3, Folder 27, Asian American Studies Library Archives, University of California, Berkeley; Doxey, *Doxey's Guide to San Francisco*, 122–124; and Todd, *The Chamber of Commerce Handbook for San Francisco*, 70. Funerals were big hits at other Chinatowns, too. See Herbert Heywood, "China in New England," *New England Magazine* 28 (June 1903): 473–483.
55. Frank Norris, "Passing of 'Little Pete'; The Funeral Rites Held Over a Famous Chinaman," *The Wave*, January 30, 1897, 7. For background on Little Pete, see Jesse B. Cook, "San Francisco's Old Chinatown" *San Francisco Police and Peace Officers' Journal of the State of California* 9:6 (June 1931): 1–2, Chinese Historical Society/San Francisco Collection, Box #3, Folder 27, Asian American Studies Library Archives, University of California, Berkeley.
56. Genthe, *Old Chinatown*, 134–136; 1908 ed., 43–44.
57. "A CHINESE DOCTOR," *The San Francisco Medical Press*, edited by Henry Gibbons and R. Beverly Cole, 6:4 (January 1865): 186.
58. A. H. Hazen to Sun Sun Wo Company, M. Schlictmann Collection, Bancroft Library, University of California, Berkeley.
59. "Life History of Mr. Woo Gen," July 29, 1924, Oral History, Survey of Race Relations Collection, Hoover Institution Archives, Box 27, Folder 183, 7–8.
60. Untitled article, no publication, August 27, 1933. Chinese Historical Society, San Francisco Collection, Box #3, Folder 92, Asian American Studies Library Archives, University of California, Berkeley.
61. Loo Yee Kern, "Chinatown Goes Dial," *Pacific Telephone Magazine* (1949): n.p. In 1911, the exchange had 474 business subscribers and 660 residential subscribers. See Thomas W. Chinn, *Bridging the Pacific: San Francisco Chinatown and Its People* (San Francisco: Chinese Historical Society, 1989), 40.
62. Todd, *The Chamber of Commerce Handbook for San Francisco*, 73. For a discussion of how the Chinese used the American legal system to fight their isolation, see Charles J. McClain, *In Search of Equality: The Chinese Struggle against Discrimination in Nineteenth-Century America* (Berkeley: University of California Press, 1994).

63. Links to the mainstream world did not stop with communication. Letter from Nowland C. Hong, president, Los Angeles lodge, CACA, to *East/West Chinese American Journal* (San Francisco), February 17, 1971; reprinted in Cheng-Tsu Wu, ed., *"Chink!"* 256. For a brief history of the association, which later changed its name to the Chinese American Citizen's Alliance, see Sue Fawn Chung, "Fighting for Their American Rights: A History of the Chinese American Citizens Alliance," in *Claiming America: Constructing Chinese American Identities during the Exclusion Era*, edited by K. Scott Wong and Sucheng Chan (Philadelphia: Temple University Press, 1998), 95–126.
64. Frank Norris, "Cosmopolitan San Francisco: The Remarkable Confusion of Races in the City's Quarter," *The Wave*, Christmas ed., 1897, 4.
65. Genthe, *Pictures of Old Chinatown*, 33.
66. Eaton, "Sui Sin Far, The Half Chinese Writer, Tells of Her Career," *Boston Globe*, May 5, 1912; reprinted in *Mrs. Spring Fragrance*, 290, 295.
67. See "In the Land of the Free," reprinted in *Mrs. Spring Fragrance*, 93–101; "The Land of the Free," *Montreal Daily Witness*, reprinted in *Mrs. Spring Fragrance*, March 15, 1890, 179, and "Chinatown Needs a School," *Los Angeles Express*, October 14, 1903, reprinted in *Mrs. Spring Fragrance*, 202–203.
68. Sui, *Leaves*, 223. See also the tombstone the Chinese community in Montreal and Boston erected for Sui: in Chinese characters at the top it says, "Yi bu wong hua,"—"The righteous or loyal one does not forget China." Translation in Amy Ling, *Between Worlds*, 32–33.
69. Eaton, "The Chinese in America: Part IV," 251. Ferens, *Edith and Winifred Eaton*, pins Edith's alignment with dominant values largely on missionary texts; see 57–60.
70. Edith Eaton, Sui Sin Far to Robert L. Park, October 15, 1909, Box 21, Folder 15, Chinese Historical Society Collection, Asian-American Archives, University of California, Berkeley. I find no mention of this letter in any of the Sui biography or criticism.

Conclusion

1. Danzy Senna, *Caucasia* (New York: Riverhead Books, Penguin, Putnam, 1998), 334.
2. Ibid., 334.
3. David Walker, *Appeal: To the Coloured Citizens of the World, but in Particular, and Very Expressly, to Those of the United States of America* (1829); reprinted edition by Charles M. Wiltse (New York: Hill and Wang, 1965), 63n.
4. André Malraux, "The Cultural Heritage" (1936), as quoted by F. O. Matthiessen, *American Renaissance: Art and Expression in the Age of Emerson and Whitman* (New York: Oxford University Press, 1941), xv, n5.

   This cult of the conquering individual guides the myth of the west that opened this study, and it bleeds through to literary studies in general. Matthiessen, for example, claimed that frontier humorist George Washington Harris (1814–1869), creator of Sut Lovingood, brought "us closer than any other writer to the indigenous and undiluted resources of the American language." *American Renaissance*, 637. C. K. Patell, "Comparative American Studies: Hybridity and Beyond," *American Literary History* 11:1 (Spring 1999): 166–186, gives a brief history of the frontier and individual cult and its impact on American literary studies. See also R.W.B. Lewis,

The American Adam: Innocence, Tragedy, and Tradition in the Nineteenth Century (Chicago: University of Chicago Press, 1955), and Harold Bloom. For a more recent enactment of this cult of the individual, see Bloom's, "Mr. America," *New York Review of Books*, November 22, 1984, 19–24.

5. Bhabha, "Commitment to Theory," *The Location of Culture*, 34. Gary Y. Okihiro claims that the margins' critique defines the center, and they thus become the mainstream; see *Margins and Mainstreams*.
6. Matthiessen, *American Renaissance*, 656.
7. For discussions on reworking the canon and threading together many cultures, see, for example, Carolyn Porter, "What We Know That We Don't Know: Remapping American Literary Studies," *American Literary History* 6 (1994): 467–526, and Gregory S. Jay, "The End of 'American' Literature: Toward a Multicultural Practice," *College English* 53:3 (March 1991): 264–281.

SELECTED BIBLIOGRAPHY

Archives

American Antiquarian Society
Bancroft Library, Library Collection, M. Schlictmann Collection
Beineke Rare Books Library, Yale University
Boston Public Library Rare Books and Manuscripts
Dartmouth University Archives
Hoover Institution of War, Revolution, and Peace Archives, Stanford University
 Library Collection
 Survey of Race Relations Collection
Houghton Library, Harvard University
Oberlin College Archives
Stanford University Medical Center Rare Books and Manuscripts Collection
Stanford University Rare Books and Manuscript Collection
University of California, Berkeley
 Asian American Studies Library Archives
 Chinese Historical Society Collection
 Chinese Historical Society/San Francisco Collection
University of Texas at Austin, Harry Ransom Research Center
Watkinson Library, Trinity College
Williams College Archives

Major Newspaper Runs

Anglo-African Magazine, New York, 1859
The Christian Recorder, Philadelphia, Pennsylvania, 1861–1870
Freedom's Journal, New York, New York, 1827–1829
The National Era, Washington, D.C., 1847–1860
The North Star, Rochester, New York, 1847–1851
The Rights of All, New York, New York, 1829
The Wave, San Francisco, 1897
The Weekly Advocate and *The Colored American*, New York, New York, 1837–1841

Selected Other Sources

Abzug, Robert H. *Cosmos Crumbling: American Reform and the Religious Imagination.* New York: Oxford University Press, 1994.

Alexander, Elizabeth. "'We Must Be about Our Father's Business': Anna Julia Cooper and the In-Corporation of the Nineteenth-Century African-American Woman Intellectual." *Signs: Journal of Women in Culture and Society* 20:2 (Winter 1995): 336–357.

Alger, William Rounseville. *Life of Edwin Forrest, the American Tragedian.* 2 vols. Philadelphia: J. B. Lippincott, 1877.

Allen, Theodore W. *The Invention of the White Race,* Vol. 1: *Racial Oppression and Social Control.* New York: Verso, 1994.

———. Vol. 2: *The Origin of Racial Oppression in Anglo-America.* New York: Verso, 1997.

Apess, William. *On Our Own Ground: The Complete Writings of William Apess.* Edited by Barry O'Connell. Amherst: University of Massachusetts Press, 1992.

Appiah, K. Anthony. *In My Father's House: Africa in the Philosophy of Culture.* New York: Oxford University Press, 1992.

Babb, Valerie. *Whiteness Visible: The Meaning of Whiteness in American Literature and Culture.* New York: New York University Press, 1998.

Bailyn, Bernard. *The Ideological Origins of the American Revolution.* Cambridge: Harvard University Press, 1967.

Bank, Rosemary K. "Staging the 'Native': Making History in American Theatre Culture, 1828–1838." *Theatre Journal* 45:4 (December 1993): 461–487.

Barnes, Charlotte M. S. *The Forest Princess; or, Two Centuries Ago in Plays, Prose, and Poetry.* Philadelphia: E. H. Butler, 1848.

Barthes, Roland. *Mythologies.* New York: Hill & Wang, 1972.

Bascom, John. "Consciousness: What Is It?" *American Presbyterian Review* 18 (July 1869): 478–491.

———. *Philosophy of Literature.* 1874. Reprint, New York: G. P. Putnam's Sons, 1895.

———. *Things Learned by Living.* New York: G. P. Putnam's Sons, 1913.

Baym, Nina. "A Refusal to Be Other." *American Quarterly* 46, No. 3 (September 1994): 434–440.

———. *American Women Writers and the Work of History, 1790–1860.* New Brunswick, N.J.: Rutgers University Press, 1995.

Beard, George M. *American Nervousness: Its Causes and Consequences.* New York: G. P. Putnam's Sons, 1881.

Bederman, Gale. *Manliness and Civilization: A Cultural History of Gender and Race in the United States, 1880–1917.* Chicago: University of Chicago Press, 1995.

Bell, Howard. *A Survey of the Negro Convention Movement, 1830–1861.* New York: Arno Press, 1969.

———. *Minutes of the Proceedings of the National Negro Conventions, 1830–1864.* New York: Arno Press, 1969.

Benes, Peter, ed. *The Dublin Seminar for New England Folklife Annual Proceedings 1991.* Boston: Boston University, 1991.

Berkhofer, Robert F., Jr. *The White Man's Indian: Images of the American Indian from Columbus to the Present.* New York: Vintage Books, 1979.

Bhabha, Homi K. *The Location of Culture.* New York: Routledge, 1994.

Blight, David W. "In Search of Learning, Liberty, and Self-Definition: James McCune Smith and the Ordeal of the Antebellum Black Intellectual." *Afro-Americans in New York Life and History* 9:2 (July 1985): 7–25.

Blumin, Stuart M. "The Hypothesis of Middle-Class Formation in Nineteenth-Century America: A Critique and Some Proposals." *American Historical Review* 90:2 (April 1985): 299–338.

Brodhead, Richard H. "Introduction." *The Journals of Charles W. Chesnutt.* Edited by Richard H. Brodhead. Durham, N.C.: Duke University Press, 1993.

Bulfinch, Ellen Susan, ed. *The Life and Letters of Charles Bulfinch, Architect, with Other Family Papers*. Boston: Houghton Mifflin, 1896.

Calloway, Colin G., ed. *After King Philip's War: Peace and Persistence in Indian New England*. Hanover, N.H.: University Press of New England, 1997.

Campbell, Karlyn Kohrs. *Man Can Not Speak for Her,* Vol. 1: *A Critical Study of Early Feminist Rhetoric*. New York: Greenwood Press, 1989.

———. *Man Can Not Speak for Her,* Vol. 2: *Key Texts of the Early Feminists*. New York: Greenwood Press, 1989.

Carby, Hazel V. *Reconstructing Womanhood: The Emergence of the Afro-American Woman Novelist*. New York: Oxford University Press, 1987.

Carr, Helen. *Inventing the American Primitive: Politics, Gender, and the Representation of Native American Literary Traditions, 1789–1936*. Cork, Ireland: Cork University Press, 1996.

Cawelti, John. *Apostles of the Self-Made Man*. Chicago: University of Chicago Press, 1965.

Cheng-Tsu Wu, ed. *"Chink!" A Documentary History of Anti-Chinese Prejudice in America*. New York: World Publishing, 1972.

Chinn, Thomas W. *Bridging the Pacific: San Francisco Chinatown and Its People*. San Francisco: Chinese Historical Society, 1989.

Clifford, James. *Routes: Travel and Translation in the Late Twentieth Century*. Cambridge: Harvard University Press, 1997.

Cmiel, Kenneth. "'A Broad Fluid Language of Democracy': Discovering the American Idiom." *Journal of American History* 79:3 (December 1992): 913–936.

———. *Democratic Eloquence: The Fight over Popular Speech in Nineteenth-Century America*. New York: William Morrow & Co., 1990.

Condit, Celeste Michelle, and John Louis Lucaites. *Crafting Equality: America's Anglo-African Word*. Chicago: University of Chicago Press, 1993.

Conner, Torrey. "A Western View of the Chinese in the United States." *Chautauquan* 32 (January 1901): 373–378.

Cooper, Anna Julia. *A Voice from the South*. 1892. Reprint, New York: Oxford University Press, 1988.

———. "The Third Step (Autobiographical)." Mimeograph. Moorland-Spingarn Collection, Howard University.

———. *The Voice of Anna Julia Cooper, Including A Voice from the South and Other Important Essays, Papers, and Letters*. Edited by Charles Lemert and Esme Bahn. New York: Rowman and Littlefield, 1998.

Cottrol, Robert J. *The Afro-Yankees: Providence's Black Community in the Antebellum Era*. Westport, Conn.: Greenwood Press, 1982.

Crummell, Alex. "The Need of New Ideas and New Aims." In *Africa and America: Addresses and Discourses*. Springfield, Mass.: Willey, 1891.

Curry, Leonard P. *The Free Black in Urban America, 1800–1850: The Shadow of a Dream.* Chicago: University of Chicago Press, 1981.

Dann, Martin E. *The Black Press, 1827–1890: The Quest for National Identity.* New York: G. P. Putnam's Sons, 1971.

Davidson, Cathy N., ed. *Reading in America: Literature and Social History.* Baltimore: Johns Hopkins University Press, 1989.

Davis, David Brion. "At the Heart of Slavery." *New York Review of Books* 43:16 (October 17, 1996): 51–54.

———. *The Problem of Slavery in the Age of Revolution, 1770–1823.* Ithaca, N.Y.: Cornell University Press, 1975.

———. *The Problem of Slavery in Western Culture.* Ithaca, N.Y.: Cornell University Press, 1966.

Davis, Natalie Zemon. "Narrative as Knowing: Stories and the Hunger to Know." *Yale Journal of Criticism* 5:2 (1972): 159–163.

Deloria, Philip J. *Playing Indian.* New Haven: Yale University Press, 1998.

Denning, Michael. "The End of Mass Culture." *International Labor and Working-Class History* 37 (Spring 1990): 4–18.

———. "'The Special American Conditions': Marxism and American Studies." *American Quarterly* 38:3 (1986): 356–380.

di Leonardo, Micaela. "White Ethnicities, Identity Politics, and Baby Bear's Chair." *Social Text* 41 (1994): 5–33.

Dicker, Laverne Mau. *The Chinese in San Francisco: A Pictorial History.* New York: Dover, 1979.

Douglas, Ann. *Terrible Honesty: Mongrel Manhattan in the 1920s.* New York: Farrar, Straus & Giroux, 1995.

Douglass, Frederick. *My Bondage and My Freedom.* 1855. Reprint, New York: Dover, 1969.

———. *Narrative of the Life of Frederick Douglass.* 1845. Reprint, New York: Doubleday, 1989.

Doxey, William. *Doxey's Guide to San Francisco and the Pleasure Resorts of California.* San Francisco: W. Doxey, 1897.

Du Bois, W.E.B. *Black Reconstruction.* Philadelphia: A. Safer, 1935.

———. *Dusk of Dawn: An Essay toward an Autobiography of a Race Concept.* 1940. Reprint, in *Writings.* New York: Library of America, 1986.

———. *Souls of Black Folk.* 1903. Norton critical edition, edited by Henry Louis Gates, Jr., and Terri Hume Oliver. New York: W. W. Norton, 1999.

duCille, Ann. *The Coupling Convention: Sex, Text, and Tradition in Black Women's Fiction.* New York: Oxford University Press, 1993.

Dyer, Richard. "White." *Screen* 29:4 (Fall 1983): 44.

Eaton, Edith Maude (Sui Sin Far). *Mrs. Spring Fragrance and Other Writings.* Edited by Amy Ling and Annette White-Parks. Urbana: University of Illinois Press, 1995.

Elkins, Stanley, and Eric McKitrick. *The Age of Federalism.* New York: Oxford University Press, 1993.

Farwell, W. B., John E. Kunkler, and E. B. Pond. "Official Map of 'Chinatown' in San Francisco." In "Report, Special Committee on Chinatown." 1885. Bancroft Library holdings, University of California, Berkeley.

Fields, Barbara. "Ideology and Race in American History." In *Region, Race, and Recon-*

struction: Essays in Honor of C. Vann Woodward, edited by S. Morgan Kaurser and James McPherson. New York: Oxford University Press, 1982. 143–177.

———. "Slavery, Race, and Ideology in the United States of America." *New Left Review* 181 (May/June 1990): 95–118.

———. "The Advent of Capitalist Agriculture: The New South in a Bourgeois World." In *Essays on the Postbellum Southern Economy*, edited by Thavolia Glymph and John J. Kushma. College Station: Texas A&M University Press, 1985.

———. "The Nineteenth-Century American South: History and Theory." *Plantation Society and the Americas* 2:1 (April 1983): 7–27.

Fishkin, Shelley Fisher. "Interrogating 'Whiteness,' Complicating 'Blackness': Remapping American Culture." *American Quarterly* 47:3 (September 1995): 428–466. Reprint in *Criticism and the Color Line: Desegregating American Literary Studies*, edited by Henry B. Wonham. New Brunswick: Rutgers University Press, 1996.

———. *Was Huck Black?: Mark Twain and African-American Voices*. New York: Oxford University Press, 1993.

Fishkin, Shelley Fisher, and Carla Peterson. "'We Hold These Truths to Be Self-Evident': The Rhetoric of Frederick Douglass's Journalism." In *Frederick Douglass: New Literary and Historical Essays*, edited by Eric J. Sundquist. Cambridge: Cambridge University Press, 1990. 189–204.

Fitch, John A. *The Steel Workers*. New York: Russell Sage Foundation, 1910.

Fliegelman, Jay. *Declaring Independence: Jefferson, Natural Language, and the Culture of Performance*. Stanford: Stanford University Press, 1993.

Foner, Eric. *Reconstruction: America's Unfinished Business, 1863–1877*. New York: Harper & Row, 1988.

———. "The Meaning of Freedom in the Age of Emancipation." *Journal of American History* 81:2 (September 1994): 435–460.

Forbath, William E. "The Ambiguities of Free Labor." *Wisconsin Law Review* 4 (1985): 767–817.

Forbes, Jack D. *Black Africans and Native Americans: Color, Race, and Caste in the Evolution of Red-Black Peoples*. New York: Basil Blackwell, 1988.

Foster, Francis Smith. *Written by Herself: Literary Production by African American Women, 1746–1892*. Bloomington: Indiana University Press, 1993.

Frankenberg, Ruth, ed. *Displacing Whiteness: Essays in Social and Cultural Criticism*. Durham, N.C.: Duke University Press, 1997.

———. *White Women, Race Matters: The Social Construction of Whiteness*. Minneapolis: University of Minnesota Press, 1993.

Franklin, John Hope, and Alfred A. Moss, Jr. *From Slavery to Freedom: A History of Negro Americans*. 6th ed. New York: McGraw-Hill, 1988.

Fredrickson, George M. *The Black Image in the White Mind: The Debate on Afro-American Character and Destiny, 1817–1914*. Hanover, N.H.: Wesleyan University Press, 1971.

Fuller, Margaret. *Summer on the Lakes in 1843*. 1844. Reprint, Urbana: University of Illinois Press, 1991.

Gaines, Kevin K. *Uplifting the Race: Black Leadership, Politics, and Culture in the Twentieth Century*. Chapel Hill: University of North Carolina Press, 1996.

Gates, Henry Louis, Jr. *Figures in Black: Words, Signs, and the "Racial" Self*. New York: Oxford University Press, 1987.

———. *The Signifying Monkey: A Theory of African-American Literary Criticism*. New York: Oxford University Press, 1988.

———, ed. *"Race," Writing, and Difference*. Chicago: University of Chicago Press, 1986.

Genthe, Arnold. *As I Remember*. New York: Reynal and Hitchcock, 1936.

———. *Old Chinatown, with Text by Will Irwin*. New York: Mitchell Kennerley, 1912.

———. *Pictures of Old Chinatown with Text by Will Irwin*. New York: Moffat, Yard, and Company, 1908.

Gilbert, Sandra M., and Susan Gubar. *The Madwoman in the Attic*. New Haven: Yale University Press, 1979.

Gilman, Charlotte Perkins. *The Charlotte Perkins Gilman Reader: The Yellow Wallpaper, and Other Fiction*. Edited and introduced by Ann J. Lane. New York: Pantheon Books, 1980.

Gilroy, Paul. *The Black Atlantic: Modernity and Double Consciousness*. Cambridge: Harvard University Press, 1993.

Giroux, Henry A. "White Squall: Resistance and the Pedagogy of Whiteness." *Cultural Studies* 11:3 (1997): 376–389.

Glickstein, Jonathan A. *Concepts of Free Labor in Antebellum America*. New Haven: Yale University Press, 1991.

Gould, Stephen J. *The Mismeasure of Man*. New York: W. W. Norton, 1981.

"Greenough the Sculptor, and His Last Production." *Bulletin of the American Art-Union* (September 1851).

Guha, Ranajit. "On Some Aspects of the Historiography of Colonial India." In *Selected Subaltern Studies*, edited by Ranajit Guha and Gayatri Chakravorty Spivak. New York: Oxford University Press, 1988. 37–49.

———. "The Prose of Counter-Insurgency." In *Selected Subaltern Studies*, edited by Ranajit Guha and Gayatri Chakravorty Spivak. New York: Oxford University Press, 1988. 45–84.

Gustafson, Sandra. "Nations of Israelites: Prophecy and Cultural Autonomy in the Writings of William Apess." *Religion and Literature* 26:1 (Spring 1994): 31–53.

Hall, Stuart. "Negotiating Caribbean Identities." *New Left Review* 209 (January/February 1995): 3–14.

———. "Notes on Deconstructing the Popular." In *People's History and Socialist Theory*, edited by Raphael Samuel. London: Routledge and Kegan Paul, 1981. 227–240.

Halttunen, Karen. *Confidence Men and Painted Women: A Study of Middle-Class Culture, 1830–1870*. New Haven: Yale University Press, 1982.

Harding, Vincent Gordon. "Wrestling toward the Dawn: The Afro-American Freedom Movement and the Changing Constitution." *Journal of American History* 74:3 (December 1987): 718–739.

Haynes, Carolyn. "'A mark for them all to . . . hiss at': The formation of Methodist and Pequot Identity in the Conversion Narrative of William Apess." *Early American Literature* 31:1 (1996): 25–44.

Hedrick, Joan D. *Harriet Beecher Stowe: A Life*. New York: Oxford University Press, 1994.

Hepburn, A. D. *Manual of English Rhetoric*. Cincinnati: Wilson, Kinkle and Co., 1875.

Herman, Tom. "Tax Report, Briefs." *Wall Street Journal*, March 17, 1999, 1.

Hevner, Carol Eaton. "The Paintings of Rembrandt Peale: Character and Conventions." In *In Pursuit of Fame: Rembrandt Peale, 1778–1860*. Washington, D.C.: Smithsonian Institution Press, 1992.

Heywood, Herbert. "China in New England." *New England Magazine* 28 (June 1903): 473–483.

Higginbotham, Evelyn Brooks. "African-American Women's History and the Metalanguage of Race." *Signs* 17:2 (1992): 251–274.

———. *Righteous Discontent: The Women's Movement in the Black Baptist Church, 1880–1920.* Cambridge: Harvard University Press, 1993.

Higgs, Robert. *Competition and Coercion: Blacks in the American Economy 1865–1914.* Cambridge: Cambridge University Press, 1977.

Hill, Adams Sherman. *The Principles of Rhetoric.* 1878. Reprint, New York: American Book Co., 1895.

Hinks, Peter P. *To Awaken My Afflicted Brethren: David Walker and the Problem of Antebellum Slave Resistance.* University Park: Pennsylvania State University Press, 1997.

Horseman, Reginald. *Race and Manifest Destiny: The Origins of American Racial Anglo-Saxonism.* Cambridge: Harvard University Press, 1981.

Horton, James Oliver. *Free People of Color: Inside the African American Community.* Washington, D.C.: Smithsonian Institution Press, 1993.

Howard-Pitney, David. *The Afro-American Jeremiad: Appeals for Justice in America.* Philadelphia: Temple University Press, 1990.

Hutchinson, Louise Daniel. *Anna Julia Cooper: A Voice from the South.* Washington, D.C.: Smithsonian Institution Press, 1981.

Hutton, Frankie. *The Early Black Press in America, 1827 to 1860.* Westport, Conn: Greenwood Press, 1993.

Ignatiev, Noel. *How the Irish Became White.* New York: Routledge, 1995.

Jacobs, Harriet A. *Incidents in the Life of a Slave Girl, Written by Herself.* Edited by L. Maria Child. 1861. Reprint. Edited by Jean Fagan Yellin. Cambridge: Harvard University Press, 1987.

Jacobson, Matthew Frye. *Whiteness of a Different Color: European Immigrants and the Alchemy of Race.* Cambridge: Harvard University Press, 1998.

Jameson, Fredric. "Cognitive Mapping." In *Marxism and the Interpretation of Culture*, edited by Cary Nelson and L. Grossberg. Urbana: University of Illinois Press, 1988. 347–357.

———. "Postmodernism and Consumer Society." In *The Anti-Aesthetic: Essays on Postmodern Culture*, edited by Hal Foster. Port Townsend, Wash.: Bay Press, 1983. 111–125.

———. "Postmodernism, or the Cultural Logic of Late Capitalism." *The New Left Review* 146 (July-August 1984): 59–92.

———. "Reification and Utopia in Mass Culture." *Social Text* 1 (1979): 130–148.

Jaynes, Gerald David. *Branches without Roots: Genesis of Black Working Class in the American South, 1862–1882.* New York: Oxford University Press, 1986.

Jefferson, Margo. "On Defining Race, When Only Thinking Makes It So." *New York Times*, national edition, March 22, 1999, B2.

Jefferson, Thomas. *Notes on the State of Virginia.* 1787. Reprint, *Writings.* New York: Library of America, 1984.

———. "Rockfish Gap Report." 1818. Reprint, in *Theories of Education in Early America*, edited by Wilson Smith. Indianapolis: Bobbs-Merrill, 1973. 319–339.

Johnson, Nan. *Nineteenth-Century Rhetoric in North America.* Carbondale: Southern Illinois University Press, 1991.

———. "The Popularization of Nineteenth-Century Rhetoric." In *Oratorical Culture in*

Nineteenth-Century America: Transformations in the Theory and Practice of Rhetoric, edited by Gregory Clark and S. Michael Halloran. Carbondale: Southern Illinois University Press, 1993. 139–157.

Jones, Sally L. "The Original Characters of Edwin Forrest and His American Style." Ph.D. diss., University of Toronto, 1992.

Jordan, Winthrop. *White over Black: American Attitudes toward the Negro, 1550–1812*. Chapel Hill: University of North Carolina Press, 1968.

Katznelson, Ira. "Working-Class Formation: Constructing Cases and Comparisons." In *Working-Class Formation: Nineteenth-Century Patterns in Western Europe and the United States*, edited by Ira Katznelson and Aristide R. Zolberg. Princeton: Princeton University Press, 1986. 3–41.

Kelley, Robin D. G. "People in Me: On the Polycultural Nature of Blackness." Lecture delivered at the University of Texas at Austin, December 4, 1997.

———. "Race and Racism: A Symposium." *Social Text* 42 (Spring 1995): 3.

———. *Race Rebels: Culture, Politics, and the Black Working Class*. New York: Free Press, 1994.

———. "'We Are Not What We Seem': Rethinking Black Working-Class Opposition in the Jim Crow South." *Journal of American History* 80 (June 1993): 75–112.

Kenny, Kevin. *Making Sense of the Molly Maguires*. New York: Oxford University Press, 1997.

Kincheloe, Joe L., Shirley R. Steinberg, Nelson M. Rodriguez, and Ronald E. Chennault, eds. *White Reign: Deploying Whiteness in America*. New York: St. Martin's Press, 1998.

Kingston, Maxine Hong. "San Francisco's Chinatown." *American Heritage* 30:1 (1978): 36–47.

Kirker, Harold, and James Kirker. *Bulfinch's Boston, 1787–1817*. New York: Oxford University Press, 1964.

Kolchin, Peter. "Whiteness Studies: The New History of Race in America." *Journal of American History* 89:1 (June 2002): 154–174.

Konkle, Maureen. "Indian Literacy, U.S. Colonialism, and Literary Criticism." *American Literature* 69:3 (September 1997): 457–486.

Kraditor, Aileen S. *Means and Ends in American Abolitionism: Garrison and His Critics on Strategy and Tactics, 1834–1850*. New York: Pantheon, 1967.

Krupat, Arnold. *For Those Who Come After: A Study of Native American Autobiography*. Berkeley: University of California Press, 1985.

———. *The Voice in the Margin: Native American Literature and the Canon*. Berkeley: University of California Press, 1989.

Lanham, Richard A. *A Handlist of Rhetorical Terms*. 2d ed. Berkeley: University of California Press, 1991.

Lapsansky, Emma Jones. "'Since They Got Those Separate Churches': Afro-Americans and Racism in Jacksonian Philadelphia." *American Quarterly* 32 (1980): 54–78.

Leach, Douglas Edward. *Flintlock and Tomahawk: New England in King Philip's War*. New York: Macmillan, 1958.

Lemert, Charles, and Esme Bahn, eds. *The Voice of Anna Julia Cooper, Including A Voice from the South and Other Important Essays, Papers, and Letters*. New York: Rowman and Littlefield, 1998.

Lepore, Jill. *The Name of War: King Philip's War and the Origins of American Identity*. New York: Alfred A. Knopf, 1998.

Levine, George. *The Possessive Investment in Whiteness: How White People Profit from Identity Politics*. Philadelphia: Temple University Press, 1998.

Levine, Robert S. "Disturbing Boundaries: Temperance, Black Elevation, and Violence in Frank J. Webb's *The Garies and Their Friends*." *Prospects*. Cambridge: Cambridge University Press, 1994. 349–374.

———. *Martin Delany, Frederick Douglass, and the Politics of Representative Identity*. Chapel Hill: University of North Carolina Press, 1997.

Lewis, David Levering. *W.E.B. Du Bois: Biography of Race*. New York: Henry Holt, 1993.

Light, Ivan. "From Vice District to Tourist Attraction: The Moral Career of American Chinatowns, 1880–1940." *Pacific Historical Review* 43:3 (August 1974): 367–394.

Lindsay, Arnett G. "The Economic Conditions of the Negroes of New York Prior to 1861." *Journal of Negro History* 6, no. 2 (1921): 190–199.

Ling, Amy. *Between Worlds: Women Writers of Chinese Ancestry*. New York: Pergamon Press, 1990.

———. "Edith Eaton: Pioneer Chinamerican Writer and Feminist." *American Literary Realism*, 16 (1983): 287–298.

———. "Revelation and Mask: Autobiographies of the Eaton Sisters." *Auto/Biography Studies* 3:2 (1987): 46.

———. "Winnifred Eaton: Ethnic Chameleon and Popular Success." *MELUS* 11:3 (Fall 1984): 5–15.

———. "Writers With a Cause: Sui Sin Far and Han Suyin." *Women's Studies International Forum* 9:4 (1986): 411–419.

Lipsitz, George. "Listening to Learn and Learning to Listen: Popular Culture, Cultural Theory, and American Studies." *American Quarterly* 42:4 (December 1990): 615–636.

Litwack, Leon. *North of Slavery: The Negro in the Free States, 1790–1860*. Chicago: University of Chicago Press, 1961.

Loggins, Vernon. *The Negro Author: His Development in America to 1900*. 1931. Reprint, Port Washington, N.Y.: Kennikat Press, 1964.

Lorde, Audre. *Sister Outsider: Essays and Speeches*. Trumansburg, N.Y.: Crossing Press, 1984.

Lott, Eric. *Love and Theft: Blackface Minstrelsy and the American Working Class*. New York: Oxford University Press, 1993.

Lowe, Lisa. "Heterogeneity, Hybridity, Multiplicity: Marking Asian American Differences." *Diaspora* 1:1 (Spring 1990): 24–44.

Lowe, Pardee. *Father and Glorious Descendant*. New York: Council on Books in War-Time, 1943.

Lubiano, Wahneema, ed. *The House That Race Built: Black Americans, U.S. Terrain*. New York: Pantheon Books, 1997.

Lutz, Tom. *American Nervousness, 1903: An Anecdotal History*. Ithaca, N.Y.: Cornell University Press, 1991.

Majors, M. A. *Noted Negro Women: Their Triumphs and Activities*. Chicago: Donohue and Henneberry, 1893.

Marable, Manning. "The Black Radical Congress: Revitalizing The Black Freedom Movement." *Black Scholar* 28:1 (Spring 1998): 54–70.

Martin, Waldo E., Jr. *The Mind of Frederick Douglass*. Chapel Hill: University of North Carolina Press, 1984.

Matthiessen, F. O. *The American Renaissance*. New York: Oxford University Press, 1941.

McClain, Charles J. *In Search of Equality: The Chinese Struggle against Discrimination in Nineteenth-Century America*. Berkeley: University of California Press, 1994.

McClintock, Anne, Aamir Mufti, and Ella Shohat, eds. *Dangerous Liaisons: Gender, Nation, and Postcolonial Perspectives Cultural Politics,* Volume 11. Minneapolis: University of Minnesota Press, 1997.

McCoy, Drew R. *The Elusive Republic: Political Economy in Jeffersonian America*. Chapel Hill: University of North Carolina Press, 1980.

McElrath, Joseph R., Jr. *Frank Norris and the Wave: A Bibliography*. New York: Garland, 1988.

McFeely, William S. *Frederick Douglass*. New York: W. W. Norton, 1991.

McHenry, Elizabeth. *Forgotten Readers: African-American Literary Societies, 1830–1940*. Durham, N.C.: Duke University Press, 2002.

McQuaid, Kim. "William Apes, Pequot: An Indian Reformer in the Jackson Era." *New England Quarterly* 50 (December 1977): 605–625.

Michaels, Walter Benn. "The Victims of New Historicism." *Modern Language Quarterly* 54:1 (March 1993): 111–121.

Miller, Floyd J. *The Search for a Black Nationality: Black Emigration and Colonization, 1787–1863*. Urbana: University of Illinois Press, 1975.

Morgan, Edmund S. *American Slavery, American Freedom: The Ordeal of Colonial Virginia*. New York: W. W. Norton, 1975.

Morrison, Toni. *Playing in the Dark: Whiteness and the Literary Imagination*. New York: Vintage Books, 1992.

Mosell, Mrs. N. F. *The Work of Afro-American Women*. 2d ed. Philadelphia: Geo. S. Ferguson Company, 1908.

Moses, Wilson J. *Classical Black Nationalism: From the American Revolution to Marcus Garvey*. New York: New York University Press, 1996.

Nash, Gary B. "Black Americans in a White Republic." In *Race and Revolution*. Madison: Madison House, 1990. 57–87.

———. *Forging Freedom: The Formation of Philadelphia's Black Community, 1720–1840*. Cambridge: Harvard University Press, 1988.

———. *The Urban Crucible: Social Change, Political Consciousness, and the Origins of the American Revolution*. Cambridge: Harvard University Press, 1979.

Nell, William. *Colored Patriots of the American Revolution*. 1855. Reprint, New York: Arno Press and The New York Times, 1968.

Nelson, Dana D. *National Manhood: Capitalist Citizenship and the Imagined Fraternity of White Men*. Durham, N.C.: Duke University Press, 1998.

———. *The Word in Black and White: Reading Race in American Literature, 1638–1867*. New York: Oxford University Press, 1992.

Noah, Major Mordecai. "She Would Be a Soldier or The Plains of Chippewa." 1819. Reprint. In *Dramas from the American Theatre, 1762–1919*, edited by Richard Moody. New York: World Publishing Company, 1966. 123–142.

Norris, Frank. *Works*. New York: John Lane Company, 1909.

———. *Vandover and the Brute*. 1914. Reprint, Lincoln: University of Nebraska Press, 1978.

O'Connell, Barry, ed. *On Our Own Ground: The Complete Writings of William Apess*. Amherst: University of Massachusetts Press, 1992.

Okihiro, Gary Y. *Margins and Mainstreams: Asians in American History and Culture*. Seattle: University of Washington Press, 1994.

Olmsted, Frederick Law. *A Journey in the Back Country* Vol. 2. 1860. Reprint, New York: G. P. Putnam's Sons, 1907.

Omi, Michael, and Howard Winant. *Racial Formation in the United States from 1960s to the 1980s*. New York: Routledge, 1986.

Parton, James. *The Life of Horace Greeley, Editor of the New York Tribune*. New York: Mason Brothers, 1855.

Patell, C. K. "Comparative American Studies: Hybridity and Beyond." *American Literary History* 11:1 (Spring 1999): 166–186.

Patterson, Orlando. *Freedom*. New York: Basic Books, 1991.

Peale, Rembrandt, *Portrait of Washington*. Philadelphia: 1824.

Pearce, Roy Harvey. *The Savages of America: A Study of the Indian and the Idea of Civilization*. 1953. Revised edition. Baltimore: Johns Hopkins University Press, 1965.

Pease, William H., and Jane H. Pease. *They Who Would Be Free: Blacks' Search for Freedom, 1830–1861*. New York: Atheneum, 1974.

Penn, I. Garland. *The Afro-American Press and Its Editors*. 1891. Reprint, New York: Arno Press and The New York Times, 1969.

Pennington, James W. C. *Text Book of the Origin and History &c. &c of the Colored People*. Goodell Anti-Slavery Collection No. 60. Hartford: L. Skinner, Printer 1841.

Perlman, Daniel. "Organizations of Free Negroes in New York City, 1800–1860." *Journal of Negro History* 56:3 (1971): 181–197.

Peterson, Carla L. *"Doers of the Word": African-American Women Speakers and Writers in the North (1830–1880)*. New York: Oxford University Press, 1995.

Pfeil, Fred. "Sympathy for the Devils: Notes on Some White Guys in the Ridiculous Class War." In *Whiteness: A Critical Reader*, edited by Mike Hill. New York: New York University Press, 1997. 21–34

Pfister, Joel. "The Americanization of Cultural Studies." *Yale Journal of Criticism* 4:2 (1991): 191–229.

Place, Charles. *Charles Bulfinch: Architect and Citizen*. Boston: Houghton Mifflin, 1925.

Pomeroy, R. W. [supposed author]. *The Young Merchant*. Philadelphia: Published by R. W. Pomeroy, No. 3, Minor Street, 1839.

Porter, Carolyn. "What We Know That We Don't Know: Remapping American Literary Studies." *American Literary History* 6 (1994): 467–526.

Pratt, Mary Louis. *Imperial Eyes: Travel and Transculturation*. New York: Routledge, 1992.

Quarles, Benjamin. *Frederick Douglass*. New York: Atheneum, 1969.

Quitslund, Toby. "Arnold Genthe: A Pictorial Photographer in San Francisco, 1895–1911." Ph.D. diss., George Washington University, 1988.

Rael, Patrick. *Black Identity and Black Protest in the Antebellum North*. Chapel Hill: University of North Carolina Press, 2002.

Reed, Harry. *Platform for Change: The Foundations of the Northern Free Black Community, 1775–1865*. East Lansing: Michigan State University Press, 1994.

Reynolds, David S. *Beneath the American Renaissance: The Subversive Imagination in the Age of Emerson and Melville*. Cambridge: Harvard University Press, 1988.

Robinson, Cedric J. *Black Movements in America*. New York: Routledge, 1997.

Rodgers, Daniel T. "Republicanism: The Career of a Concept." *Journal of American History* 79:1 (June 1992): 11–38.

Roediger, David, ed. *Black on White: Black Writers on What It Means to Be White*. New York: Schocken Books, 1998.

———. *Towards the Abolition of Whiteness: Essays on Race, Politics, and Working Class History*. London: Verso, 1994.

———. *The Wages of Whiteness: Race and the Making of the American Working Class*. New York: Verso, 1991.

Rogin, Michael Paul. *Fathers and Children: Andrew Jackson and the Subjugation of the American Indian*. New York: Alfred A. Knopf, 1975.

Ryer, Washington M. *The Conflict of Races: The Migration of the Manufacturing Industries of the United States and Europe to the Eastern Shores of Asia*. San Francisco: P. J. Thomas, Printer and Publisher, 1886.

Sacks, Karen Brodkin. "How Did Jews Become White Folks?" In *Race*, edited by Steven Gregory and Roger Sanjek. New Brunswick, N.J.: Rutgers University Press, 1994. 78–102

———. "Toward a Unified Theory of Class, Race, and Gender." *American Ethnologist* 16:3 (1989): 534–550.

Said, Edward. *Orientalism*. New York: Random House, 1978.

Saillant, John. "Lemuel Haynes's Black Republicanism and the American Republican Tradition, 1775–1820." *Journal of the Early Republic* 14 (Fall 1994): 293–324.

Saxton, Alexander. *The Indispensable Enemy: Labor and the Anti-Chinese Movement in California*. Berkeley: University of California Press, 1971.

———. *The Rise and Fall of the White Republic: Class Politics and Mass Culture in Nineteenth-Century America*. New York: Verso, 1990.

Scheffaner, Herman. "The Old Chinese Quarter." *Living Age* 254 (August 10, 1907): 359–366.

Schwartz, Barry. *George Washington: The Making of an American Symbol*. New York: Free Press, 1987.

Scott, Joan Wallach. *Gender and the Politics of History*. New York: Columbia University Press, 1988.

Sellers, Charles. *The Market Revolution: Jacksonian America, 1815–1846*. New York: Oxford University Press, 1991.

Senna, Danzy. *Caucasia*. New York: Riverhead Books, Penguin, Putnam, 1998.

Shilton, Katherine. "'This Scholarly and Colored Alumna:' Anna Julia Cooper's Troubled Relationship with Oberlin College." *http://www.oberlin.edu/external/EOG/History322/AnnaJuliaCooper/AnnaJuliaCooper.htm* (accessed July 14, 2003).

Sklar, Kathryn. *Catharine Beecher: A Study in American Domesticity*. New Haven: Yale University Press, 1973.

Sklar, Martin J. *The Corporate Reconstruction of American Capitalism, 1890–1916: The Market, the Law, and Politics*. New York: Cambridge University Press, 1988.

Slotkin, Richard. *Fatal Environment: The Myth of the Frontier in the Age of Industrialization*. Middletown, Conn.: Wesleyan University Press, 1985.

Smith, Henry Nash. *Virgin Land*. 1950. Reprint, Cambridge: Harvard University Press, 1971.

Smith, James McCune. "Introduction." In Frederick Douglass, *My Bondage and My Freedom*. 1855. Reprint, New York: Dover, 1969.

Smith-Rosenberg, Carroll. *Disorderly Conduct: Visions of Gender in Victorian America*. New York: Oxford University Press, 1985.

Sollors, Werner. *Beyond Ethnicity: Consent and Descent in American Culture*. New York: Oxford University Press, 1986.

———. "A Critique of Pluralism." In *Reconstructing American Literary History*, edited by Sacvan Bercovitch. Cambridge: Harvard University Press, 1986. 250–279

———. "Introduction: The Invention of Ethnicity." In *The Invention of Ethnicity*. New York: Oxford, 1989.

———. *Neither Black Nor White Yet Both: Thematic Explorations of Interracial Literature*. New York: Oxford University Press, 1997.

Stampp, Kenneth, and Leon F. Litwack, eds. *Reconstruction, an Anthology of Revisionist Writings*. Baton Rouge: Louisiana State University Press, 1969.

Stange, Maren. *Symbols of Ideal Life: Social Documentary Photography in America, 1890–1950*. Cambridge: Cambridge University Press, 1989.

Steinberg, Stephen. *The Ethnic Myth: Race, Ethnicity, and Class in America*. Boston: Beacon Press, 1982.

Stepto, Robert B. *From behind the Veil: A Study of Afro-American Narrative*. 2d ed. Urbana: University of Illinois Press, 1991.

Stone, John Augustus. *Metamora*. In *Metamora and Other Plays*, edited by Eugene R. Page. Princeton: Princeton University Press, 1941.

Stuckey, Sterling. *The Ideological Origins of Black Nationalism*. Boston: Beacon Press, 1972.

Sumida, Stephen H. *And the View from the Shore: Literary Traditions of Hawai'i*. Seattle: University of Washington Press, 1991.

Sundquist, Eric, ed. *Frederick Douglass: New Literary and Historical Essays*. Cambridge: Cambridge University Press, 1990.

———. *To Wake the Nations*. Cambridge: Harvard University Press, 1993.

Sweet, Leonard I. *Black Images of America, 1784–1870*. New York: W. W. Norton, 1976.

Swift, David E. *Black Prophets of Justice: Activist Clergy before the Civil War*. Baton Rouge: Louisiana State University Press, 1989.

Tate, Claudia. *Domestic Allegories of Political Desire: The Black Heroine's Text at the Turn of the Century*. New York: Oxford University Press, 1992.

Taylor, Charles. *Multiculturalism and "The Politics of Recognition."* Princeton: Princeton University Press, 1992.

Tchen, John Kuo Wei. *Genthe's Photographs of San Francisco's Chinatown, Photographs by Arnold Genthe*. New York: Dover, 1984.

Terrell, Mary Church. *A Colored Woman in a White World*. Washington, D.C.: Ransdell, 1940.

The Tenth Annual Report of the American Society for Colonizing the Free People of Colour of the United States, with an Appendix. Washington, D.C.: Way Gideon, Printers, 1827. Daniel A. P. Murray Collection, 1818–1907, Library of Congress.

Tiro, Karim M. "Denominated 'SAVAGE': Methodism, Writing, and Identity in the Works of William Apess, A Pequot." *American Quarterly* 48:4 (1996): 653–679.

Todd, John. *The Young Man: Hints Addressed to the Young Men of the United States*. Northampton: Published by J. H. Butler, 1844.

Tripp, Bernell. *Origins of the Black Press: New York 1827–1847*. Northport, Ala.: Vision Press, 1991.

Vizenor, Gerald. *Manifest Manners: Post Indian Warriors of Survivance*. Hanover, N.H.: Wesleyan University Press, 1994.

Volosinov, V. N. (Mikhail Bakhtin). *Marxism and the Philosophy of Language*. Translated by Ladislav Matejka and I. R. Titunik. New York: Seminar Press, 1973.

Waldstreicher, David. *In the Midst of Perpetual Fetes: The Making of American Nationalism, 1776–1820*. Chapel Hill: University of North Carolina Press, 1998.

Walker, Cheryl. *Indian Nation: Native American Literature and Nineteenth-Century Nationalisms*. Durham, N.C.: Duke University Press, 1997.

Walker, David. *Appeal: To the Coloured Citizens of the World, but in Particular, and Very Expressly, to Those of the United States of America*. 1829. Reprint, edited by Charles M. Wiltse. New York: Hill and Wang, 1965.

Walters, Ronald G. *The Antislavery Appeal: American Abolitionism after 1830*. New York: W. W. Norton, 1978.

Washington, Booker T. *Booker T. Washington Papers*. Edited by Louis R. Harlan. Champagne: University of Illinois Press, 1975.

———. *The Story of My Life and Work*. Atlanta: J. L. Nichols, 1901.

Wells-Barnett, Ida B. *Crusade for Justice: The Autobiography of Ida B. Wells*. Edited by Alfreda M. Duster. Chicago: University of Chicago Press, 1970.

———. *A Red Record: Lynchings in the United States*. 1895. Reprint in *On Lynchings*. Salem, N.H.: Ayer, 1991.

White, Hayden. *Metahistory: The Historical Imagination in Nineteenth-Century Europe*. Baltimore: Johns Hopkins University Press, 1975.

White-Parks, Annette. *Sui Sin Far/Edith Maude Eaton: A Literary Biography*. Urbana: University of Illinois Press, 1995.

Wilentz, Sean. *Chants Democratic: New York City and the Rise of the American Working Class, 1788–1850*. New York: Oxford University Press, 1984.

Williams, Raymond. "Base and Superstructure in Marxist Cultural Theory." *New Left Review*, November–December 1973: 3–16.

———. *Marxism and Literature*. New York: Oxford University Press, 1977.

Wills, Garry. *Cincinnatus: George Washington and the Enlightenment*. New York: Doubleday, 1984.

———. *Inventing America: Jefferson's Declaration of Independence*. New York: Vintage Books, 1979.

Wilmeth, Don B. "Noble or Ruthless Savage?: The America Indian on Stage and in the Drama." *Journal of American Drama and Theater* 1 (1989): 38–78.

Winant, Howard. "Behind Blue Eyes: Whiteness and Contemporary U.S. Racial Politics." In *Off White: Readings on Race, Power, and Society*, edited by Michelle Fine, Lois Weis, Linda C. Powell, and L. Mun Wong. New York: Routledge, 1997. 40–53.

Winch, Julie. *Philadelphia's Black Elite: Activism, Accommodation, and the Struggle for Autonomy, 1787–1848*. Philadelphia: Temple University Press, 1988.

Wong, K. Scott. "Chinatown: Conflicting Images, Contested Terrain." *MELUS* 20:1 (Spring 1995): 3–15.

———, and Sucheng Chan, eds. *Claiming America: Constructing Chinese American Identities during the Exclusion Era*. Philadelphia: Temple University Press, 1998.

Wonham, Henry B., ed. *Criticism and the Color Line: Desegregating American Literary Studies*. New Brunswick, N.J.: Rutgers University Press, 1996.

Wood, Gordon S. *The Creation of the American Republic, 1776–1787*. New York: W. W. Norton, 1972.

———. *The Radicalism of the American Revolution*. New York: Vintage Books, 1991.

Woodward, C. Vann. *The Strange Career of Jim Crow*. 1954. 2d ed. New York: Oxford University Press, 1966.

Wright, Nathalia, ed. *Letters of Horatio Greenough, American Sculptor*. Madison: University of Wisconsin Press, 1972.

Young, Robert J. C. *Colonial Desire: Hybridity in Theory, Culture, and Race*. New York: Routledge, 1995.

Yung, Judy. *Unbound Feet: A Social History of Chinese Women in San Francisco*. Berkeley: University of California Press, 1995.

Zafar, Rafia. *We Wear the Mask: African Americans Write American Literature, 1760–1870*. New York: Columbia University Press, 1997.

Ziff, Larzer. *Writing in the New Nation: Prose, Print, and Politics in the Early United States*. New Haven: Yale University Press, 1991.

INDEX

ABOUT THE AUTHOR

Todd Vogel is a visiting assistant professor of English and American studies at Trinity College, Connecticut. He edited *The Black Press: New Literary and Historical Essays* (Rutgers University Press). His journalistic work has appeared in *Business Week*, the *Washington Post*, the *Boston Globe,* and the *Dallas Morning News*.